Religion
in the Old South

Chicago History of
American Religion

A Series Edited by
Martin E. Marty

Religion
in the Old South

Donald G. Mathews

The University of Chicago Press Chicago and London

DONALD G. MATHEWS is professor
of history at the University of North
Carolina. He is the author of
*Slavery and Methodism: A Chapter
in American Morality, 1780–1844*
and the editor of *Agitation for
Freedom: The Abolitionists*.

The University of Chicago Press, Chicago 60637
The University of Chicago Press, Ltd., London

© 1977 by The University of Chicago
All rights reserved. Published 1977

Printed in the United States of America

Library of Congress Cataloging in Publication Data

Mathews, Donald G
  Religion in the old South.

  (Chicago history of American religion)
  Bibliography: p.
  Includes index.
  1. Christianity—United States—Southern States.
2. Evangelicalism—United States—Southern States.
I. Title.
BR535.M37   277.5   77–587
ISBN 0–226–51001–8

For Jane

The Spirit of the Lord God is upon me; because the Lord hath anointed me to preach good tidings unto the meek; he hath sent me to bind up the broken-hearted, to proclaim liberty to the captives, and the opening of the prison to them that are bound; to proclaim the acceptable year of the Lord, and the day of vengeance of our God.

Isaiah 61: 1–2

Contents

Foreword by
Martin E. Marty   ix

Preface   xiii

1. "Disallowed Indeed of
   Men, but Chosen of
   God, and Precious"   1

2. "To Set in Order the
   Things that are
   Wanting"   39

3. "An Enlightened
   and Refined People"   81

4. "We Who Own Slaves
   Honor God's Law"   136

5. "The Trumpet Sounds
   within-a My Soul"   185

6. "To Proclaim Liberty
   to the Captives"   237

Notes   251

Note on Sources   265

Index   269

Foreword

During the third quarter of the twentieth century the population of the American North grew by 32 percent, from 102,641,000 people to 135,470,000. Meanwhile, the growth rate in the South was almost double that, from 48,865,000 to 77,651,000, or 59.5 percent. This "Sun Belt," as it came to be known, includes southern California and a Southwest that historically shared little with the nation's Old South. Yet as a region, this new South has attracted attention for the power of its politics, economics, racial attitudes, entertainment, athletics—and its religion.

Almost any conjuring of southern images is bound to include religion near the center. To those who despise the southern style, its faith makes up a "Bible Belt" of ignorance, emotionalism, and prejudice. To the nostalgic it is chiefly southern spirituality that is referred to as "that Old-Time Religion." Two of the most potent forces in late twentieth-century American religion, the Evangelicalism associated in the public mind with the name of Billy Graham and the black religion that inspired much of the movement for justice and equality in society, have their deepest roots in the southern past. In some ways, southern religion merits study because the region that is its host is itself larger than most nations. At the same time, that religion "trickles up" into the North and beyond it into much of the world, so it has cosmopolitan significance.

Despite the vividness of southern religious imagery in the public mind, few books have set out to isolate southern faith, church life,

or spiritual impact. Those we have are largely devoted to the life of
single denominations or single issues. Fine studies exist to set forth
relations of white Methodists to slavery, Presbyterians to the Negro,
Baptists to social issues. Others have dealt with recent or brief time
periods, as they discuss the crisis of contemporary religion or a few
days in the life of a colonial cleric.

What was the Old South, in its religious dimension, that Old
South that did so much to produce today's Sun Belt and its shadows
elsewhere? Until Donald Mathews drew together strands from
many monographs and a wide range of original sources, answers to
such a question could be found only with great difficulty. Seldom
does an introducer have an opportunity to write a foreword to an
obviously necessary book, not one wedged in between competitive
studies. I know nowhere else to direct readers if they seek a compact, yet in its own way comprehensive, view of this topic. Yet
if this is a pioneering work, it is not sketchy, random, or
idiosyncratic. Those who have read widely in the sources will, I have
no doubt, feel confident that Professor Mathews is at home in them
and is a most judicious and clear synthesizer or introducer of fresh
themes.

Tellers of the South's religious story cannot rely on some of the
familiar topics or devices available to many historians of faiths
elsewhere. With notoriously rare exceptions, they are not likely to
stumble upon first-rate theological minds. There are no figures
comparable to Jonathan Edwards, Ralph Waldo Emerson, Horace
Bushnell, Walter Rauschenbusch, or the brothers Reinhold and H.
Richard Niebuhr. The South had few cultural centers from which
emanated important architectural styles or religious art.

Lacking high-cultural monuments, however, a historian like
Mathews is free to do something that many scholars neglect. He
can, indeed he must, get up close to his subjects, the people of the
South. They did produce impressive churchmen, institutionalists,
and evangelizers. From their collective souls welled Negro spirituals
and white Gospel music, the people's sound down into our own
time. The South was full of geniuses at the art of persuasion,
conversion, crowd-control, the building of structures for caring
about people. If formidable theologians were absent, effective
pastors were not. They conspired with the people to come up with

plausible and deeply held interpretations of a history that included many elements of the tragic dimension, the factor so often overlooked by northern religionists in their search for progress and the Kingdom.

Professor Mathews found a way to bring together materials from this popular culture and to help readers find their way through the southern maze. While much of his book deals with the white people, Mathews does not neglect to see how they related to black America, and devotes long sections to the slaves' appropriations and innovations in the realm of faith. Since the black-white theme dominates the history of the South and still touches most aspects of the lives of most Americans today, it is fortunate that he has devoted so much attention to this theme. But if the Old South was the Cotton Kingdom and the slave empire, its people had topics other than slavery and race relations on their minds.

While what Mathews calls the Evangelical style, one which accented both personal turning and then communal identity, spread across the nineteenth-century United States and shared features with Protestant Christianity elsewhere, nowhere was it as pervasive or as deeply rooted as in the South. A hundred and more years later revivalism, evangelism, and the religion of the personal experience of Jesus Christ are a part of the lives of Presidents, legislators, athletes, entertainers, millionaires, and poor Appalachians alike. No one is likely to comprehend their scope or depth unless he knows his way around the South in the crucial period of Evangelical development. Mathews is concerned both to define this Evangelicalism and to do justice to its internal varieties.

Roman Catholicism plays little part in this history, for Catholics were rare in the South, and to this day their community there is dwarfed by a Baptist-Methodist-Presbyterian-Church of Christ culture with an Episcopalian underlay. While the author is careful to keep the lines of denominationalism clear, he is more interested in doing what has not been done before: to speak of southern religion as a gestalt, a whole, a belief system that helped many sorts of men and women make sense of a world. Since the search for meaning and belonging had to be intense in the South during the years of its modern formation, and since that search goes on everywhere today, this is a case study in religious experience for those who did not know they were interested in the South. And for those who come to the study or the enjoyment of the South bringing only their secular spectacles, not trained to look at the webbing and knotting that religion provides, these pages will be an eye-opener. If this book depends upon several generations of specialized studies, it is also certain to help inspire more inquiry in the future.

Martin E. Marty
The University of Chicago

Preface

This essay suggests in broad outline how and why Evangelical Protestantism became the predominant religious mood of the South. Religion and the American South are fused in our historical imagination in an indelible but amorphous way. Southern politics, social relations, and literature easily command our attention, propelling us through time in search of that essential insight into the South that will reveal something significant about our national experience—and perhaps about the human condition. We transform the religious dimensions of southern sensibilities into abstractions of sin, guilt, tragedy, irony, and soul. The writing of southern history has often become in itself a religious expression of the author and a moral Rorschach test for the reader. Despite this fascination with evil, sin, and guilt, however, there have been few attempts to present an historical overview of the place of religion in southern society. The few scholars who have written on various aspects of southern religious history have preferred the limitations of the specialized monograph, the denominational history, or the narrative biography, of which so few have been written that there is not sufficient material from which to fashion a convincing synthesis. Thus we have a phenomenon which everyone agrees must have affected southern history because it has been so pervasive, but which has escaped the queries How? and Why?

In the chapters that follow, I have attempted to explain the *why* by tracing the *how*. This book is not the last word on southern religion, but a first word, an invitation to further discussion of the character, functions, and significance of religion in shaping and defining the South as a distinct part of the new American nation. But even more specifically we will be concerned only with the single most influential strain of religious activity in the South during the formative years before 1860—Evangelicalism. The emphasis upon Evangelicalism is justified by the primacy of that mode of Protestantism in the Old South. This is not to demean the contributions of non-Evangelical religious groups, but to underscore the fact that this book is not a history of all the southern religious. It is not a history of the churches, nor of the denominations, nor of the theology, nor of the religious culture of the Old South—although all of these would be worthwhile subjects, and although a little of each impinges upon the task undertaken here. Rather, the book is concerned with how southern society was affected by Evangelical values and institutions. The reason for limiting discussion to the Old South, instead of scanning the whole process of southern history, is simply to establish as clearly as possible the social and religious base from which the region has proceeded since the War for Southern Independence.

The burden of this task has been to focus as consistently as possible upon that invisible nexus where the individual, family, class, and society are defined and expressed in the predominant religious mood of the Old South. Theology and formal idea-systems, therefore, are not the raw material from which this book has been crafted. The religious-social continuum has been emphasized as steadfastly as the sources and the ability of the writer would allow, a posture which will account for the bias of the presentation and explain its limitations as well as its achievements. Keeping this focus in mind, we may proceed with a cautionary reminder that any book is a series of hypotheses, some closer to the conventional historical wisdom than others, which may or may not eventually be verified. It is hoped, however, that these hypotheses will call attention to one of the most important and least understood historical processes that have shaped our nation, the creation of a large southern social constituency that was not quite a class—although it was first expressed as a class movement—nor quite strictly a religious mood apart from social conflict, institution-building, and class consciousness.

My argument can be expressed in two sentences: As a social,

historical process, Evangelical Protestantism in the Old South enabled a rising lower-middle/middle class to achieve identity and solidarity, rewarding its most committed religious devotees with a sense of personal esteem and liberty. From interaction with and participation in this process, blacks created the measure by which southern Evangelicalism itself could be judged, and through their appropriation of Evangelical Christianity expressed a religious-social ethos that could best convey its significance in the Evangelical promise to "preach liberty to the captives." It is obvious from this statement that southern Evangelicalism is not to be thought of as *white*. The book begins with the white Evangelicals' social movement of the late eighteenth century. It ends as many antebellum blacks thought History itself would end, with the envelopment and transformation of the meaning of white Evangelicalism through the unfolding of black Christianity. There may be as much poetry as truth in conceiving of black-white religious interaction in this fashion, but it is much truer to the historical record than is the traditional reluctance to take black religion seriously. Moreover, such a view attempts to make sense of the undeniable participation of blacks and whites in common religious exercises, a fact which made southerners "more religious" than nonsoutherners and made southern religion different from that of the rest of the nation.

One important side effect of discussing the participation of both whites and blacks in southern religion is to demonstrate the essentially frivolous nature of the nineteenth-century debate—still carried on in various manifestations—about whether or not historians should or can avoid making value judgments. If one's perspective is broad enough to include all classes and significant groups in historical analysis, the problem disappears, since historical figures make value judgments upon themselves as well as each other. To take an example from this book: historians' righteous indignation at a Christian proslavery argument has prevented a calm, sensible analysis of the slaveholding ethic which was as natural an extension of Evangelicalism as was abolitionism—a conclusion which historians have resisted for years. The reason is that the fight over slavery enlisted partisans from both sides of the Mason-Dixon line even after Emancipation, and the antislavery historians won. Consequently, northern Evangelicalism has been viewed as being consistent with its highest principles in attacking slavery; southern Evangelicalism has been scorned as a distortion for the opposite reason. This mischievous dichotomy has persisted because the model for explaining southern Evangelicalism has been shaped by the moral sensibility of liberal historians and their alter egos, the radical abolitionists. By taking black Christianity seriously, however, and by including slaves as well as slaveholders in southern religion, the issue of Evangelical impact is seen in a new light, for there is no historical reason to argue that the blacks' religion was any less an extension of Evangelical Protestantism than that of whites. Black Christians' moral accomplishments and commitment are powerful evidence in themselves. To accuse southern Christianity of being distorted and hypocritical is to share the tacit assumption that white people and their experiences are the standard of judgment in our history. That assumption did not dictate the argument of this book.

At this point it must be admitted that the manner in which the term *Evangelicalism* is used will annoy those who like clean-cut and precise definitions. The anarchy of historical experience, which often blurs categories and boundaries, is no vindication of untidiness in historians, but definitions—even those which are merely operational—tend to reify dynamic processes into speciously discrete periods or stages and to that extent distort reality. Besides, Evangelicalism changed from one generation and social challenge to the next, so that the entire book is a definition of Evangelicalism in the Old South.

A few comments can be made, however, about the generic marks of Evangelicalism which were in evidence throughout its history. The first is an elaboration of the Protestant perspective that the Christian life is essentially a personal relationship with God in Christ, established through the direct action of the Holy Spirit, an action which elicits in the believer a profoundly emotional conversion experience. This existential crisis, the *New Birth* as Evangelicals called it, ushers the convert into a life of holiness characterized by religious devotion, moral discipline, and missionary zeal. To achieve this remarkable transformation, Evangelical preaching rejects the appeal to reason and restrained sensibilities for a direct, psychological assault upon sin and the equally direct and much more comforting offer of personal salvation. The style, suited as it is to the democracy of emotion rather than the hierarchy of intellect, destroys the psychological and social distance between preacher and people, often evoking tearful, passionate outbursts. These marks of Evangelicalism were, as we shall see, institutionalized in the Baptist, Methodist, Presbyterian, Disciples of Christ, and Protestant Episcopal denominations, but even in these churches—with the exception of the Methodists—there were non-Evangelicals. And there were also Evangelicals in denominations not specifically mentioned here. Thus the terms *Evangelicals* and *Evangelicalism* as employed here will have a frequently imprecise and abstract quality to them. That this is deliberate does detract from the annoyance it may cause; but perhaps it will demonstrate why this essay proceeded on the conviction that Evangelicalism was a social process as well as a religious perception, and as such can be understood only in historical, as opposed to definitional, terms.

As social process, Evangelicalism enveloped the South in the following fashion. It first broke into the South as an extension of revivals throughout the British world, a volatile social movement providing a value system to raise converts in their own esteem, give them confidence in themselves and their comrades, and create the moral courage to reject as authoritative for themselves the life-style and values of traditional elites. As a result of this act of rebellion they began to form a sense of bondedness and special mission, which at one time led most of their radical spokesmen to seal the authenticity of their revolution by attacking slavery. This revolutionary and romantic gesture failed to achieve social change because Evangelicals themselves wanted prestige and influence and wanted also to achieve power on the basis of their own estimation of themselves and the economic tools at their command. Unfortunately for blacks, one of these tools was slavery, and most Evangelicals channeled their resentment against non-Evangelical slaveholders by claiming that they could, at least in theory, make the slaves a more integral and stable part of the community than could nonbelievers. Through creating their own institutions and networks of communication, white Evangelicals finally achieved—in their own minds at least—the pinnacle of refinement and respectability. They had come a long way from their origins as sturdy religious folk who had attacked the pretensions of a previous aristocracy. Through the religious institutions they shared with whites, black Christians became a movement within a movement, a community within a community, a society within a society'. Ironically, however, these shared institutions became as important as specifically black institutions, even as they had once been important as specifically lower-middle-class institutions. The religious-social continuum of black Christianity created a mode of survival and sense of victory that was much closer to the original message of Evangelicalism than the mood and institutions of whites.

The research from which these themes emerged was done in libraries throughout the South. Private papers, journals, newspapers, biographies, and secondary literature have been used, as have a great many local and regional church records which reveal the provincial drabness, minor tragedy, and earnest pride of human life so important to the understanding of religion in its social context. I am grateful to the staffs of the following institutions: Amistad Research Center, Dillard University, New Orleans, Louisiana; Archive Department, University of the South, Sewanee, Tennessee; Baptist Historical Collection, Wake Forest University; Dargan-Carver Library, Baptist Historical Commission, Nashville, Tennessee; Department of Archives and History, Montgomery, Alabama; Department of Archives and History, Raleigh, North Carolina; Department of Archives, Louisiana State University, Baton Rouge; Duke University Library; Emory University Library; Furman University Library; Historical Foundation of the Presbyterian and Reformed Churches, Montreat, North Carolina; Howard-Tilton Memorial Library, Tulane University; Library of Congress; Methodist Publishing House Library, Nashville, Tennessee; Millsaps College Library; Presbyterian Historical Society, Philadelphia; Princeton University Library; Samford University Division of Manuscripts, Birmingham, Alabama; South Caroliniana Library, the University of South Carolina; Southern Historical Collection, the University of North Carolina at Chapel Hill; Tennessee State Archives, Nashville, Tennessee; Union Theological Seminary Library, Richmond, Virginia; University of Alabama Library; University of Virginia Library; Vanderbilt University Library; Virginia Baptist Historical Society, University of Richmond; Virginia Conference Historical Collection, Randolph-Macon College, Ashland, Virginia; Virginia Historical Society, Richmond; Virginia State Library, Richmond; Wofford College Library.

I am also indebted to the National Endowment for the Humanities for providing funds to travel to many of the archives mentioned above and for giving me a research project grant (with Robert M. Calhoon of the University of North Carolina at Greensboro) to develop my ideas.

The findings and conclusions presented here do not necessarily represent the views of the Endowment. Nor do they represent the views of the trustees of the University of North Carolina, who granted me time to write through a Kenan Leave, awarded on the basis of a generous and effective recommendation by my chairman, Professor George V. Taylor.

Many friends have graciously helped me prepare the manuscript. Robert Zenowich has probably forgotten that he suggested I write it; Martin Marty made it possible for me to do so. Marty's enthusiastic support and gentle prodding have, I hope, paid off. I have received invaluable criticism, conversation, and encouragement from scholars who have read portions of the manuscript— Anne Firor Scott of Duke University; Rhys Isaac of Latrobe University; Alice Mathews of Western Carolina University; members of the Department of Religion at the University of North Carolina; members of the Homewood Seminar in American Religious History at the Johns Hopkins University and its generous chairman, Timothy L. Smith. I am grateful to these people for their interest, questions, and corrections. John Scott Strickland and William Hay also deserve mention. Secily Jones typed the manuscript and was gracious enough to talk with me about portions of it.

Jacques and Julie—very special friends with a wicked sense of humor—helped keep both history and historians in perspective.

I owe a very special professional and personal debt to two people who, although they have not read the manuscript, made me want to write it in the first place. One is just beginning his career, the other is one of the most distinguished scholars and teachers in his field—Robert F. Engs and H. Shelton Smith, who grace their calling as few people ever do.

Three colleagues read the entire manuscript. Linda Kerber of the University of Iowa not only cautioned me about certain extravagances and asked the kind of questions I expected of her, but also, with the kind of insight that helped to refine it, responded to the essay as a whole. Donald M. Scott of North Carolina Sate University was also generous with his time and his talent. He has a rare analytical capacity for teasing out ideas and seeing implications that characterizes the best kind of historical criticism.

Jane De Hart Mathews of the University of North Carolina read the manuscript with her usual care and intelligence. But she also had to hear it phrase by phrase before it was even written, endure the pangs of its development, and finally to read it as if it were new to her. Few colleagues can do as much. As her husband, I have been especially graced, for she, much more than the Evangelicals I have studied, has taught me the meaning of love and redemption.

1   *"Disallowed Indeed of Men, but Chosen of God, and Precious"*

The first white southerners—before there was a South or a nation or even very much of a Virginia—lived under the rule of religion. Limited at first to public worship and the pastoral care of a saintly priest, religious discipline was imposed with unforgiving severity by Virginia's governors in 1610-11 in order to create the moral rigor and social solidarity so desperately needed to guarantee the survival of the fragile community. For three years the vanguard of English invasion had struggled to the point of physical and moral exhaustion with famine, pestilence, Indians, and each other. Preparing at last to scurry back to the mother country, where life was safe and more predictable, they were stopped by Governor Thomas West, Lord De La Warre, who arrived at the eleventh hour with fresh supplies, colonists, and courage. The latter, a quality as important to the collective as to the individual, De La Warre attempted to inject into his bedraggled colony through the familiar offices of the church and her ministry. "Almighty God be duly and daily served," he commanded, thus articulating what was, after all, the bounden duty of every Englishman and one which was to begin with daily attendance at morning and evening prayer.

There was much more to be considered, too, for a failure of nerve, from which De La Warre had just rescued his people, is deadly to any collective. To whip Virginians into shape, the governor thought it necessary to remind them of the solemnity of their mission into the New World and of the ultimate source of their strength. Let no one blaspheme or curse, he commanded, lest he reveal a despair which once had pushed the community to the edge of destruction. Let no one "speak impiously or maliciously" of the Christian religion, its doctrines, or its clergy, lest authority be undermined. And let no disrespectful violation of the sabbath with profane "gaming" subvert the seriousness with which Virginians were to pursue the common task of serving God and saving the commonwealth. The governors of Virginia were determined to bind their subjects, on pain of corporal or capital punishment, into a cohesive community with rituals of divine service. Relations among members of the community, responsiveness to authority, and the daily round of work were to be ordered according to the ritual and doctrine of the Church of England. If they had been carried out, the rules of the early governors would have imposed upon the infant colony a solidarity which would have interpreted social deviation as heresy, blasphemy, or schism. In colonial Virginia, religion and community were very nearly synonymous.

De La Warre's Draconian laws, "exemplified and enlarged" by his deputy, Sir Thomas Dale, were a natural enough expression of the seventeenth-century English view of man's actions in God's universe. In that view, communities were held together in part by ritual and beliefs about the nature and destiny of man, theoretical concepts which were legitimated by the dramatic myth of the Protestant faith then unfolding in England. Personal decisions about matters as diverse as marriage and financial investment were wrestled with in terms of God's will, just as the historic destiny of the colony was explained as part of God's plan of salvation. Indeed, to Protestant Englishmen who lived under the mysterious providence of Almighty God and explained history in religious terms, contact with peoples of other cultures and conflicts with nature and the forces of social disintegration were explained in Christian concepts. Private as well as public statements about the Virginia venture could therefore justify it as a mission to spread faith and civilization to the New World wilderness by fusing English expansionism with the apostolic command to preach the Gospel to all creatures. It was not that Virginia was in fact a mission, but that it could meaningfully be interpreted as one. It was not that Virginians were uniquely religious, but that they were conventionally so, and that in their conventional way they turned to the church to keep the community together.[1] The process was different from that which developed later in New England, where a religious ideology had established principles of social cohesion even before Pilgrim and Puritan left for America. A sense of belonging to each other reinforced by conflict with authority and devotion to a theology of intense self-discipline gave the New England venture a cohesiveness and sense of destiny from the beginning. Virginians had come to their first social crisis without a common commitment to a unique ideology; but they did know that the doctrines and ritual of their church could help to provide order, without which society is impossible. The irony of the 1610-11 crisis was that the church could exercise its functions only under martial law.

When the crisis passed and martial law was suspended, religious rituals and beliefs were no longer called upon to be the primary bonds of social solidarity. Instead, they became gradually formalized as the established church, which in turn took its place as one of several institutions of government in the primitive New World order. A legislative assembly, counties, and parishes were developed to supervise Virginians as they scattered up the rivers to plant the tobacco that was to transform the colony into an increasingly complex society. With tobacco came wealth and with wealth came new immigrants to exploit the wealth or be exploited by the wealthy for their labor. With new immigrants came confusion about status—the place of each new arrival in the society—and how each person was to be treated, whether a heathen African (by ascription) or an English gentleman (by aspiration). To help prevent confusion endemic to the colonial social situation, therefore, the Church of England provided an ideal model of stability. Social convention and differences of wealth would of course help to ease some of the confusion, but an established church was important, too, as authorities in the southern colonies realized when they set about to create one. Individual laws could not create a church all at once, but Virginians (1632), Marylanders (1649), and Carolinians (1706) began a process of establishment soon after settlement. Ministerial support, vestry government, church attendance, and many other matters were provided for in attempts to establish a rule of religion within the primitive and fragile social system.[2]

The church was to fill three important functions. First of all it was to provide a means of transforming geographically scattered farms into a community. The interaction of mutual claims and expectations and contributions to the common life could be judged and approved by the community's leaders through churchwardens, whose job it was to bring profane, disorderly people before the county court. The duties of churchwardens symbolized the responsibility of scattered individuals and families to a moral order which was both abstract and specific. The fact that every Virginian, for example, was required by law to attend church services each week was designed to reinforce the moral policing of the churchwardens by bringing people together within sight and touch of each other to hear the moral precepts of the community explained. The reminder may not have visibly altered behavior, but regular participation in divine service should have functioned as an important ritualistic enactment of community. Simply by providing a place for people to meet and renew acquaintances, church services could theoretically have helped to create a sense of belonging.

Identification with the community is impossible, however, unless a person believes that it cares for him or her. The church provided a very important means of expressing that care, a second aspect of its function in society. It consecrated the important transitions and traumas of life, and set itself the task of taking care of orphans, widows, paupers, and others who could not take care of themselves. The experiences of each individual were to be circumscribed by the expectations of the whole community: infants were not simply born, they were baptized; children did not simply grow, they were catechized; men and women were not simply brought together to begin the life process all over again, they were wed with the blessings of the church. This ritualization of life was supposed to establish stability and provide security for each individual even if he had not been thoroughly catechized; it was to signify his importance to other individuals.

A third process was also at work in the church. The isolated parishes had to be brought into some sort of relationship with each other in order to create the society, just as isolated individuals and families had to be brought into an integral relationship to create communities from parishes. Family connections, county courts, and the House of Burgesses were in varying degrees complementary and often superior to the church in their creation and maintenance of communal and societal relationships. But the church was designed to fulfill the same functions, and was considered important in doing so, despite its supplementary role. Theoretically, uniformity in worship, catechetical instruction, and moral surveillance would help to provide a uniformity in basic values and behavior throughout the colony. Ministers were to report to authorities at the capital the vital statistics, state of moral government, and general vitality of the parish. As the man responsible for catechizing, exhorting, and guiding the community, the minister was to be an important link in the colonial chain of authority. He was therefore protected by law from "disparagement," lest authority itself be disparaged. In return, he was expected to be an authentic priest, a man whose credentials, as presented to the governor, proved him to have been ordained according to the rites of the Church of England. A society could not afford to have men in positions of moral authority who were at odds with the conventions and beliefs upon which it relied for social harmony. It is quite obvious that in binding community to society through religious and clerical uniformity, colonial authorities did not make a clear distinction between sacred and profane society. Consequently, religious dissent was looked upon not as a mere difference of opinion, but as a challenge to authority and therefore a disruption of community.

Expectations of institutional performance rarely coincide with reality, but for the established churches in the southern colonies, differences between thought and act were almost disastrous. Although the Church of England in America was gradually taken under the care of the Bishop of London and the Society for the Propagation of the Gospel in Foreign Parts, it never achieved the independence and power to which its legal position as established church should have entitled it. It was an episcopal church without diocese and bishop. Consequently, generations of colonists grew up and died within the church without ever having been confirmed, and priests were ordained for the New World in pathetically small numbers. Even worse for the church, no ecclesiastical machinery securely bound its congregations together, disciplined its priests, or sastisfactorily supported its missionary parishes. The remarkable feature of the establishment was probably that it existed at all, especially in North Carolina, where in 1765 there were only six priests to serve twenty-nine country-wide parishes in a population of over one hundred thousand people. The South Carolina church was merely the low country planter aristocracy at prayer; the backcountry was left to dissenters and the Devil, between which Anglican missionaries could not distinguish. The Chesapeake area was little better served. In 1724, Virginia had twenty-eight priests for about 140,000 people and Maryland, even while providing its priests with handsome livings, fared little better. Despite the aid of laymen who read the liturgy and conducted the affairs of the churches in the place of ordained priests, the network of parishes designed to watch behavior, educate Christians, and hold society together operated incompletely and inadequately.

Churchmen knew their problems only too well, or at least knew from personal experience that problems existed. American priests complained of overbearing and independent vestries, niggardly and reluctant support, immense and sparsely populated parishes, and insolent dissenters. Vestries were the sometimes elected and often self-perpetuating bodies of laymen, members of the ruling elite, who assumed responsibility for running the affairs of the parish, which included caring for church buildings and dependent persons, and calling the minister. The last responsibility was a particularly sensitive issue. Some vestries refused to induct ministers into their livings, preferring instead to reappoint them year by year, thus depriving them of a secure tenure and guaranteeing that priests would be subservient neither to the Bishop of London, nor to his special representative, the commissary, nor even perhaps to the governor, but to the local gentry. In fact, very few church laymen in the southern colonies supported the move to appoint a bishop in America because they feared a loss of their autonomy. The phrase, "established church," may have a fine ring to it, denoting power and respectability, but in the case of the southern colonies, the established church was what each locality allowed it to be. There were, to be sure, independent Anglican missionaries supported by the Society for the Propagation of the Gospel, and there were also a few well-organized and well-supported parishes, but the power of the church depended on the support and good will of local elites. Although colonial assemblies might set aside public monies for clerical salaries and church buildings, vestrymen were responsible for carrying out the laws, and their relationship with the minister determined the quality of the latter's support, including the quality of the glebe land set aside for his use. The priest's own ability as a farmer and businessman dictated whether or not he could exploit the glebe effectively. If he were a bad farmer he might just avoid poverty; if he were too successful he might be tempted to devote most of his energy to his most rewarding occupation.

Independence of the canons and rubrics of the church was reinforced in many areas by the geographical size of the parish, the difficulty of transportation, and the consequent inability of priests to keep in contact with their parishioners. Parishes could be 120 miles long and 40 miles wide. Priests of parishes sprawled over the vast backcountry confronted everything that churchwardens and vestrymen were supposed to prevent: pregnant brides, wildly uncontrollable children, and ignorant, profane adults—all living without the order and stability promised by laws establishing the church. "Had a large congregation," recorded one priest, "but according to Custom, one half of them got drunk before they went home."[3] In such a chaotic situation, rituals which were supposed to maintain contact between individual and society became nothing more than official sanctions that scarcely betokened respectability. Even more frustrating for priests, the infrequently performed rituals may have helped to kindle a smoldering resentment by reminding scattered and partially isolated parishioners of the aloofness of authority. Certainly the priests' response to their "riotous and Lewd" people must have communicated a censoriousness and sense of superiority which would have made their role as moral leaders almost impossible to perform.

As if matters were not bad enough with nominal Anglicans, churchmen also had to face the problem of religious dissent. In some backcountry parishes dissenters were even a majority of the vestry, a condition which did little to consolidate the establishment. As immigrants from Ulster, Germany, Wales, and New England filtered into the southern colonies, they naturally brought their own religious beliefs and institutions with them, although the Presbyterianism of the Scotch-Irish was often more a lingering memory than an active faith. Quakers presented the first challenge to religious conformity in the seventeenth century, but as new tracts of land became available, they and the Baptists, Presbyterians, and Lutherans were allowed the privileges of public worship so long as they did not disturb the peace or threaten the position of the established church. To guarantee the dissenters' good behavior, they were subjected to certain restrictions: weddings were to be performed only by an Anglican priest; meetinghouses were to be registered with the authorities; nonconformist ministers were to be licensed for specific localities but forbidden to itinerate. Such laws could be ignored or loosely construed as long as dissenters proved to be law-abiding, thus fragmenting the rule of religion as enclaves of non-Anglicans established their own beliefs and practices as superior to those of a distant and foreign authority. Churchmen did not like this state of affairs, but there was nothing they could do about it. Their ideal of the English church's holding communities and society together through a rule of religion was much more a dream than a reality.

Churchmen could not effectively change their situation because of the way in which they understood it. To be sure, there were objective reasons why their task was so difficult; the dispersed population, jealous vestrymen, and recalcitrant dissenters presented real challenges to the power and prestige of the Church of England. The ecclesiastical limitations of having no diocesan machinery also damaged the effectiveness of the church. But other communions suffered the same limitations and won over the population of the South, whereas the Church of England steadily declined almost to the point of oblivion. The establishment could not shape the religious history of the South because its problems were conceived of as problems in organization and power. It was argued that if diocesan machinery, complete with a bishop, existed in the New World, priests, freed of their vestries, would gain status, a fact which would in turn draw more and better men to vacant livings, thus guaranteeing every parish a moral and spiritual leader. With an independent priesthood, moral discipline could presumably be tightened in communities, and Episcopal vistations would link communicants and priests alike to a smoothly running ecclesiastical system.

Efficiency and increased communication, however, would have done little more than agitate the primary problem of the establishment: its identification with and commitment to the class system. As an extension of the powerful men in each locality, the Anglican church was quite naturally incapable of eliciting intense devotion from folk who felt powerless and insignificant. Society in the English New World may have been bereft of a nobility, but it was not lacking an aristocracy, which, while possibly base-born in the dimly remembered past, was by the eighteenth century sure of the rightfulness of its high position. Even if the upper class was replenished from below, it was nevertheless distinct from other, lower ranks in the social hierarchy, exercising authority through the court and vestry systems and maintaining careful distinctions between itself and its less wealthy countrymen. Through distinguishing dress, education, leisure activities, and place at public worship, the better sort could very easily emphasize their superior rank in society, a rank which elicited a deferential manner—and sometimes fear—from social inferiors. The ranks of the better sort, the middling classes, the vulgar, and the slave were carefully ordered in the minds of colonial Americans, and in the minds of most, the church stood with the gentry.

Churchmen believed that the church's primary mission in the New World was to bring all inhabitants—Indians, Africans, Europeans—under the rule of religion as outlined in the Thirty-Nine Articles and the Book of Common Prayer. If they had stopped there, they might have been more successful in America; but they did not. They identified their church with the perpetuation of a hierarchial social system. This in itself would not have doomed their future communicants to minority status if churchmen had not been so concerned with the definition and maintenance of the upper order. But almost everything about the church prevented its eliciting meaningful participation in common devotion and Christian equality. The organization of the local church was itself a constant reminder of social distinctions, as the wealthy sat in their private pews musing about how they should run the church and dispense the social services of the parish. From the pulpit, a careful, lifeless preaching informed parishioners about proper behavior, appropriate attitudes, and a comely deference to social convention. Such a style conveyed the sense of the lower orders as unruly and disobedient persons, or even worse, as the "enemy" to be subdued and domesticated, rather than as the Lost Sheep of Israel to be brought into a saving relationship with Christ Jesus. The result was an adversary relationship between churchmen and lower-class people that was impossible to overcome.

The church failed to make a serious attempt to associate members of the community with each other on the basis of shared personal and religious experiences. Contacts between persons were governed primarily by their presumed ranking in the social system, and morality was characterized not so much by the concept of self-discipline demanded of all, as by obedient orderliness that identified Christian humility with social deference. The messages of the church and clergy seemed to travel in only one direction—from authority down to those whose proper response was to listen attentively and submit dutifully. Rather than evoking an elemental feeling of commonality, the sermons stated as clearly as possible the rules of social conduct. When the Virginia General Assembly decreed in 1662 that the baptism of enslaved Africans in no way altered their social standing, it might also have emphasized that the same held true for white Virginians and for future colonists everywhere in the New World. The Anglican church simply tried to fit everyone snugly into a social system where individuals were valued not on the basis of their own merit but on their family background and social station. No tinkering with ecclesiastical machinery could repair this fatal flaw.

The flaw was becoming ever more apparent to southern colonists by the 1750s, especially with the provocative and portentous expansion of the Evangelical movement. At the time, the movement appeared to be a disorderly and potentially dangerous confrontation between constituted authorities and contentious, emotional, and presumptuous rabble. From the perspective of a revolutionary age, the confrontation seems tame indeed. No leaders were violently displaced; no Bastille destroyed; no soviets created; no communes founded. In fact, institutions we usually think of as primarily political were largely untouched by a movement which nevertheless furrowed the brows, disquieted the thoughts, and aroused the anger of many members of the traditional aristocracy. This uneasiness, expressed in private conversation and exhibited in public attempts to restrict or suppress itinerant preachers, was part of a growing concern about orderliness in society and especially about maintaining a proper respect for traditional authority. To persons anxious to preserve their place in society, the Evangelical movement seemed to lack both order and proper respect—and to a threatening degree. What was perceived as a threat to some people was, however, to others the promise of a new way of looking at themselves, the community, and their place in society.

The Evangelical movement in the South was part of a more general, widely dispersed trend toward intense religious commitment in Atlantic Protestant civilization. Embracing thousands of people from the Germanies to the British Isles to New England, Evangelicalism brought a theology of personal experience and √ individual importance to a culture whose intellectual leaders had exalted the impersonal aspects of history and the cosmos. The formal liturgy of the churches, which emphasized ritual acts without engaging personal involvement, nicely paralleled the scholastic theology that pushed God just beyond the reach of human understanding without allowing for the real possibility of divine revelation. Of course men could know God through nature and reason, but the man who aspired to such knowledge was usually a theologian or philosopher. The ordinary man or woman who might claim to have a knowledge of God was as likely as not to be thought a little deranged. The exaltation of reason in an age which was probing the universe through the exciting and revolutionary theories of Sir Isaac Newton is certainly understandable. The idea of the mechanistic universe which could be comprehended by understanding its laws was so attractive that soon every aspect of human knowledge was subjected to a search for its peculiar laws. By thus objectifying the very cosmos itself and making its mysteries subject to the analytical powers of the human mind, the irrational aspects of human existence were not only ignored but discounted. It was a sign of the age that a pro-Christian tract should be entitled *Christianity not Mysterious.*

When Christians hastened to rest their case on the ability of the mind to probe the many revelations of God in Nature, it is not surprising that others should simply dispense with God's presence, as did the Deists. They did not deny the existence of God, they simply considered Him irrelevant; He had not made Himself known in a specific revelation—such a thing was contrary to reason and the working of nature—but in continuous, general revelation which rational men could understand by studying nature. For the Deists, nature was much more exciting and believable than an unfortunately mysterious God.

With the exclusion of God from direct contact with people came a disquieting effect upon those Christians who were also concerned about the tendency to justify their faith solely on the ground of reason. In response, a few Christians early in the eighteenth century began to form small devotional groups within the churches of western Europe. Their most urgent concern was to recapture the dynamic quality of life which was thought to have motivated the ancient church. They prayed for the Holy Spirit to descend upon them so that the God Who had been so persistently pushed away from them by theologians, philosophers, and scientists would break through the wall of Reason and touch their hearts; intellectually they repudiated a universe characterized essentially by nonpersonal forces. In social terms they affirmed the importance of Christian love in bonding people together and claimed that through the grace of God they had been chosen out of the world to be disciplined followers of Christ Jesus. He was not far off, but present in their small groups, and by His presence elicited an outpouring of prayer, devotion, and mutual affection. The proof of His care for them was not to be found in nature but in history, and not only in ancient and mighty acts, but in the miraculous transformation of their own lives. In personal terms they had in their small groups of intimate friends and fellow worshipers found a community which cared for them, and they knew that that community was more important than all other social relationships because God Himself had touched them in a profoundly personal experience. Others had had that same experience, and as they discussed this wonderful phenomenon with each other, confessing their sins and professing their faith in God and love for each other, they were doing two important things—affirming their own personal worth and sharing their affirmation with others. New standards of social participation were being introduced. Social rank, learning, intelligence—most of the bases for making invidious distinctions among people—were cast aside.

The movement did not enlist all Christians, of course, and those whom it did affect did not automatically agree with all other converts. English Evangelicals, for example, varied drastically in the way in which they tried to explain themselves, some with the theology of John Calvin and others with that of Calvinism's chief apostate and opponent, Jacobus Arminius. What divided them,

however, was not so important as what united them: an overwhelming sense of the presence of God, a belief in the entire
transformation of the personality through an intense religious
experience (as opposed to rational analysis), and the consequent
emphasis on the integrity of each person. It may seem strange that a
movement which emphasized the total depravity of man, the wrath
of God, and the necessity of repentance should have attracted men
and women by the thousands. It may seem stranger still to
emphasize that such a movement should be considered as one
which placed high value upon each individual. And yet in the
context of the time it was not strange at all because of the promised
renewal of self and the reordering of values. In the conversion
experience, Evangelicalism brought God down from His aloofness
into human life in a most dramatic and personal way which no
reason could deny. His condemnation of sin, awful as it was, was
also a sign that He was involved with humanity. As Evangelicals
turned away from a world which so obviously had repudiated God,
they were brought into a relationship with people who cared for
them and gave them a sense of belonging. The quality of this
relationship is best captured in the phrase they used to describe
it—the New Birth. They were renewed individuals, but celebration
of this renewal did not erupt in panegyrics to individualism. Their
personal renovation was the foundation of a new community.

   Like most movements, American Evangelicalism began and grew
in spurts. Outbursts of intense religious excitement would break
out here and there in isolated areas to be bound together initially in
the person of an itinerant evangelist and eventually in some kind of
ecclesiastical relationship. The greatest itinerant was the renowned
George Whitefield, a Calvinist, Evangelical Anglican priest who
berated traditional ecclesiastical leaders for their impersonal,
rationalist theology and damnably inadequate piety. Whitefield's
visit to New England and the middle colonies in 1740–41 helped to
focus the dissatisfaction with traditional religious life which had
already erupted into several local revivals. The conditions which
made Whitefield so attractive to thousands of people encouraged
other evangelists to follow him in challenging traditional authority—a challenge which usually led to conflicts, some of them
severe. The scenario was played out over and over. An itinerant
Evangelical preacher would issue an emotion-laden call to repent of

false subjection to the world and worldly ministers who knew not
the power of the Holy Spirit. Having entered another man's parish
uninvited, the interloper would argue that clergymen could not be
authentic Christians for all their education, propriety, and appeals to
reason unless they had had a conversion experience themselves and
preached doctrines which would lead to that experience in others.
In reply, traditionalists petulantly attacked the illegitimacy and
schismatic tendencies of Evangelical preaching. It shattered social
harmony and peace, they complained. It seduced unstable people
into following ignorant men whose low opinion of an educated
clergy was all the evidence needed to demonstrate that these
ill-mannered rowdies had no regard at all for the sacred office which
they professed to occupy. That they attacked a clergy which could
not elicit a broken-hearted repentance and an experience of saving
grace, argued the traditionalists, revealed the Evangelicals' readiness
to unleash the dangerous passions of the people and thus to destroy
the order of society. That they demanded all Christians have a
conversion experience like their own revealed their untutored and
egotistic presumption. At issue were the legitimacy of traditional
leadership, the appropriate psychological posture of Christian faith,
the nature of Christian commitment, and the relative importance
of reason and faith in the Christian life. Without immediate
resolution these issues broke Presbyterian and Congregational
churches into two camps—New and Old Lights (Presbyterians) and
New and Old Sides (Congregationalists).

Far more important than mere ecclesiastical division was the way
in which Evangelicalism was becoming a new mode of social
organization. As a movement which expressed dissatisfaction with
authority, it recruited men and women who for some reason had
cut their emotional ties with traditional ways of assigning prestige
and commanding respect. Uneasy with the various ways in which
they had come to terms with themselves and persons around them,
these people were also looking for a way to affirm their own
significance and that of their children by repudiating conventional
measures of personal worth and developing new ones in the most
meaningful framework of thought available to them. In the search
which led to Evangelicalism they found ways of creating new bonds
between themselves and their neighbors through the shared emotions of the conversion experience. It is not surprising that in their

repudiation of the past they should have been thought of as potential revolutionaries in their time.

Nowhere was the process more clear than in the southern provinces. And yet in that region it was virtually impossible to duplicate the kind of dramatic tour that shot George Whitefield like a comet through the New England firmament. Few crowds gathered to hear the orator in that sparsely populated land, but many read his sermons in front of the open fire at night and longed for the emotional catharsis and personal fulfillment he and others like him offered. Two social trends began to take shape which would soon make possible the marshaling of isolated but expectant people into an Evangelical movement. The more subtle trend was the internal strain within society, a generalized, pervasive dissatisfaction with the way in which people were esteemed and with the lack of meaningful personal relations in the community. Putting the matter in this fashion immediately submerges it in a morass of subjectivism, for *dissatisfaction*, *esteem*, and *meaningful* are such imprecise, value-laden words. And yet these are the very words which best capture the sense of frustration with traditional religion, which was, after all, supposed to tie the individual, community, and society together. The second and more obvious trend was the migration of thousands of people into the southern colonies during the generation before the American Revolution. They came with little or no attachment to the Anglican church and its hypothetical place in the social system, preferring communal relationships much different from those honored by local elites and provincial leaders. With these two trends complementing each other in their social impact, it is not surprising that many people should have been susceptible to the preaching of Evangelicalism.

The experience of dissenters in Hanover County, Virginia, is an excellent example of the quest for new modes of expression and meaning. In fact, the Hanover disaffection from the established church is often cited as the beginning of the Evangelical movement in the South, although it would be more accurate to see it not as the first of many events, but as an indication of an increasing malaise that was to afflict society in the southern colonies and make the Evangelical movement possible. Sometime in the late 1730s, Samuel Morris, whose occupation as bricklayer did not place him among the local gentry, began to lead a group of his neighbors in prayer and Bible study, when by law they should have been in the back pew of the church listening to the Reverend Patrick Henry. But Henry's sermons were dull and "not savouring of experimental piety"; they could not provide the ideas nor elicit the responses that Morris and his friends discovered from reading Luther's commentary on Galatians and Whitefield's sermons on repentance and conversion. Soon Morris's little group became several little groups, the very existence of which belied the presumed harmony of the community and forced Governor William Gooch to summon dissenting leaders to Williamsburg to find out who they were and what they were up to. Morris and his friends were already a little concerned about the problem, since while they knew what they were not—Anglicans—they did not know what they were. For a while they called themselves "Lutherans" because of their affinity for the great reformer's ideas. Further inquiry and a lengthy conversation with Governor Gooch, who had been raised a Presbyterian, convinced them that they were Presbyterians.[4]

The search for communal identity was just begun. The dissenters now needed to find out what Presbyterianism meant, so they asked the Evangelical Presbyterian Synod of New York to send them a pastor. In response, the synod sent a series of preachers, none of whom settled permanently in Hanover, but all of whom helped to solidify the base of Evangelicalism in one small part of Virginia. The growth of a dissenting community might have been disturbing enough in itself, but the itinerants in Hanover and in some of the German settlements in the West sometimes attacked the morality, competency, and authenticity of the established church and its clergy. The implications were only too clear to Governor Gooch and to lesser colonial officials—attacks upon established clerical authority were attacks upon all established authority. The "censoriousness" and "bigotry" of the New Light evangelists was a constant complaint of their opponents, who occasionally fined New Light leaders for nonattendance at church or simply forbade preaching by itinerants who were not attached to any licensed meetinghouse. The authorities could not abide the idea of a public leadership's being developed outside the orderly patterns prescribed by law and convention. Preachers were not authentic unless licensed by the civil authorities, argued Gooch, who demanded orderliness and proper deference in direct proportion to the increase in New Light preaching. In reply, the New Lights argued that preachers were not authentic unless they satisfied the needs of the people. And their defense of the right to follow whom they would was a stubborn refusal to defer to established authority; deference would have been tantamount to admitting that they were deviants and therefore not members of a community which rested on sound principles. They knew otherwise.

The man who brought the first impulse of Evangelicalism to maturity and made the Hanover dissenters acceptable was Samuel Davies. The young widower from Delaware was well equipped to take charge of the Evangelical community in Virginia. He was a graduate of one of the academies or "log colleges" which Evangelical Presbyterians had organized to provide pious education for potential ministers. Somewhere he must have learned diplomacy as well as Greek and Latin, for he managed to combine respectability with Evangelical independence when he came to Virginia as a New Light pastor in 1748. The first thing Davies did was to prove his responsibility by asking Governor Gooch for a license to preach in the four dissenting meetinghouses of Hanover county. The next thing he did was to prove his authenticity as a preacher of the Word by enlarging the dissenting community.

These two actions were indicative of Davies's abilities as a politician. A careful man who persistently emphasized his and his people's responsibility, he avoided confrontation with authority save through the sacrosanct procedures of the law. Since New Light itinerants had not been in the habit of requesting licenses to preach, Davies's application seemed to affirm his trustworthiness. Trust turned to suspicion, however, when authorities learned that Davies was organizing new congregations and attempting to have an assistant licensed. For a few years after his entry into Virginia, therefore, Davies found himself trying to justify the dissenting community in terms of the Act of Toleration passed by the English Parliament in 1689. Instead of denouncing the government from the pulpit, as had previous New Light preachers, he argued for the extension of the Toleration Act to Virginia and for the right of dissenters to build as many meetinghouses as they wished and to call as many pastors as they needed. The authorities viewed such

actions as potentially subversive and attempted to limit dissenting
clergymen to one pulpit each. They failed. Davies seems to have
worn his opponents down with argument, legal appeals, and
dignified behavior. Authorities would not molest responsible dissenters at worship even when the preacher directing that worship
was unlicensed. After a decade of growth, New Light Presbyterians
were begrudgingly allowed to exist without harassment from
traditionalists, thanks to the political ability of Samuel Davies.

The demand on Davies's political talents was created by his
ability to develop and lead an Evangelical community. An expression of his own talent, this ability was also an extension of his
people—as much a social function as an individual accomplishment. The Evangelical surge was a classic reform movement in the
manner by which it selected its leaders and authenticated them.
Varying in the extent and intensity of opposition to traditional
institutions, such movements nevertheless share a determination to
replace present leaders with persons more responsive to the needs of
their members and more expressive of members' wishes and
feelings. In one sense, therefore, reform movements are a return to
the primitive process of creating institutions from scratch, selecting
leaders outside formal channels, where objective standards are
established to legitimate those who measure up. Leaders of movements are selected in a more subjective fashion; chosen because
they say what the community wants to hear, and more important,
wants to say, and perhaps more important still, wants to feel. The
feelings of trust, propriety, and necessity when directed to leadership and social institutions make possible the smooth operation of
society. If people begin to feel restless about the propriety and
trustworthiness of traditional leadership, they will respond positively to persons who can articulate their uneasiness. And if those
same persons can give them a sense of doing something to
improve the situation and elevate their own sense of worth, a new
leadership emerges. Such leadership is charismatic in the sense that
it ignores the stamp of approval from formal, licensing bodies and
demands instead the mutual identification of community and
leader established through actual contact and responsiveness.
Responsiveness is measured by the dynamic life of the community
itself, its growth, activity, interest in common ventures, and
willingness to hear what the leadership has to say.

People were very willing to hear Davies, so willing in fact that his conservative opposition accused him and his fellow New Lights of seeking unwarranted power and influence. The warrant for power and influence, however, was perceived differently by establishment priests and New Light clergy. Davies's warrant, for example, came from his ability to speak directly and personally to each of his hearers in the congregation and to get them to change their lives. Two things were involved in this process: the New Light manner of preaching, and its role in developing a new community. Davies's preaching was a radical departure from the formalism of either the Anglican Church or the Old Side Presbyterians, a departure most clearly exemplified in Davies's second-person direct address to his people, with its accompanying sense of urgency. He did not preach about abstract moral principles or an abstract universe or an abstract God, but about *your* life and *your* relationship to God, who seeks *you* out of a condemned world. The *you* in Davies's mind became a *me* in the mind of many of his hearers. He preached to *me* about Christ's love for *me*, the awfulness of *my* sin and guilt, and *my* salvation through Christ's sacrifice. Davies could persuade people to "search" themselves with such intensity that they would leave themselves open to having attitudes, indeed their whole orientation, changed in a dramatic catharsis of emotions. The process through which Davies tried to lead his congregations was common to all Evangelical preaching. First "convict" the people of sin—make them so aware of their own guilt that they feel utterly helpless. This despair becomes repentance, which makes the subject susceptible to the act of faith. Faith, said Davies, presupposes " a deep sense of our undone, helpless condition," the sense of which was preliminary to the essential act of conversion which set each person on a new way of life.[5] After conversion, the thrust of Evangelical preaching was to encourage and instruct the Christian in a new life of discipline and prayer.

It might be thought that Evangelicalism, with its emphasis on personal guilt and the need for a radical decision on conversion was the religious discovery of individualism. In a sense, of course, Evangelicalism did isolate the individual from his surroundings and demand an act which would validate his entire existence; but it did not leave him alone, nor did it celebrate his isolation. It brought him immediately into a community established on rules and

regulations quite unlike those of "the world." Evangelical literature is filled with repudiations of the world and persistent affirma-
tions of the necessity of doing God's will. To do God's will one did
not simply fix his attention upon heaven, but became a part of
the Evangelical community which supported him in his daily
struggle to overcome temptation and doubts. In the act of repudiating the world and joining a new community, distinctions
between the true believer and the worldlings became very important
as others became less so. For example, whether or not a person was a
member of the gentry and had fine clothes and a position of
worldly authority was not important because these distinctions were
based on ephemeral things. Thus, when Evangelicals refused to
gamble, wear ostentatious clothing, dance, or otherwise engage in
activities that emulated those of the gentry, they were saying that
the conventional distinctions of society were not authoritative
for them. Behavior which once denoted respectability and prestige by almost universal agreement was now being attacked as
improper.

The Evangelical call to come out of the world, a call to create new
social distinctions on the basis of religious commitment, was clear
and unmistakable. Davies, diplomatic in political matters, was
quite abrupt in his distinctions between the world and the
Evangelical community, the damned and the saved. All humanity
stood before the judgment and condemnation of God as nations
and as individuals, Davies emphasized. Virginia was no exception,
for there "the generality [was] impenitent, unreformed, and
prayerless," many in "high places have been suspected of treachery
or cowardice, or at least bad conduct," and others were afflicted
with a "spirit of security, sloth, and cowardice."[6] "Our Country,"
accused Davies, "has sinned on securely for above one hundred and
fifty years; and one age has improved upon the vices of another."
Surely, he said, God must be expected to punish a nation where
"swarms of prayerless families" were scattered across the landscape,
and where there were "ignorant vicious children unrestrained and
untaught by those to whom God and nature hath entrusted their
souls." A peaceful society was no sign of God's pleasure, Davies
warned. Indeed, he attacked the conventional patterns of deference
which held his society together as "more than enough of cringing
compliance of worms to worms, of clay to clay, of guilt to guilt."[7]

Individuals' sins, too, revealed the corruption which merited God's condemnation: "insatiable desires after things below, . . . the lethargy of carnal security, . . . the fever of lust." According to Davies, more common was the apathy of people who ate no "spiritual food," or even worse, having eaten, became "nauseated."[8]

If society were pregnant with evil, were not all men children of the Devil? Only if they chose to be, said Davies, only if they refused to admit their guilt, only if they remained outside the Evangelical community. All men were justly condemned, argued Evangelicals, but some were graciously saved from paying the price of their corruption by throwing themselves on the mercies of the Lord Jesus Christ. "He that believeth in him is not condemned; but he that believeth not is condemned already." The terrible insistence on universal sin and guilt did not dictate a common fate for all men, but cast in bold relief the distinction between those who could not escape their just condemnation and those who could. The result was a radical cleavage between Evangelicals and worldlings. A person was either saved or not; there could be no middle group or lingering devotion to old ways or friends. "Break off all friendship with his enemies," commanded Davies, for Christ demanded nothing less than total commitment. The demand was a complete reorientation that began with a moral and mental crisis wherein a person almost literally broke down under the weight of his own sin. At this point, having assumed an appropriate "humility and self-abasement," Evangelicals believed that God "implants the principles of life in your souls." The culling process had begun, and through his New Birth the Evangelical had become a new man, no longer "senseless" to God, but now "*fervent in spirit*," praying, praising God, and denying himself the "trifling" pleasures of the world: sensuality, clever conversation, horse races, and extravagant display.[9] The words used to distinguish between one's pre- and and post-conversion life reveal also the distinctions between Evangelicals and worldlings. Once dead to God, they were now alive; once blind, now able to see; once lost, now found; once in rebellion against God, now contrite; once stupid and ignorant of divine things, now faithful; once condemned, now saved. To non-Evangelicals, who were content to allow life to proceed without religious intensity and felt no need to introduce more invidious distinctions into society, the Evangelical movement seemed bother-

some and pretentious. To those who believed that the emotional breakdown of the contrite sinner was as irrational as the joyous exuberance that followed it, the movement seemed to arouse the common folk dangerously. But all could agree that the Evangelical
√ community was creating a new mode of social organization.

The sense of separateness was not easily sloughed off, especially by Evangelicals themselves. Even while speaking to his people of their civic responsibilities during the French and Indian War, Davies reminded them of the difference between the rest of society and themselves. Presbyterian historians have liked to think that Davies assumed an important public role as publicist and unofficial recruitment officer during the war, but in their haste to portray him as a public figure, they ignore the fact that he spoke as the leader of a community that thought of itself as being apart from the rest of society. This is made abundantly clear by reading carefully one of his best-known sermons, "Religion and Patriotism, the Constituents of a Good Soldier." One of the means God had created for making men's salvation sure, said Davies, was to have them engage in a righteous cause, and surely everyone could agree that the British cause was righteous. But Davies separated the cause of fighting for British "liberties" from the "sinful and impenitent" country which did the fighting. And he further separated the Evangelical soldier from the sins of the country. Even if God permits the country to fail because of its corruption, he told his congregation, "be assured that you at least have done *your* part conscientiously." According to Davies, Virginia society was in rebellion against God, and it was doubtful if even "an army of saints or heroes" could "defend a guilty, impenitent people ripe for the judgment of God." Since Evangelicals could not change God's providence or judgment, Davies held that they should repent their sins, do their best, and trust in the Lord. In this moment, as in all others, Davies did not forget that his congregation was a "select company."[10] He was a loyal Britisher to be sure, and intensely patriotic, but he knew that he and his people were different from other Virginians and thankful to God for it!

The restlessness and dissatisfaction evident in Evangelical Presbyterian growth soon erupted in a more dramatic and widespread outburst of activity that made Davies and his followers appear almost respectable. The new Evangelicals were New Light or Separate Baptists from New England, whose leaders began to sift into North Carolina and Virginia in the 1750s, and who soon began to establish their own churches and create new ones. Baptists had appeared in the South earlier in the century—Charleston had had a Baptist congregation since 1695—but they were quiet, well-mannered folk who were not active proselytizers. The New Lights, however, were neither quiet nor well-behaved even by Evangelical Presbyterian standards, for they openly attacked the Anglican clergy, ordained semiliterate men as ministers, stubbornly refused to apply for licenses to preach, and valued emotional outbursts in their meetings as a sign of God's presence and favor. Through these actions, the Baptists managed to attack most of the underpinnings of colonial order. They denied the authority of the Crown to direct the moral life of the community through the Church of England, as well as the right of the Crown to legitimate religious leadership. Samuel Davies, after all, had applied for a license to preach, thus admitting the right of the civil authorities to make him do so. But Separate Baptists were not so compliant; nor were they as insistent as the well-educated Davies, who became president of the College of New Jersey, that education should be a prerequisite for ordination. Education, as the privilege of the few, was, for the Baptists, a sign of worldly but not heavenly approval. The Baptists, far more than the New Light Presbyterians, were scornful of traditional prerequisites for spiritual leadership and did their best to repudiate all traditional forms, which, in their view, shackled the common folk in their approach to the throne of Grace. The social implications were extremely important, for with the Baptists, the Evangelical movement took on momentum and with explosive and frightening clarity served notice of a major revolution.

Shubal Stearns was the first New Light Baptist leader in the South. Coming from Connecticut in 1754, he established a Separate Baptist Church at Sandy Creek in Orange County, North Carolina. The Separates were the creation of the Great Awakening in New England, where they had first been "Strict" Congregationalists, but had finally professed themselves Baptists in their quest for the pure church, a quest which was something of an obsession with them. The Separates thought they had approximated that goal, by insisting, difficult though it was to achieve, upon three distinguishing characteristics of the true Christian. First and most important, they said, the convert must have had a personal religious experience of overpowering emotions rooted in a specific time and place. So powerful were the emotions released at Separate meetings as people passed from the world into the Kingdom that they were often characterized by seizures, convulsions, and uncontrollable weeping. The preaching which brought on these responses, recalled one Baptist minister, was a "warm and pathetic address," a comment which was at the very least a masterful understatement.[11] Samuel Davies's simple but carefully prepared addresses were formal indeed when compared to the shrill harangues and chants, called the "holy whine," which were delivered to elicit emotional responses of their hearers.

The second characteristic of the converted Christian, as far as Separates were concerned, was the immersion in living water of adults who professed faith in Christ Jesus. The Bible, they argued, mentioned no other kind of baptism; the sprinkling or christening of infants was a worldly corruption which did not make a clear distinction between the converted and unconverted, since the infant could not speak for himself to affirm faith in the Christ.

A third mark of the Christian life for the Separatists was submission to the authority of the church to scrutinize carefully the personal as well as public life of each Christian. The fervency which Davies had insisted upon was of equal importance to Separates, who suspected their conservative Baptist opponents of worldliness because of their "superfluity of apparel." Separate fervency included surveillance not only of dress, but also of speech and manners, for in all things Christians were to display the glory of Christ. A cynical Anglican might have observed that such scrutiny was just as well, since Baptists had no glory or status to flaunt, nor vast fortunes to waste on expensive dress, but he would have mistaken strength for weakness. The gospel preached by Stearns and his itinerant colleagues quite clearly rejected values that made invidious distinctions between people on the basis of political power, wealth, or family background. The community created by personal experience, baptism, and discipline was a reproach to the old order and a promise of a new one.

Many people believed the promise. Within four years (1758) of his settling in North Carolina, Stearns and his itinerants had converted enough people to enable six churches to form an association on New Light principles. Still aloof were General Baptists, who tended toward free-will doctrines of Arminianism, and Regular Baptists who, although Calvinistic, were also very suspicious of emotional excesses and revivals. The response of more traditional Baptists merely meant, however, that Separates would win the field because of their persistent aggressiveness and joyful disregard of traditional procedures. Gradually they pushed to the coast and into Virginia and South Carolina, preaching to the thousands of people filling up the southern backcountry as well as to those in more established areas. To a transient population, New Lights offered orderliness through discipline and a sense of belonging through the conversion experience and baptism. To the more settled areas, Separates offered an alternative to the established church or to no church at all, for in many places they were the only religious leadership available. In both situations they offered a way of organizing people into groups that cared for them and provided guidelines for personal as well as public life.

Probably the most important aspect of the New Light Baptist movement was its radical experimentation. The very act of moving from one place to another meant that many Americans were willing to try new places, climates, crops, and modes of social organization. In the uncertainty of moving, traditional loyalties and ways of doing things were necessary, too, to provide enough security to support the travelers in their search for the promised land. The balance between tradition and innovation which formed the needs and goals of eighteenth-century southerners made the Separates important to an increasing number of people. Separates offered the comforts and supports of church life, but offered them without the encumbrances of patterns which reminded people of a highly stratified society or of unresponsive and arrogant clerical elites.

Separates' experimentation revealed a commitment to equality which, although not absolute, was certainly foreign to conventional social values. Their nine rituals which objectified and reinforced this commitment were homely but significant attacks upon the maintenance of social distance among Christians through the intimacy of physical contact and personal involvement in each other's spiritual lives. They instituted three new kinds of rites, additions to the traditional Protestant sacraments of the Lord's Supper, and baptism, to express the newness of their community. First of all, there were those symbolic acts which emphasized the community's concern for persons in special circumstances either because of age, health, or official duties undertaken on behalf of the church: devoting children to Christ, anointing the sick, and the laying on of hands. Second, there was the ritual interaction of individuals and community in expressing publicly their sense of God's love for them, a kind of testimony meeting or love feast. Third, there were the acts which reaffirmed their Christian commitment to each other: the right hand of fellowship, the kiss of charity, the washing of feet. Separates claimed scriptural warrant for their actions, but in the context of time and place, these rites were innovations and as such emphasized that the old world was cast off and that a new one was at hand. Even the short-lived radical experiment of allowing women to testify to their own religious experience in public was a significant part of the probing, questioning, and reordering that was attractive to large numbers of people.

Perhaps one of the most important, revolutionary innovations of these rituals was their use of physical contact to convey the love of Christians for one another. Separates touched each other with hands, arms, and lips, actions which were completely at odds with conventions that maintained invidious distinctions among people in part by maintaining social distance. Thus the intimacy of Baptist meetings condemned the false social ranking of the world even as it reinforced communal solidarity and conveyed the meaning of God's love for His children. With this kind of social basis, it is not surprising that the young, energetic, and illiterate preachers who berated authority should have sensed their eventual victory over the forces of the Devil and the world.

Separates did not explode into a movement of irresistible power. Although there were sometimes great bursts of activity in which large numbers were converted, the process of growth was usually slow and undramatic. No centralized agency such as Methodists later used was required; but a parallel development in all Southern Baptist churches revealed a splendid determination to create a community of love and discipline for all ranks in society. Mother churches would send out itinerants to convert a few families, who might eventually constitute a church of perhaps fifteen or twenty-five members. These churches would grow steadily over a decade or until migration or a revival in religious interest brought new converts. As their churches grew, members needed to know if they were thinking, doing, and anticipating the right things, and in order to help each other settle these and other problems, they formed associations which were soon assuming responsibility for sending out itinerants as well as for maintaining orthodoxy. And with the strength of union, Baptists began to proliferate. The "revival" in the Sandy Creek association meeting of 1785 gave courage and motivation to Separates, but they did not constitute a church in Virginia until 1760, nor did they extend their preaching efforts north of the James River until 1767. But between that date and 1774 there was an explosion which created almost fifty Separate churches. The years of itinerant preaching and visitation had interested hundreds of families in the new gospel and prepared them for a period of rapid organization. The same kind of process was at work throughout the populated South among all sorts of Baptists by the 1770s. In South Carolina, for example, three centers of Baptist activity—the Charleston, Welsh Neck, and Congaree areas—dispatched missionaries to the shifting population around them. By the early 1770s the rapid growth of New Light Baptists had seized the initiative rather rudely from Evangelical Presbyterians, making the latter almost respectable in the eyes of a concerned aristocracy.

To men anxious about social ranking, power, and stability, Baptists seemed troublesome at best and dangerous at worst. Although the gentry did not universally take direct action against the Separates, enough did so to reveal the doubts and fears which beset many traditionalists who feared their customary rule was nearing an end. Baptists broke all the canons of deferential etiquette. They did not apply for licenses from the authorities to preach. They did not take care to compliment the Bishop of London and his clergy, as had Davies. They did not mince words in attacking as immoral and illegitimate the men who represented the apostolic succession rather than the apostolic message. Their ministers attacked education, which many Baptists lacked, as a sign of gentility; rather than a valued achievement to be envied and respected, education was more often than not scorned as a proud, worldly accomplishment which stood in the way of true, Christian knowledge. The Baptists in effect excommunicated most of the ruling classes, an act which brought upon them a great deal of verbal abuse and many accusations of bigotry and fanaticism.

Because their words and acts indicated a refusal to live by inherited modes, Baptists suffered jail sentences for disturbing the peace in Virginia. In North Carolina the troops of Governor William Tryon, seeking Regulators who had recently been in rebellion against constituted authority, naturally assumed that Baptist communities were seedbeds of sedition and dispersed many of them. Unlike Davies, the Baptists were not politic; they confronted authority and sometimes refused to obey it. From their jail cells they preached to large crowds, who indicated by their presence that they, too, stood against traditional authority.

In 1774, just as Baptists were beginning to reap a spectacular harvest from years of preaching, they encountered the Methodists. Followers of John Wesley, Methodists avowed their leader's devotion to the Church of England even as they carried on a campaign which would eventually destroy the influence left to that church by the Baptists and Presbyterians. Actually, when Methodists arrived in the South they were welcomed, for a moment at least, by Devereaux Jarratt, Anglican rector of Bath parish in Dinwiddie County, Virginia. Jarratt had already shocked his parishioners into the Evangelical movement by what was for them a new, radical kind of preaching quite unlike the "cool, dispassionate manner" of his predecessor, who encouraged his parishioners, as Jarratt recalled, "to walk *in the primrose paths of a decided, sublime*, and elevated virtue."[12] The concept of virtue, exclaimed Jarratt, was "heathenish"; what his people needed was conviction of sin, conversion, and a new life in Christ. Although successful at first only with the "middle ranks" of society, he was soon able to persuade the poor to come to him for instruction, as he went to their houses to organize prayer societies. Soon he was itinerating beyond Bath parish into the border counties of Virginia and North Carolina. The fatiguing work was exhilarating, and because of the large crowds he gathered, very satisfying to his ego; but Jarratt could not satisfy the demands of his own revival.

He was limited by his own priorities, since in a choice between satisfying expressed needs of his people and his own sense of what was fitting he opted for order, deference, and propriety. All his life he had stood in awe of rank, and it is very easy to conclude from his autobiography that he entered the ministry of the establishment rather than that of the Presbyterians who converted him because he believed that being an Anglican priest would stamp him as a gentleman. Baptists, he recalled as an old man, had disrupted society; but the Methodists did worse. They accepted his aid (but not his direction), abandoned him, and enticed many of his converts into schism. He bitterly remembered Methodist preachers as ''multitudes of ignorant and inexperienced men, of all ranks and colours'' whose ''jargon,'' ''wild notions,'' and ''furious gestures'' made a mockery of religion.[13]

Thousands of people thought otherwise. They were not converted at one time in a massive outpouring of emotion, but in various bursts of activity which brought the Methodists over four thousand southern converts between about 1768 and 1776. Frustrated by the mother church's stolid refusal to support them, Methodist preachers soon began to act as priests by celebrating the sacraments. Devereaux Jarratt was aghast, and so, for the moment, was Francis Asbury, the man who more than any other person would establish American Methodism. But even as the latter herded the schismatic Virginians back into the fold, he must have known that his movement would soon break its institutional connection.

Why one group of Evangelicals yielded influence to another is not at all clear. The conventional suggestion that Methodist organization won the day is clearly inadequate, since during the first months of Methodist participation in the southern Evangelical movement, Wesleyans were little better organized than Baptists. Perhaps Methodists' style made them seem slightly less confrontational than Baptists. They did their best to avoid open conflict with authority; and even if they did not spare the Anglican priesthood for its ''cold,'' ''careless'' manner of life, they may have commended themselves to people who were ready to profess Evangelical beliefs but not ready to avow Calvinist doctrine. Perhaps Baptist doctrines seemed to many to be too harsh in their predestinarian assumptions; perhaps the Baptist belief that one could not fall from grace once one was saved ran counter to experience; perhaps immersion and adult baptism seemed to require too great a repudiation of the past; perhaps the Methodists simply preached to people that other Evangelicals had missed. For whatever reason, Methodists joined the Evangelical movement with an intensity equaled by few and surpassed by none.

Methodists provided essential elements to the Evangelical movement. If they did not sweep all other Evangelicals from the field with their efficient organization, they were soon to demonstrate to both Presbyterians and Baptists the advantages of institutional flexibility. Three major groups had regional organizations—Methodist conferences, Baptist associations, Presbyterian presbyteries—to lend support to individual churches; and both Baptists and Presbyterians had dispatched itinerant missionaries on an ad hoc basis. The Methodists demonstrated the advantage of a permanent itineracy which could provide a ministry for much greater numbers of laymen than the settled pastors of the Presbyterian churches or even the missionary plans of Baptist associations. Methodist preachers rode large circuits, preaching in houses, barns, or other denominations' churches, organizing classes to make up societies, which joined with other societies of the circuit to make up a quarterly meeting conference. The genius of the developing system was its utilization of laymen as class leaders, lay preachers, and exhorters. Baptists also developed a leadership that emphasized the grave responsibilities of the laity, but the Methodists as a lay movement within the established church were the very model of anticlericalism, and as such provided yet another way to repudiate authority, a feature which attracted many who could not bring themselves to become Baptists.

In terms of ideas, too, Methodists contributed something important to the Evangelical movement. Presbyterians and most Baptists, even when most hostile to worldly authority, were still exclusivist in their theological attachment to the doctrines of election, final perseverance of saints, and personal passivity in the work of salvation. The framework of thought which structured religious experience after a Calvinist model of strict theological reasoning was undoubtedly forbidding for many people who simply had no patience with the paradoxes, ambiguities, and abstractions of Calvinism, even when presented in a homely, semiliterate fashion.

Methodists, for example, rejected the Calvinist God who demanded strict obedience to an impossible ethic, left the sinner
without assurance of salvation all his life, and then, despite the
marks of grace he might exhibit, nonetheless consigned him to
Hell. There was no credit given for a good try. The caricature was of
course unfair to Presbyterian and Baptist theology, but it was
nevertheless the way in which many Methodists understood
Calvinism.

A God who condemned morally unconscious infants, religiously
uninformed adults, and persons struggling valiantly with sin was
not in the Methodists's view moral. Morality had to be reasonable
in the homespun philosophy of Methodist preachers, who did not
see the reasonableness or fairness of God's making persons unable
to decide to be children of God, and then condemning them for
failing to do so. If God freely offered salvation, the Methodists
argued, He could make all men able to accept it in His prevenient
grace, a formula which was twisted by uninformed but receptive
Americans into the belief that man had an active part in his own
salvation. Although not strict Arminianism, the theory did result
from John Wesley's Arminian predilections and was transformed by
the needs of people who wanted a religion to save them, rather than
one which reaffirmed the ambiguity of human existence. Consistent with this desire, Methodist doctrine offered people an endless
number of chances to receive God's grace, for although the doctrine
emphasized that a person might be assured of final salvation, it also
allowed for the real possibility of backsliding. Contradictory as
these two positions might seem, they reflected the psychological
need for ultimate reassurance and the practical experience of falling
from the state of grace, subjective realities which orthodox Calvinism could not really take seriously.

This focus on theological differences, however, is misleading. One
of the mistakes which historians have made in discussing denominationalism in the United States has been to settle on debate about
points of doctrine as a way of distinguishing between various
religious groups. In attempting to define differences between
Methodism and Calvinism within the context of Evangelicalism,
the mistake is particularly mischievous because it ignores the way in
which the two sides actually disagreed. The major distinctions
between Methodists and other Evangelicals must not be sought

within debates about doctrine, but in the relative importance to the parties involved of engaging in such debate in the first place. To emphasize doctrinal differences as a way of keeping tabs on Methodists, Baptists, and Presbyterians is to ignore the fact that throughout their history, American Methodists have been severely criticized by theologically oriented opponents and scholars for nourishing an anti-intellectual, antitheological bias. This perception proceeded from early Methodists' obvious discomfort in the heat of theological controversy. Conflict did not offend Methodists—they could fight Calvinists over institutional procedures and structures—but abstractions which detracted from practical matters such as saving souls were to be avoided, as far as the Methodists were concerned.

Baptist theological conflict in eastern North Carolina and southern Virginia during the last twenty-five years of the eighteenth century provides a case in point. Baptists had been in the area since 1729, living in relative theological tranquility until they were confronted by Separates in the 1760s. The latter raised the issue of regeneration and grace, Christian commitment, and baptism within a biblical and theological context, and the end result was a decision among all contending parties that baptism was valid only if administered to adults who had had an experience of the saving power of Jesus Christ. In other words, Separates won the debate. Baptists who were unsure as to whether or not they had had such an experience were persuaded to be receptive to an authentic work of God; and when they were able to convince others that they had been overpowered by the Holy Spirit and could testify to an experience of grace, they were rebaptized.[14] The entire debate was conducted on a solid theological platform. The community of believers, their relation to each other, and their hope for the future had been defined by theological symbols familiar to the participants, if not to outsiders.

Methodists never engaged in such prolonged theological discussion. They seemed to have attracted people who found the endless controversy over who we are, what we shall be, and what we believe a lot of nonsense. What they found to be much more significant than this endless self-definition was self-expression. Those who were susceptible to Methodist preaching were apparently people who had very little interest in the tight, closed communities of Baptists. They wanted to participate in a meaningful and secure Christian life, to be sure, and if they had a quarrel with Baptists' theology, it was superseded by their even more intense distaste for Baptists' interest in theology as the rigid definition of community. The most obvious difference between the two sects, the practice of baptism, displays the two styles in conflict. Baptists would not and could not sanction infant baptism, a stand which Methodists believed to border on unreasonable and stubborn bigotry. A preference for total adult immersion Methodists could have understood; but in their view, insistence upon it verged on hysterical fanaticism. Conversely, the Methodist practice of baptizing anyone at anytime in his life with as much water as was necessary—a moist hand, a pitcher, or a river—was to Baptists a sign of the intellectual and theological anarchy of their Methodist brethren. Methodists were more pragmatic, less demanding in their requirements to define the self theologically, more open to communion with other Christians, less harsh in their view of the place of infants in the social system. Francis Asbury summed up the early Methodist view on theological debate in his journal: "Matters which are the least disputed in religion are the most essential; and those who are most fond of controverted trifles have the least real religion."[15]

Admittedly this attitude betokens a theological position. Theological structure was acceptable to Methodists if you were interested in that sort of thing, but for them it was not the most important aspect of Christian thought. More important was whether or not you had had an experience of the saving power of Jesus Christ and had become committed to experimental Christianity. If you had done this, or had had this happen to you—Methodists could put the matter either way with no embarrassment—Methodists were willing to admit, quite apart from doctrine, that you were a Christian. Such an attitude infuriated Baptists on one side and scandalized Presbyterians on the other. Whereas these two denominations disagreed with each other and among themselves over theological issues, Methodists did not spend one-tenth the time in ferreting out theological error. They engaged in semihumorous taunting of Calvinist pretension and contradictions, to be sure, and occasionally wrote a tract against Calvinism or imported one from

England. But this activity usually took place in an area where theological controversy was a traditional, cultural rite of definition, such as in New England.

Within the Methodist fold itself, discussions were over politics (power within the church) and morality (slaveholding and drinking). On that rare occasion when a Methodist minister appeared to be preaching heretical doctrine, his clerical brethren would investigate the charges—always vague—and point out to their erring brother where he was wrong. In reply, he would usually blurt out something compliant, such as "I'm sorry. I'll be happy to say the right thing because nothing should get in the way of the Mission."[16] If on the other hand he had been charged with insubordination or slaveholding, the fight would have been drawn out and bitter. Methodists did not batter each other about theology, as did Baptists and Presbyterians; they had better things to do, such as saving the world and "reforming the nation." This was an ideological position which distinguished them from Calvinists, to be sure, but it was arrived at not by embracing theological definition as much as by avoiding it.

Distinctive as the three Evangelical churches were, they were part of the same general movement, and their members were very much alike. But just who these people were and why they burst into the public life of the skeptical, rationalist, empiricist southern colonies of the eighteenth century are difficult questions to answer. The first place to look for evidence is in the cluster of ideas, values, and appeals—the ideology—which attracted them to Evangelicalism. By far the most significant aspect of Evangelical ideology was its demand for a radical conversion experience to set Evangelicals off as a separate community. Entry into the community was initiated by a moral crisis of profound, ego-shattering repentance, an acknowledgment of justly condemned sin and guilt for past associations and loyalties, which might have included dancing, horse racing, levity, and the desire to wear ostentatious clothing. Spiritual biographies of young Evangelicals record painful struggles to subdue sensual pleasures which, as they confessed it, aped fashionable society and affirmed the superiority of the aristocracy and its invidious distinctions of rank and status. Such standards of conduct were not, Evangelicals maintained, appropriate for the children of God; but they did not rest the matter merely on behavior. They challenged the most cherished values of the aristocracy, especially the hegemony of reason and its stewards, the educated elites. The conversion experience rested not on one's reason or that of the minister, nor upon assent to doctrines affirmed either by nature or revelation, but in the immediate intuition of God's will and in complete surrender to it. In that moment, the wisdom of men, the ranking of society, and the superiority of the wise were confounded, and one left the world to join the people of God. "Disallowed indeed of men," preached Asbury's itinerants, "but chosen of God, and precious."[17]

In that one phrase was revealed the resentment and aspiration of people who defined themselves as being above conventional social distinctions. To be important to God, one did not have to possess wit, learning, wealth, family connections, or even a white skin. Although wealthy people became converts, and neither race nor class nor sexual distinctions were universally eradicated among Evangelicals, previous social distinctions were consciously demeaned and often rejected in the actions and values of the movement. The conversion experience through which one entered the community was itself a rejection of reason and learning and the high status with which these otherwise highly valued qualities were identified. The postconversion life of holiness introduced a new standard by which to judge people, one more appealing than that supported by social convention. The old distinction of family and class was rejected for the new distinction of piety and morality. In the world, people were judged by whether or not they were respectable or vulgar. In the Evangelical community the words persisted, but they took on a new meaning interpreted in moral rather than social terms. *Respectable* came to mean "pious" or "moral," rather than "capable of eliciting respect by reason of social rank"; and *vulgar* came to mean "impious" or "immoral," rather than indicating commonness or "low social rank." All men and women were not equal in the Evangelical view of the world, but they could be made equal through rejecting conventional canons and accepting Evangelicalism.

Aside from ideology, there were other clues as to who Evangelicals were. Their aristocratic opponents often described them as

uneducated rabble who were ruled by passion rather than reason
and were therefore dangerous. Baptist refusals to apply to the state
for licenses to preach, and persistent Evangelical attacks upon
Anglican clergymen cast the former in the role of incendiaries at
worst and hypocrites at best. The charge of hypocrisy, often hurled,
probably was an expression of resentment at the effrontery of
people who, at least according to the aristocracy, pretended to be
better than they actually were in social as well as in moral terms. In
the gentry's view, Evangelicals were disruptive, ill-mannered
people who simply did not know their place. But this view was not
that of the gentry alone. Often those at the lower ranges of society
attacked Evangelicals with brickbats, stones, and curses, as if these
passionate and aggressive religious folk were as much a threat to the
peace and well-being of the lower classes as they were perceived to
be to the aristocracy. Why this should have been true is something
of a mystery, unless Evangelical attempts to set themselves off from
others of their own class and background appeared to push the latter
even farther down the scale of power, status, and prestige. The
charges of censoriousness and bigotry, leveled almost universally
against Evangelicals, were the angry responses of people who had
been attacked as being beyond the pale of social and moral
acceptability; they reveal a deep and bitter resentment against those
who were perceived as setting themselves off as special—worse, as
superior—to other people. This Evangelical self-aggrandizement,
seemingly so presumptuous and disruptive to the gentry, must have
been particularly galling to people who could not dismiss Evangelical claims on the basis of a superior education or social standing.

Evangelicals also tell us something about themselves in their
memoirs and church records. Their memoirs recall parents who
were neither wealthy nor desperately poor—certainly not the
rabble. They were hardworking and sometimes successful enough
to own rather large farms and a few slaves. They were often a
restless lot, however, and many moved several times in their search
for a stable, secure, and rewarding life. They were usually not
members of the gentry, but there is often a defensiveness in their
children's memoirs that marks a people who think that they have not
been valued as highly by society as they ought to have been.
Evangelical preachers often identified themselves and their congre-

gations as "poor" people whose value was not truly appreciated by the gentry, but their poverty was perceived in relation to the wealthy, with whom they wished to be identified, and not to the landless, unambitious folk who in the Evangelicals' view had no aspirations whatsover. Francis Asbury, the ubiquitous founder of American Methodism, revealed a ferocious pride in his low status and that of his circuit riders, while at the same time expressing a deep resentment at the gentry's hostility and aloofness, which he attributed to class consciousness. But he had time to jot down such thoughts because he was a frequent guest in the homes of slaveholding Methodists; and although he bitterly regretted Methodists' involvement in human bondage, he was as proud of his coreligionists' material prosperity as he had once been of their low estate. Baptists were very much like their Wesleyan friends, urging each other to bring their servants to worship and encourage their conversion and submission to gospel discipline.

Who, then, were these "poor" people, some of whom owned slaves, most of whom owned farms, and all of whom dramatically repudiated the world for a new life in Christ's community? They were independent folk who had been successful enough to resent the invidiousness of the distinction between them and the aristocracy, but humble enough to take certain stubborn pride in the inadequacy of traditional social distinctions to define them. They were moving not only through space (to better farms) and time (to a better status) but also through eternity, that is, to a community which replaced the traditional ethic with a new one. Whichever aspect of movement one emphasizes, these people were moving away from old social ties to new ones. The fact that a majority of white members were women and that blacks were converted in such great numbers, at least by comparison with past membership, strengthens the impression that Evangelicalism attracted people who were dissatisfied with conventional society. Both women and blacks were consciously appealed to: "God," they were told, "is no respecter of persons." And both groups were assigned a higher status within the Evangelical community than elsewhere. Christian testimony, discipline, and love theoretically knew no bounds, and in the early stages of movements, theory reigns supreme.

Evangelicalism therefore was a means through which a rising

''new'' class sought authentication outside the archaic social hierarchy. It is tempting to say that Evangelicals were the middle class,
developing consciousness through the historical process. But the
word *middle* represents a certain intellectual confusion, since it
connotes position between either up and down or left and right; it
therefore does not quite represent Evangelicals' anger with the
social system or repudiation of it, or their emphasis upon the New
Birth. They were trying to replace class distinctions based on wealth
and status—they called it worldly honor—with nonclass distinctions based on ideological and moral purity. They tried, if they did
not succeed, to go outside the social system by rejecting its claims
upon them. Their ideology emphasized their radical but nonpolitical perception: it was radical for its rejection of traditional
authority and deferential habits; it was nonpolitical in its rejection
of political means to attain authenticity and influence. And it was
attractive enough to create a new community which would help to
create the South. Whatever name we give to this process, therefore,
it produced a new social reality.

2

"To Set in Order the Things that are Wanting"

Evangelicalism has often been thought of as the religious mood of individualism. The idea of community, which celebrated fraternal bonds and social responsibility, seems foreign to the Evangelical ideal of the free individual's wrestling with the demons of his own soul until set free by a mighty surge of the will. The sense of community which seemed so powerful among the converts of Samuel Davies, Shubal Stearns, and Francis Asbury is seen as ephemeral in the conventional view, suppressed as it was by the subjective tyranny of the conversion experience. Furthermore, the traditional view holds that the individualism sparked by the elemental and emotional transfiguration of personal loyalties was strengthened by the subsequent life of personal struggle between conscience and the world. The private war with oneself presumably allowed no time for creating and sustaining an openness to the tragedies, needs, and hopes of other people. Thus locked into an overriding concern with self, the convert was supposedly further disabled from developing a sense of community by the institutional arrangements of his religion. In the conventional view, the rejection of an established church is seen as preventing the convert from realizing the intimate relationship between religion and the social order and thus the civic responsibilities to which a Christian was rightfully called. The primacy of local churches over national bodies presumably reinforced this tendency, as did the competitive proselytization of his sect, which set him against people with whom he should have been compatible.

This traditional view is quite accurate up to a point. It deftly exposes the individualistic implications of Evangelical thought, for no one can fail to be impressed and perhaps a little startled at the intense introspection, subjectivism, and voluntarism of faithful Evangelicals. Equally characteristic of such people, however, was their insistence on initiating the individual into a permanent, intimate relationship with other people who shared the same experience and views of the meaning of life and who were committed to the goal of converting the rest of society. The polarity of "community" and the "individual" simply did not exist for Evangelicals. But polarity did exist between the beloved community and the rest of the world, and it was very important for the religious to keep the contrast in mind. The distinction was be-between true believers, who were united in the bonds of love, and worldlings, who were "senseless" to divine things and "careless" for their own lives. Evangelicals' personal letters, sermons, tracts, and diaries leave the ineradicable impression that these people were obsessed not only with living a holy life in a close, personal relationship with God, but also with replacing the disorder of the world with the order of "Christian society."

To appreciate fully the communal character of Evangelicalism, it is necessary to remember who Evangelicals were and what they did and said. When their words are understood against the background of their actions, it is easier to see the way in which the Evangelical community became so important, for words often mean very little unless one knows who is speaking them and why.

If the hypothesis of the first chapter is correct, Evangelicals were people who for one reason or the other were dissatisfied with traditional modes of authority and behavior, modes which were affirmed by inherited religious institutions and identified with the elites of a relatively stratified society. Although a few genteel men and women entered their ranks, Evangelicals were, for the most part, honest, hardworking folk, who aspired to become more esteemed by their fellows than they had been, but who had neither the family connections nor the wealth to enable them to do so. This is not to ascribe to them ulterior motives nor to cast any doubt at all on the sincerity and depth of their faith, but to suggest why they were more likely to be converted than people who had already achieved or inherited an enviable place in society. Indeed, the integrity of their faith may be indicated in part by the fact that they did not attempt to scramble up the social ladder so much as to replace traditional standards of ascribing personal worth with other measurements—those of the Evangelical religion.

That they did not develop a sophisticated social ethic immediately was probably as much a function of their social position as it was an extension of an individualistic ideology. In social and intellectual limbo by reason of their relatively low social standing, Evangelicals were not terribly concerned with maintaining, in customary ways and for customary reasons, the solidarity of the larger society. Had they lived in New England, where Evangelicalism had a generic identity with a theory of civic responsibility, their ethic might have contained the seeds of a more organic social ideal. The Puritans who founded New England had bequeathed a legacy of social responsibility in the form of covenants, by which people bound themselves together by oath and declaration. Church, town, and colony all assumed an organic identity in which the individual was constantly reminded of social responsibility and in which he was linked with his fellows for better or for worse in God's providental design. Evangelicals in New England could never really slough off the corporateness bound so tightly by ideas, the simple existence of towns, and the relative power of the churches. Southern Evangelicals inherited neither institutions nor ideas to facilitate the development of a social ethic. In the southern colonies, social solidarity was justified not in the religious and secular extensions of the covenant theology, but in the pretensions of a flaccid Anglicanism and the weak, decaying shell of a ramshackle establishment.

As people at odds with a social system that demeaned or ignored them, Evangelicals could not be expected to subordinate the individual to the larger society, which had in many ways already trampled him in the dust. Instead they placed him in a community which cared about him, for in the Evangelical view, care was the one thing in which society was most deficient. Social and geographical distance isolated individuals in the eighteenth-century South. Social rank was maintained by a cool formality between classes, an ascending elegance of dress, and such niceties as special pews in parish churches. Geographical isolation of the scattered

population helped to reinforce the feeling of being alone and
uncared for. It is not surprising, therefore, that Evangelicals
rejected society—they called it "the world"—and redefined social
relationships in terms of social intimacy, mutual respect, and
communal discipline. Intimacy was most dramatically expressed by
the many ways in which Evangelicals touched each other, offering
the right hand of fellowship almost universally. They often prayed
through personal crises with their arms around each other, and
some greeted their brothers and sisters in Christ with a kiss. Many
Baptists even washed each others' feet. Perhaps even more intimate
than ritualistic touching, however, was public confession of sin and
sharing with others the deepest, most private thoughts about
oneself and his relationships with other people and with God.
Under such conditions, the great social distance valued by the world
could not be sustained, at least within the communion of the
faithful.

   To guarantee the nonworldly character of interpersonal relationships, Evangelicals submitted to a loving discipline. Indeed, *order*
and *discipline* were probably the most universally applicable words
which Evangelicals used to describe the Christian life. That the
subject of discipline was the individual there is little doubt; a
member was expected to restrain his natural tendency to lust after
the careless pleasures of the world. But he was not expected to fight
against "the World, the Devil, and Tom Paine"—apathy, evil,
and infidelity—all by himself. If preoccuaption with private
morality helped to support a "theology of individualism," the
convert's submission to "the edification, comfort, loving instruction, watchful care, and faithful admonitions of fellow-members"
helped to support the bonds of communality. Church records of the
early Evangelical movement without exception reveal a people
unwilling to accept the idea of a solitary Christian. Indeed,
Evangelicals believed that the individual if left alone was likely to
lapse too easily into worldly association; friendships with the
unregenerate (non-Evangelicals) would likely undermine his frail
loyalty to eternal things. The Evangelical community confirmed the
importance of the individual convert by offering him compassionate fellowship with people who, like himself, needed help and
guidance. In the Evangelical view, the "world" did not care what
one did, and therefore did not care for people with the intensity

and persistence which most Evangelicals wanted. To be sure, discipline was not always welcomed, but members saw it as preferable to the chaos from which thousands had been saved.

"Watchful care" over members was concerned with both the private and public, personal and collective aspects of life. It is admittedly difficult to determine whether discipline should be thought of as focusing on the individual or community; but the view most faithful to the Evangelicals themselves would emphasize a persistent concern with the social character of private acts in which community and individual each had a stake. So important was this √ concern that disciplinary cases were part of the regular life of the church from the very beginning of the Evangelical movement. Solemnly, church members would meet at stated intervals to do, as Baptists at Mattrimony church put it, "the work of the lord and to set in order the things that are wanton."[1] The invocation was not quite scriptural, since the original verse (Titus 1:5) required the apostle to set in order the things that were "wanting," but the North Carolina Baptists knew better than anyone else what they were up against. Whether wanton or wanting, the world was a disorderly place, and Evangelicals were called out of it to establish proper social relations. The establishment of these relations required, first of all, strict inquiry into behavior which affected only individuals, and second, careful surveillance of antisocial behavior which threatened to disrupt the community or to give it a bad name.

The scrutiny of individuals was by all accounts a serious and scrupulously precise procedure. Each denomination published various guides to church discipline—Methodists, the *Doctrines and Discipline*; Presbyterians, the *Book of Discipline*, following the Westminister Standard. Baptists printed various forms of discipline, which differed very little from association to association or even from those of other denominations. To be sure, Baptists did not recognize a judicatory higher than the local church, but even communions organized with an ascending hierarchy from the local church to national assembly believed discipline was essentially the responsibility of local congregations. This fact meant that Evangelicals were called to account by people who knew them well and who were concerned, as Presbyterians said, "for edification not for destruction."[2] To this end, the church as a redemptive community scrutinized conduct with great caution, allowing the accused every opportunity to demonstrate either innocence or repentance. Representative offenses identified most readily were swearing, lying, gambling, and attending races, circuses, theatres, or dances. By far the most popular form of misconduct was intemperance.

Even behavior which seems within one context to be primarily of concern to individuals had social implications. Evangelicals believed that actions of church members represented the seriousness and devotion of the entire fellowship, so when one Christian relaxed his struggle with the world, he brought disgrace upon all his fellows. For the Evangelicals, there could be no such thing as behavior which was of only private concern; a Christian's every action was social and therefore under the jurisdiction of the church. Some actions, however, were viewed as being more explicitly antisocial than others. Attending a horse race, for example, only ''wounded'' the reputation of the Evangelical community by evoking charges of ''hypocrisy,'' but the bonds of communal solidarity were actually weakened by other activities. Evangelicals were painfully aware of this, for the very few data available to historians suggest that the most frequent cases of discipline dealt with threats to social order. Among these were nonattendance at worship, which weakened the sense of communal identity, and actions which disturbed the harmony of the group by pitting members against each other— slander, assault, fraud, litigiousness, ''sowing dissension.'' In the Evangelical view, the disruption of family life was by far the greatest threat to community order. From the beginning of the Evangelical movement, preachers emphasized that the family was the foundation of Christian piety, knowledge, and solidarity. Crimes against the family were therefore very serious because, to the Evangelicals, fornication, adultery, and marital squabbles were indicative not merely of private failings but of disregard for the good order of the community as well. Nothing was more symbolic of the conjunction of private and social morality in Evangelicalism than sexual misconduct because it elevated license above order, temporal pleasure above eternal commitment, and individual gratification above communal responsibility.

In the struggle against disorder, Evangelicals were constantly on their guard. To be sure, the number of people formally tried,

acquitted, censured, or excommunicated in each church at any time
was very small, but the process of scrutiny and discipline was known
to every person associated with the church, whether a member or
not, and its impact was not limited to a few malcontents or
recidivists. A careful scrutiny of church records in one area and a
survey of other records throughout the South reveals that discipline
could include any member of the church, a deacon at odds with a
brother over a land transaction, as well as a woman who drank too
much or a man who failed to come to communion. Parties who
were confused and upset by personal or family disputes could
submit themselves to the discipline of the church; individuals
whose private sins gnawed at their consciences and alienated them
from their fellows could confess without being accused, knowing
that by doing so they would free themselves of guilt and be
reconciled to God, the community, and themselves. The greatest
number of cases appear to have been initiated by a member's
asking officials of the church to investigate a possible breach of
Christian order. In response, a committee would determine the
facts and request the accused to answer to the community if inquiry
revealed possible guilt, or publicize the accused's innocence if the
evidence absolved him.

At times it was possible for the entire church to be directly
engaged in a case of discipline, but such affairs were not witch-
hunts or psychological riots. Through at least the first quarter of the
nineteenth century, the dignity, fairness, and probity of these
investigations were remarkable. And although practices among
them varied, committees appear to have been essentially friendly to
the accused. Some churches made it a point to assign committees of
the same sex, and a few even allowed investigating committees of
the same race, although most inquiries into the behavior of black
people were conducted by whites. In these as well as in all other
cases, however, discipline was intended to be educational, for
penalties were designed to keep persons once converted within the
sphere of the church. The severity of the penalty was therefore
dependent upon the gravity of the offense and the attitude of the
offender, and ranged from reproof, censure, and probation to
expulsion. But even those who were excommunicated—Baptists
used the word more than Methodists—were brought back into the

church upon evidence of sincere repentance, a restitution Evangelicals worked very hard to achieve.[3]

Discipline was intended to keep people within a caring community and not to drive them out, and was, therefore, designed to be part of the life of every church member. Each case brought to the attention of the church, each step in the process of inquiry, each confrontation between Gospel order and worldly disorder had a meaning for all church members, who participated vicariously in this ritual reaffirmation of group solidarity and the Evangelical resolve to push back the world. The ritual reminded Evangelicals that there were boundaries beyond which they could not go and still remain true to the community. Supported by exhortation, preaching, and prayer, the ritual of communal discipline was universal, reported in every extant southern Evangelical church record for the years 1760 through 1860. The meaning of these patterns of discipline, with their recurring cycles of intensity, is not yet totally clear. But Evangelicals did leave an unmistakable reminder that each person was so important that he or she could not be left alone in sin; both the eternal salvation of the individual and the integrity of the community were at stake.

The disciplinary process, when contrasted with the explosive quality of the conversion experience, presents the paradox of restraint and expressiveness. Each person shed the old life in a cleansing paroxysm of grief, shame, and relief, which cast him into a new life of orderly submission to Christ. The paradox did not end with the rite of initiation, however, for in the Evangelical view, Christian life was ideally expressed in a joyful exuberance that gave new meaning to the concept of discipline. Believers' tears—which were so important to Evangelical preachers as a sign of God's presence—were seen as expressions not merely of contrition and grief, but also as expressions of joy in the discovery of meaning, security, love, and hope. Restraint and release also characterized the general expansion of southern Evangelicalism, which seemed to take place in surges or phases—that of the Presbyterians (1740s), the Baptists (1750s and 1760s), and the Methodists (1770s). But the American Revolution diverted attention to more concrete enemies than Satan and sin, so that even as roving preachers continued to serve their Lord, they were disturbed by what seemed to be the

uncharacteristic restraint of the Holy Spirit. After the British threat
was gone, however, Evangelicals once again reported great numbers
of converts; by 1792—the earliest year for which an informed
estimate of the religious population is possible—Evangelicals
accounted for the majority of professing Christians in southern
states.

Conventional estimates as to the proportion of church members
in the general population usually range between 8 and 10 percent,
but the figures are too low. The most active Evangelicals—
Methodists and Baptists—boasted a total of 89,600 southern
members; 12,000 were black Methodists and 38,000 were white.
The division of Baptists between white and black is impossible to
ascertain; and Presbyterians reported no membership estimates in
1792, although they did record 55 southern preachers and over 55
vacant churches. A high estimate of membership for the three
Evangelical churches would be set at about 125,000, with no more
than 25,000 black members. The latter figure is inflated because it
is based on the assumption that other churches were only slightly
less effective than Methodists in preaching to blacks. An equally
generous estimate of remaining denominations at 25,000 members,
most of whom would be white, allows for a figure of 150,000 white
church members in the South in 1792 among a total white
population of 1,140,000. Church members, however, were almost
always over sixteen years of age, as were about 550,000 whites. Thus
the conventional estimate that fewer than 10 percent of the people
were church members is rather misleading. Clearly 27 percent of
the adult, white population were church members and most (83
percent) were Evangelicals. Of the total black population, probably
about 3 percent were church members, and once again most were
Evangelicals. The meaning of these figures for understanding the
total impact of the southern Evangelical movement is unclear, even
assuming the figures are correct, because the quality of the
relationship between church members and nonmembers is largely a
matter of conjecture. To take one obvious example: southern
women outnumbered men in the churches (65 : 35), though men
outnumbered women in the general population (51.5 : 48.5). This
fact may mean that the percentage of families represented in the
Evangelical community has to be revised upward. The sentimental
memories of later Evangelicals about their pious mothers may

reflect accurately the general influence of female church members who taught their children values which were not entirely scorned by worldly husbands. If we do not know the precise impact, therefore, we do know that the Evangelical movement had in a generation become a major force in southern life.

To describe Evangelicalism as a "force" is to attempt to be true to its enigmatic quality and its unquestionable power to shape people's lives individually and collectively. As participants in an expansive movement, Evangelicals valued the volatility of rapid and emotion-laden recruitment as a sign of divine favor. They therefore tried to achieve the impossible—to institutionalize the dynamic quality of their origins, the time when Shubal Stearns and Francis Asbury had first dispatched missionaries to the perishing people of the southern colonies. During that period, preaching seemed to have been a supernatural gift, for through evocative cadences and tender appeals "the Lord had poured out His Spirit" over and over again in special seasons or in general outbursts of conversion. In private homes, taverns, meetinghouses, and courthouses, Baptist and Methodist itinerants carried on a constant battle with Satan and the world, even when they were blessed by only a few converts here and there. The preachers' work was difficult, exacting thousands of hours on horseback in heat and cold, dust and mud, and with just enough opposition—they called it persecution—to reinforce their identification with the New Testament apostles. The foundations of southern Evangelicalism were not laid out with the dramatic suddenness of great revivals driving down gigantic piles upon which to build the church. Rather the base was built by laying many bricks, carefully aligned by prayer, and cemented with the mortar of discipline and "pathetic preaching." But because the excitement and drama of revivals was so vivid and evocative, it was the revival which enabled the original Evangelicals to convey the emotional power of their faith to the generations which followed them.

As they worked their way throughout the post-Revolutionary South, preachers were encouraged by local outbursts of great religious intensity. In a few areas whole families were converted, in others a few important individuals; and there were usually reports of the renewing of old commitments, the recapturing of "vital

piety.'' Acceleration of Evangelical tempo increased steadily until
in the period from 1785 to 1792 revivals burst their local boundaries;
Methodists enjoyed dramatic gains on the Delmarva peninsula;
Baptists and Presbyterians celebrated the pouring out of the spirit
in central Virginia and central North Carolina; and Baptists built 29
new churches (total 96) in South Carolina during the 1790s, as over
a hundred thousand people rushed into the state. But by the
middle of the decade, ministers began to complain of declension:
they themselves seemed to be "dried up"; the people were silent,
and God seemed to have withdrawn His spirit from them.

It was characteristic of Evangelicals that they should have been
frustrated and despondent at the apparent dissipation of the Spirit.
Their strength as special emissaries of Christ depended, in their
view, on their ability to move people, to excite old believers and to
convert new ones by their restless, ceaseless activity. Against the
background of the mid-1790s, when the clergy began to encounter
multiple editions of Thomas Paine's deistic *Age of Reason*, to hear
that anti-Christian French prejudices had filtered into America,
and to confront unpleasant schismatics, Evangelical anxiety seems
understandable. In their uneasiness, clergymen resembled many of
their fellow countrymen, who were concerned not so much about
piety as about the Alien and Sedition Acts, the Kentucky and
Virginia Resolves, and Federalist-imposed taxes. As Republicans
tried to solve their problems by assaulting Federalists, Evangelicals
tried to solve theirs by preaching a revival. The previous sporadic
local revivals had been works of the Spirit, they believed, but they
began to reason that if they prayed enough and encouraged each
other enough, God might possibly revive the work which the
faithlessness of His people had caused to founder. Somehow,
something they did hit a responsive chord. Revival activity began to
emanate from the woods of central Kentucky in 1799 until in the
summer of 1801 at Cane Ridge in Logan County there was a Great
Revival.

No one has ever really satisfactorily explained the Great Revival.
Historians have observed that institutions (churches) conducive to
such behavior were available, and that a belief system (Evangelicalism) shared by large numbers of people shaped responses by
explaining events and feelings in a meaningful way. Sometimes

scholars have tried to explain the phenomenon as a response of Evangelicals to real and imagined enemies, but why these enemies (Deism, infidelity, apathy) should have become so imminent a threat to clergy in 1801, and whether or not the laity really shared their leaders' anxieties are still unexplained puzzles. That a great many people seized the opportunity to slough off uncertainty, isolation, and despair and to commit or recommit themselves to the Evangelical community is clear. That the contagion of revival spread from Kentucky back to the heavily evangelized areas from Virginia to Georgia, where there was considerable movement of population, is also clear. Perhaps the work of the clergy in trying to stir renewed religious activity finally paid off. Or perhaps an accelerating emotional intensity induced by the disruptions of political life and population volatility had reached some sort of critical mass. For whatever reason, the Kentucky revival of 1801 was followed by a surge of Evangelical activity on both sides of the southern highlands. Religious life became marked by highly emotional meetings frequently characterized by hysterical behavior; and new converts—most of them probably youthful—joined the movement if not in great hordes, at least in delightfully immodest numbers. A precise measure of Evangelical resurgence is impossible, but the Methodists as unofficial statisticians of the movement, or at least their own part in it, reported significant gains. From its pre-revival point in 1796, membership, as reported by circuit riders, reached 46,000 southern members in 1801, 55,000 in 1803, 68,000 in 1805, and 80,000 in 1807.[4] Other denominations were as pleased as the Methodists with their own accomplishments.

The Great Kentucky Revival became a symbol of Evangelical unity and power. Throughout the United States, even into the strongholds of New England orthodoxy, spread reports that between ten thousand and twenty thousand people of the three Evangelical sects had been engaged in religious exercises for many weeks during the late summer of 1801. Great numbers of people were affected by strange seizures of uncontrollable weeping, fainting, groaning, and "barking." Evangelicals had witnessed such spectacular phenomena before, but never in such magnitude. Crowds of from five thousand to twelve thousand people began to appear in various areas of the South, brought to the preaching by news of the events in Kentucky

and eager to participate in the same kind of ecstatic behavior. In
their susceptibility to the contagion, people in the Carolinas,
Virginia, and Georgia demonstrated the almost universal familiarity
of Evangelical ideas. Southerners knew how to respond to the
evocative, very personal preaching of Evangelicals, and they knew
how to interpret what had happened to them.

There were three important results of the revival. The first was its
shattering of Presbyterian unity. The heady sense of direct contact
with God impelled a few Presbyterian clergymen into activities that
conservatives deemed irregular; a relaxation of ministerial qualifications and an almost methodistical affinity for emotional, revivalistic
preaching was deemed especially so. The result was the creation in
1801 of the Kentucky-based Cumberland Presbyterian church,
whose members were more oriented to revivals than were their
orthodox brethern. Other Evangelicals were so taken with the spirit
of unity demonstrated during the revival that they followed two
clergymen, Richard McNemar and Barton Warren Stone, in gradual
deviation from Calvinistic principles, and in a subsequent search for
more inclusive, more universally "Christian" standards of brotherhood. The result was not unity, but a merging of McNemar's
followers with the Shakers and the development by Stone of the
"Christian" denomination. A second, much more important result
of the revival was the affirmation by Evangelicals of their common
values. Denominational differences were not repudiated of course,
but the unity of Evangelicals against the world was seen as
transcending sectarian differences. To be sure, Presbyterians
remained a little aloof from the "enthusiasm" of Baptists and
Methodists, who were thought to be theologically and educa-
tionally a little sloppy, but the revival demonstrated that what
united them all was more important than what divided them. The
third result was the institutionalization of revivalism in the camp
meeting. The idea for the camp meeting was inherent in Methodist
quarterly meeting conferences and Baptist associational meetings,
where members and clergy convened to do the business of their
appropriate jurisdictions and sometimes remained to hear a brief
flurry of preaching. But neither this custom nor that of open-air
preaching by itinerants led directly to the camp meeting. The
institution was first employed by managers of one of the outbursts

at Gasper River, Kentucky, which preceded the Cane Ridge revival by over a year. Curious people for miles around prepared to encamp near Gasper River, for days if need be, in order to find that one moment when they felt the presence of the Holy Spirit. Many found exactly what they came for. To would-be revivalists, the moral was clear, and it is not surprising that the Cane Ridge revival was well publicized in advance and prepared for as an encampment.

The results of this kind of religious promotion were so impressive that many Evangelicals believed they had found a way to keep alive the emotional intensity and sense of power that had always been their ideal, but which had eluded them during the 1790s. For awhile Presbyterians, Baptists, and Methodists cooperated in sponsoring camp meetings on both slopes of the Appalachians, but eventually the more conservative Presbyterians and the jealously independent Baptists withdrew, leaving the institution to the Methodists. The importance of this innovation and of similar activities among the Baptists was that it provided for a regular, scheduled meeting at which one could expect the revival impulse of the past to be reenacted and young people initiated into the mysteries of religious conversion and the responsibilities of becoming full members of the Evangelical community.

That the revival impulse should have been formalized is not surprising, for from the first expansion of their movement, Evangelicals had been trying to bring order and structure, as well as a sense of participation, to religious life. The Methodists developed their church through the movement process itself, although they had John Wesley's British organization upon which to model their own. As Anglican lay people, Methodists at first needed simply to establish orderly patterns of itineracy for their preachers and to ensure a regular life of worship and fellowship in "classes" of about fifteen people; several combined classes constituted a "society." After the establishment of an independent national church in 1784, Methodists developed a series of conferences at the local, regional, and national levels. Methodist organization was designed for the easiest and most efficient assignment of manpower in developing new groups and rested almost solely upon the preachers, who chaired the quarterly meeting conferences and were the only members of the annual and general conferences that directed the

denomination's business. Presbyterian organization included
laymen in important roles, and was based not on missionary
exigencies so much as on scriptural exegesis via Edinburgh and
Westminster. Seven southern presbyteries had been shaped in
forty years of careful expansion, and in 1788 they helped to form
the Presbyterian Church in the United States of America. Two
synods coordinated and guided the southern churches. Baptists,
too, developed regional institutions. As the Charleston (South
Carolina) Baptist association pointed out in 1794, discipline for
the communion of saints was paralleled by discipline for the
communion of churches. Skittish though they were about sur-
rendering local autonomy, Baptists reminded each other that they
were independent in power, not communion, and like other
Evangelicals banded together to secure the truth, order, and
discipline of the Gospel.[5]

Evangelical goals of unity, order, and expansion dictated the
functions of ecclesiastical bodies superior to local churches. As
Evangelical activity increased, the ideal of the communion of
churches developed into that of a disciplined "people" or
denomination. The latter word has been given special meaning as a
purposive, goal-oriented organization bereft of a sense of history by
its Biblicism, loosened from its ancient moorings by disestablishment, purged of intellectual rigor by revivalism, and driven by its
own logic into a fierce competition with other denominations. This
characterization, while true enough at one level of analysis, ignores
the essential process at work in the South, where denominational
development was first of all integrative. The most dramatic instance
of integration was the union of Virginia Separates and the more
orthodox Regular Baptists in 1787 under a general committee;
usually, however, the process was more gradual.

Associations, presbyteries, and conferences made possible the
forging of local, sometimes isolated churches into networks through
which flowed information, definitive regulations, interpretations,
and suggestions which helped to shape the thinking and behavior
of individuals and congregations. Local churches were frequently
unsure as to the standards of behavior (could a man marry his dead
brother's wife?) and doctrine (was salvation a matter of works,
grace, or a combination of the two?). Wishing to be orderly,

curious congregations appealed to the community of churches for clarification. The communication between churches and regional bodies was almost continuous, for Evangelicals were an articulate, or perhaps a garrulous lot. Associations, synods, and conferences regularly issued pastoral guidance on personal behavior, doctrine, procedure, and social issues, such as slaveholding. These groups also judged qualifications of ministerial candidates, provided vacant churches with preachers, and acted as courts of appeal. But above all, regional bodies acted to provide Christian solidarity—peace, harmony, unity, love, and reconciliation—or as the Georgia Baptist association suggested in 1814: *"Be perfect, be of good comfort, be of one mind, live in peace, and the God of love and peace shall be with you."*[6]

To a population which moved about in great surges from the Revolution to the Civil War, the regional associations were essential. Frequently the only sense of continuity possessed by a migrant people was that which was provided by the local church; but for the church to fulfill this need for continuity it had to be like the one its new members had left behind. The guarantee was in the denominational structure. Sometimes people from such diverse localities were thrown together that churches were compelled to consult several associations, as did the Baptist Bethel Association (South Carolina) in 1790, in order to establish standards of doctrine and practice. Methodists and Presbyterians avoided Baptist confusion, but all denominations tried to maintain a definite group identity among their people. There was no way for members of a congregation to be purposive until those members were sure who they were.

If the process of forging denominations from local congregations was integrative, it was also restrictive. For if Baptists asked associations to explain the breadth of Baptist practice and belief, they also asked what made them different from Presbyterians and Methodists. The sense of belonging to a group of people, which transcended local loyalties and experience, was circumscribed by boundaries of doctrine, practice, and persuasion that made loyalties seem more real. The need to belong to a disciplined community required definitive statements and practices. Historians may dismiss many differences between denominations as having been minor, and indeed they were in many respects, but there were also important distinctions that helped to anchor the lives of many southerners.

Communion only with one's fellows, or prayer only with those bearing tickets to class meetings, sealed the bonds of fellowship and was not, as the Georgia Baptist association emphasized in 1821, an indication of ill will toward other Evangelicals but instead was an indication of a "conscientious regard for propriety and truth."[7] Consider the Methodists, whose clergymen argued the need for developing strict rules lest the world observe that "Methodists are no different from other people." Methodists were indeed different and therefore important.

The competition resulting from this insistence upon separateness was sometimes rancorous and embarrassing to coreligionists, but it was also useful. It focused attention on the attractive qualities of each church and may have spurred people to actions in which they might otherwise not have engaged. As the result of charges from other Evangelicals that Baptists knew nothing of the scriptures or their "mother tongue, much less the original languages," one Baptist group in North Carolina urged the building of academies.[8] Methodists were often shamed into greater intellectual rigor by Presbyterian learning, and Presbyterians occasionally preached fervently because of Methodist successes. At one time, Baptist associations in Virginia, North Carolina, and Georgia even followed the example of their Wesleyan competitors and assigned itinerants to spread their Gospel where there were no regular clergymen and too few Baptists to constitute a church.[9] But such measures were only temporary expedients. Generally, competition made the sects more sensitive to their uniqueness, an awareness that facilitated coopera-tion with other denominations, since individually these denomina-tions had become confident that they knew who they were.

In their dual, almost paradoxical role as integrative and restrictive institutions, denominations supplanted the religious establishment even before passage of acts which dismantled it. Although support for Baptist and Methodist ministers was more problematic than that for Presbyterians, each group managed to carry on important pastoral and missionary work quite apart from state support. By the time of the American Revolution, the Evangelical movement had demonstrated that the coerciveness of the southern establishment was more a legal fiction than a reality and more a nuisance than an obstacle, a nuisance that was remarkably easy to suffer, avoid, or ignore, as circumstances dictated. With the Revolution upon them, state legislators, most of whom were not Evangelicals, were faced with the task of defining the proper relations between civil authority and religion. Their solution was disestablishment. In 1776 and 1777 North Carolina and Georgia guaranteed by constitutional provision that no person would be required by law to support a particular church. South Carolina tried through a "general assessment" to provide state support for all Christian denominations in 1778, but by 1790 had given up the idea for complete disestablishment.

Virginia was the focus of a great debate about the place of religion in society and the responsibility of the state to support it. The issues were discussed for over a decade after Virginia burgesses in 1776 stripped the establishment of its tax support and began the relatively slow process of giving dissenting ministers the same rights and powers as Anglican priests. Only in 1786 did the Virginia legislature finally separate church and state. In the debates accompanying these decisions, the three Evangelical groups revealed three different ways of facing the problem. For the most part, Baptists were unalterably opposed to any form of establishment in which the state supported any or all forms of Christianity. Religion, stated the Baptists, would not die out if civil authority removed its patronage; the idea that it would was based neither on Evangelical experience nor "in Scripture, on Reason, on Sound Policy; but is repugnant to each of them."[10] Methodists asked for the continuation of establishment in 1776 while they were still Anglicans, but later appear to have taken no stand on the issue, persisting in the apolitical bias inherited from John Wesley. Conservative Presbyterians, however, were ready to consider a general assessment plan in which tax income would be distributed among the Christian churches. The premise behind this view was that religion restrained the violent passions and "vicious practices" of men and, by educating the "moral sense," ensured a respect for law without which a republic could not endure. Religion enforced obligation and duty and, according to conservative Presbyterians, by making people satisfied with their station, lessened the likelihood of class warfare. "Preserve religion," pleaded a Presbyterian authority, and "stem that torrent of vice which threatens to break in upon us and to blast all those sanguine hopes, which animated us to do and

suffer so much in the cause of freedom."[11] But most Evangelicals—
even among the Presbyterians—apparently believed religion should
be preserved without state support, following James Madison's
logic that the support of all could too easily become the exclusive
support of one. The legislature finally agreed and in 1785 passed
the bill establishing religious freedom which became law the next
year.

Disestablishment did not alter the development of the Evangelical churches because in a very real sense it did not affect them.
Having already developed their institutional structure and rules of
behavior, they were not waiting with hat in hand to receive the
bounty of the state. Their power—already "established"—did not
rest upon law but upon their ability to fulfill important social
functions for their communicants. Evangelicals knew that religion
could play its vital role in society as guarantor of the people's
morality and public responsibility without the help of the state.
Indeed, most Evangelicals believed state support unnecessary,
irrelevant, and possibly dangerous. They felt that religious authority
should be based on the authenticity given it through the conversion
of true believers and the devotion of those believers to the holy life.
Evangelicals knew—and had themselves demonstrated—that
institutions which attempted to function by enforcing obligations
and belief from the top down would eventually be supplanted in a
free society by institutions operating on quite another principle.

The principle created a process of social integration based on the
self-discipline of people in religious groups which assigned great
value to them as persons. The principle has been called "voluntaryism" by nineteenth-century publicists and twentiety-century
scholars, who have emphasized its incipient individualism as well as
its repudiation of state support for religion. But the word *voluntary*,
while it reflects a later democratic tendency to celebrate individual
freedom, does not capture the element of social participation and
fellowship which lured people into the southern Evangelical movement. Nor does the concept incorporate the impact of the networks
of discipline and communications which projected social relations
and obligations beyond the will of the individual into the community, society, and next generation. The strength of the inte-
grating process lay in the way in which Evangelicals made institu-

tions responsive to the needs and hopes of people. The key concept is "participation," for the convert was offered a chance to participate with God in his own salvation; he was required to participate with his fellows in the disciplined life of the Christian community; and he was expected to participate with persons of other localities in strengthening the life of the denomination. Disestablishment did not provide participation or a sense of brotherhood within the Evangelical communions; those qualities, already provided by the movement, were quite independent of state action.

Explaining who early southern Evangelicals were and what they did has helped set the framework for understanding what they said. An enterprising and mobile people who disciplined themselves and their neighbors, built denominations, and converted thousands of people, Evangelicals also had a great many things to say. Often contradicting themselves as well as each other, and rarely as systematic or rigorous as historians would like them to have been, Evangelicals developed a view of the world which affected, although it did not completely dominate, all southerners. The discussion which follows is not based upon formal theological or religious concepts extracted from their social context, but is, rather, an exposition of ideas which characterized Evangelicals' thought about themselves and their relation to the world—not their *theology*, but their *ideology*. Never completed and frequently changing, this ideology was not a set of propositions, but a cluster of anxieties, perceptions, values, and aspirations which emanated from Evangelicals' social situation, personal experiences, and formal thought.

In 1805, a Presbyterian clergyman wrote to a northern associate asking for help against the upstart Methodists in his area. Send us, he pleaded, a "young man of *popular talents, Great Piety*, & a *strong voice*."[12] The latter was especially important to impress crowds, but all four qualifications were essential: *youth* to be strong and attractive enough to do the work and win people his age; *popularity* to evoke positive responses from all sorts of people; *piety* to commend himself as an example, and a *strong voice* to forge popular appeal and personal piety into an instrument of conversion. Nothing was said about intellect because logical argument and brilliant insight counted for very little in the final struggle for men's souls. They were important in explaining or interpreting holy writ to the converted, but worse than useless in bringing people to that complete breakdown of personal pride and self-possession which preceded conversion and commitment to a holy life. And since these two acts were the primary marks of Evangelicalism, that genre of preaching was valued which made them possible.

The conversion experience was the basis of Evangelical thought about man and God and was conceived of as both an act and an experience. As an experience, it began when the preacher of strong voice and great piety created a self-awareness afflicted by a sense of unworthiness and guilt until the tension became almost unbearable. At this point in the process the sinner felt "lost," out of control of his life, totally at the mercy of a righteous God who in all justice should condemn him. The tears and groans which Evangelical preachers reported—sometimes as indications of their success—were the natural expression of people in great personal anguish. Brought to this point by an intuitive comprehension which transcended reason but which was utterly realistic even, perhaps, to the point of affecting his body, the "converted Sinner" was ready to make his decision. And at this state of the process, the conversion experience became an act. As the person "under conviction" began to see Christ as his Mediator, One who made it possible for him to be reconciled to himself and God and who could save him from the aimless life of a sinner, he threw himself on God's mercy and in that moment was made acceptable to Him. Since the sinner's acceptablility to a righteous God was in terms of his being made just through Christ's intercession, he was said to have been justified.

Inherent in the conversion experience was the nagging problem of legitimacy—was the experience a work of God or a contrivance of man? The question was not mere speculation to conservatives of the Calvinist tradition, who wished to avoid attributing to God what appeared to them to be a rejection of good order, religious instruction, and scriptural authority. They wanted men to have a saving knowledge of Christ, of course, but they distrusted emotional shortcuts which they believed elevated man in the drama of salvation. The holy and sovereign God had elected His people from before the foundation of the earth, they believed; Christ had been sent to die for them and He would claim them as He would. Nothing humans could do—even with a strong voice and great piety—could affect Him. Equally adamant were those who believed that the universe was a rational order which one came to understand through the accumulation of knowledge and not in the immediate and intuitive perception of "truth." If rationalists admitted a God in their world view, they cast Him as aloof from His creation and certainly not so involved with it as to cause the hysteria which sometimes accompanied Evangelical conversion. In reply, Evangelicals repudiated the limitation of essential knowledge to a mere handful of people set aside either by intellect or a vengeful God. The life in Christ was free to all men, they insisted, and as good empiricists offered the proof of their own experience.

The proof was also in the act. Convicted of sin, repentant and eager to flee his wretched state, the sinner decided to follow Christ. Responsibility for the act was his from the first perception of his condition through repentance to commitment—or so Evangelicals seemed to say. To theologically informed people, this view dangerously directed attention from God's sovereign providence to man's voluntary response, the result being to make the individual's subjective experience and action the most important parts of conversion. But Arminian and Calvinist alike began the Evangelical movement determined to keep God's grace as the context within which men made their decisions. And Elder John Leland, who was so influential among Virginia Baptists immediately after the Revolution, saw arguments over the paradox as needless, since in his view, both Predestinarian and Arminian were correct. "I conclude," he wrote, "that the *eternal purposes* of God, and *freedom of the human will*, are both truths. . . . The preaching that has been most profitable to men, is *the doctrine of sovereign grace in the salvation of souls, mixed with a little of what is called Arminianism.*"[13] Try as they might, Evangelicals could not sustain the paradox any better than their critics had expected them to, and it became resolved in favor of the commonsense belief in man's ability to repent and commit himself to Christ. The question of legitimacy was therefore settled in a very pragmatic way by allowing the individual to judge his own experience in the act of commitment.

The danger of allowing the convert to evaluate his own experience and acts was obvious. Christians of all eras had dealt with Antinomians, who believed themselves free to act in any way they chose. Evangelicals—*especially* Evangelicals—would have none of this, for the second mark of their faith was a firm commitment to personal holiness. This way of life was described by various terms: some preferred "personal holiness"; others referred to "experimental piety," or "experimental" or "practical" Christianity. Some, especially Methodists, spoke of "going on to Christian perfection," and others, especially Baptists and Presbyterians, thought of "making their calling and election sure." Whatever the terminology, the attitude and values were almost universally the same and were based on traditional Christian belief that a sanctified life (sanctification) followed justification.

Evangelicals have often been thought of as possessing no symbols with which to communicate sacred, transcendent reality to humanity. They possessed no liturgy to guide the faithful through a reenactment of the resurrection of Christ Jesus. They have also been accused of having had very little appreciation of the sacramental qualities of communion and baptism in which common, ordinary objects of God's creation become channels of His grace. And to some, their aesthetic sensitivity has seemed to have been allowed to die aborning. So inclined to think in concrete, pragmatic terms were they, that they resolved the paradox of God's gift and man's receptivity in the conversion experience in a simple, rude voluntarism. If Evangelicals did not have traditional symbols to communicate God to man, they nevertheless required some way to represent Him, to communicate His being, and to show at the very least what He was like in human terms. For Evangelicals, that function was filled by the sanctified believer. Once converted, Christians received an infusion of God's holiness, "His own moral nature," into their hearts so that they could be said to be like God. Or if not like Him, at least capable through a power not their own to direct other people's thoughts to Him. The persistent use in Evangelical literature of sanctified persons as indicators of God's mercy, grace, and will is evidence of the importance attached to personal holiness as a means to guide men to Christ. Indeed, the very use of the word *holiness* to describe the Christian life indicates the seriousness with which Evangelicals viewed it, and how they related it to the very being of God. For the concept of the "holy" in most cultures refers to the awesome, terrifying, ego-shattering sense of being in the presence of mysterious, divine power.

For the Evangelicals, self-discipline was the key to personal holiness. Preachers preached it, churches demanded it, tracts described it, mothers urged it upon their absent children in intensely pious letters, and sons and daughters dutifully admitted its claims upon them in reply. The holy life was a constant and relentless struggle which, in Evangelical theory at least, consumed all available energy in restraining the dangerous passions of frail, unsteady "flesh." Human sexuality especially became a persistent and terrifying personal problem for Evangelicals, as they lashed themselves in a spiritual masochism of restraint and self-denial. Natural responses and desires became for them an ominous threat of hell-fire, as the forces of good and evil fought for possession of their immortal souls. Often the more they fought against forbidden thoughts, the more fascinated by them they became, so that there was almost a sensual enjoyment in contemplating the evil with which one fought. William McKendree, who would one day be a Methodist bishop, was one who wrestled mightily with himself about the matter:[14]

Therefore avoid the allurements of Voluptuousness, and fly every temptation that leads to her banquet as you would the devil himself. Oh how she spreads her board with delicacies. Her wine sparkles, her dainties invite, her Mirth charms. Which opens a door to more dangers. Enemies from within rise and join those without to betray. Lascivious love stands in her bower. She spreads her temptations & begins to court their regard. Her limbs are soft and delicate; her attire loose & inviting, wantonness sparkles in her eyes. She woos with her looks and by the smoothness of her tongue endeavors to deceive.

To escape great temptations it was thought best to win victories over small ones. Every action—indeed every attitude—was to be carefully dissected in the perpetual chastisement of the unruly and sinful self. So intense and obsessive could this self-scrutiny become,

that even innocent but expressive behavior would consign the
would-be saint to his own private, Protestant confessional—his
diary—with plaintive words of guilt: "O how unbecoming for a
Christian, especially a preacher, to laugh ... O Lord, give me
more grace, more holiness of heart and purity of intention."[15]

Such restraint was surely the reduction of Evangelicalism to an
absurdity, but through the antebellum period, thousands of true
believers measured themselves and each other by the injunction
"Be ye soberminded." The solemnity of life was a persistent theme
in Evangelical literature, since each act was part of the work of
salvation, each attitude a reflection of God's love, each moment an
anticipation of eternity. The Evangelical clergyman who reminded
his congregation "*to endeavor to live in preparation for death*" was
therefore not being morbid, but insistent upon the ultimate
seriousness with which each day should be faced.[16] "Act now," he
was saying, "as if every moment were the measure of your entire
life." In such a profoundly resolute commitment there was no place
for expansive unrepressed celebration of self in careless diversions,
witty conversation, or lighthearted dancing.

If this dour view of early nineteenth-century Evangelicals
resembled that of seventeenth-century English reformers, it is not
surprising, for southern children of both Calvinist and Arminian
traditions read as a guide to holy living the works of the great
Puritan divine, Richard Baxter. They were especially attached to
The Saints' Everlasting Rest, which in its various abridgments was
one of the most popular religious books in the antebellum South.
The title was deceptive and not to modern eyes very restful, for as
Baxter himself explained, the book was to guide "a person in
motion seeking rest." That the final achievement of life's restless
pilgrimage was paradoxically a gift of God did not detract from the
necessity of unremitting labor in His service, a labor which Baxter
hoped to elicit by describing the torments of the damned and the
ecstasy of the blessed.

Because of these graphic intimations of eternity, it is tempting to
label Baxter and his southern devotees as otherworldly, but such a
term borders on nonsense when viewed in the context of what
Evangelicals expected of their faith. The purpose of Baxter's book
was to create in the believer an attitude of total devotion; its

obsession was the relationship between the individual and God. Although clearly expected to be part of a loving fellowship, the saints were exhorted in this popular tract to perfect their personal lives. A social approach to the throne of grace before conversion was impossible; each person came alone to God through Jesus Christ. This meant that there could be no legitimate communal life until after conversion. Consequently, the inner psychic life of the believer was Baxter's chief concern, and no matter in what situation the believer found himself, his primary responsibility was to cultivate the proper attitude. "Afflictions," for example, were not to be avoided or fled but "sanctified" to the useful contemplation of their meaning for the soul's ultimate salvation and endured for disciplining the body and strengthening the will. If arrogance was deplored, so was a "man pleasing disposition." If the wealthy and powerful were admonished for pride, the poor and powerless were warned against envy. "Are we inferiors? how prone to grudge at others' preeminence! and to bring their actions to the bar of judgment." Each person was to respond to the social context within which he lived not by changing institutions, but by changing himself. Social responsibilities were properly seen, therefore, as the perfection of present relationships for the edification and salvation of people with whom the Christian came into contact. It was argued by Baxter and believed by thousands of southern Evangelicals that the most acceptable way for a Christian to affect the world was through pious example. Reproving "lazy professors of religion," Baxter prodded the faithful to "violent and laborious striving for salvation." "I charge thee that art a Christian," he wrote, "in my Master's name, to consider and resolve the question, 'What manner of persons ought we to be in all holy conversation and godliness?' And let thy life answer the question as well as thy tongue."[17]

By following Baxter in elevating personal example as the standard of social ethics, southern Evangelicals directed the attention of anyone who wished to be a moral, socially responsible person to their own lives. The Evangelicals' self-absorption of vigilant self-discipline was compounded by the knowledge that one was also responsible for other people's attitudes and actions by being a good influence upon them. Thus was the sphere of moral action confined to what an individual could do within the context of a given situation. Moderns may be disturbed by the Evangelical abhorrence of the world and by their inability to identify institutions and power relationships as appropriate objects of reformation, but it must be remembered that while the individual believer fought the world within the sphere of personal influence and power, he theoretically fled the world in those matters that were not under his control. It requires more intellectual and political sophistication than most Evangelicals possessed to project successfully one's personal experience with right and wrong into abstractions such as power, justice, and right, and in turn evaluate the impact of institutions upon persons through these abstractions. And yet, Evangelicals attempted just such a transformation of personal into social ethics.

The means was the communal bond. If they did not write or speak much about social responsibility, Evangelicals did act to create a disciplined community of true believers—that much is surely clear. The bondedness of the community inhered in the acts of worship, open confession of sins, public testimonials of conversion experiences, and communal disciplining of deviants. Although all these acts save one (worship) were essentially those of individuals before the beloved community, they served to maintain social solidarity, rather than support personal independence. Boundaries between worldlings and Christians were reinforced by calling attention to them in public preaching, theological debate, and disciplinary action. The sense of mutual dependency which these acts developed in their cumulative effect was articulated by the language of Evangelical piety—which made all men brothers and all women sisters—and supported by the common flight from the world. Thus, in the command to love the neighbor and the demand to obey the Lord there were opportunities to create a social ethic which could affect institutions and power relationships. Opportunity does not mean necessity, however, and for Evangelicals there were two basic matters to be resolved before a mature social ethic could be developed. They had to decide just how far out of the world they wished to come, and how that distance would be determined by the tendency to locate moral struggle in the inner life of the believer where, theoretically at least, the will was supreme.

The best way to see how Evangelicals decided these matters is to follow them through the process by which they came to terms with slavery in America. That institution presented a dramatic and embarrassing challenge to a movement which offered a moral alternative to the world, but which also was uncertain as to the ranking of priorities when accelerating expansion, personal piety, subjective experience, and human equality become too volatile to be maintained in suspension.

At the beginning of the southern Evangelical movement, of course, the potential conflict of priorities was not apparent. Evangelicals were too much impressed by the spectacular reversal of Africans' attitude toward Christianity—a change from indifference to a joyful spontaneity that commanded in return a positive response from whites. Samuel Davies urged fellow Presbyterians to give servants religious instructions as members of their households, and New Light Baptists encouraged masters to bring their servants to meeting, in order to lift them out of degradation and despair to salvation and hope. Among all Evangelicals, however, Methodist circuit riders were the most aggressive in seeking out Africans, who were often more responsive to the evocative Methodist preaching than were whites. In considering the condition of their exotic changes, Methodist preachers revealed a sentimental but compelling sensitivity to the "sons and daughters of oppression," "poor distressed Africans," "the poor Negroes," "the poor Africans." As self-appointed preachers to the poor in both England and this country, Methodists were well prepared to undertake a special mission to people who symbolized poverty itself, preaching especially to black people, giving them special instruction, and attempting to make the proclamation of Christian liberty as vivid and real as they possibly could.

This inclusion of a pariah class in almost every Evangelical community is especially remarkable if one takes into account the deep antipathy of white Americans to the color, culture, and status of blacks. At a time when one of Virginia's leading men—author of the Declaration of Independence, a person who represented the acme of political sophistication—believed that blacks could never be incorporated into society, white Evangelicals were trying to do precisely that.

One can only guess why these people, who have so often been accused of bigotry and mindless emotionalism, should have been willing to bring blacks closer to themselves. Perhaps the disorder they sought to overcome by communal and self-discipline was so evident in the lives of blacks that Evangelicals knew they could not control themselves unless they also controlled their slaves. The Africans' alien culture, their lack of Christian matrimony, self-consciousness, and self-discipline may well have served as a constant challenge to be overcome. Conversion of blacks may also have been a way of asserting the superiority of Evangelicalism as an ideology designed to provide social cohesiveness in a careless and disorderly world—a superiority demonstrated by orderliness of converted black people. For whatever reason, Evangelicals acted contrary to traditional modes of public intercourse between the two races, and broke down the social distance between blacks and whites, just as they had among white converts. The impulse was not revolutionary egalitarianism, to be sure, but it did offer blacks a means of establishing their claim upon the Christian care, respect, and love of their newfound comrades.

As with whites, the conversion experience had egalitarian implications for Africans because it was the portal of a new life offered freely to all people. The testimony of all persons had to be listened to; the religious perception of all persons had to be examined; the inner lives of all persons had to be valued. Members did not have to know theology, or the Bible, or the precious mysteries of reading and writing in order to be acceptable. They did not even have to be male and white to be powerful in the Lord. A period of instruction after conviction would provide new Christians with all the knowledge and attractiveness required to enter the new life. Entry into a community as valued persons, once closed to the illiterate and poor because of their ignorance, was now made possible through the desire to reject the past, a desire which knew neither rank nor race.

The stern moral rectitude of the Evangelical ethic and the conversion experience of zealous Africans somehow became a prelude to ardent emancipationism—at least for some extraordinary people. By extension of personal experience into the historical process, the act of redirecting one's private destiny in the ways of holiness became for a prophetic few an attack upon slavery. Indeed, historians have argued that the rise of Evangelicalism in the English-speaking world was in large part responsible for the destruction of slavery, and the conventional historical explanation of northern abolitionism in the 1830s has been its association with a recrudescent Evangelicalism that transformed private anguish over ✓sin into public expiation and social reform. The vanguard of Evangelical opposition to slavery in the New World were actually pietists—members of the Society of Friends, whose quietism distinguished them from the aggressive proselytization of Evangelicals. Quaker leadership in the generation before the American Revolution grafted opposition to slaveholding onto the main branch of their ideology. The remarkable John Woolman spent the latter part of his life nourishing this transformation, and Francis Asbury, who wanted John Wesley's Methodists to be as distinctively and rigorously pure as George Fox's Friends, admired Woolman's accomplishment as one to be emulated by his small, energetic band of preachers. The little Methodist leader had already been affected by the manner in which blacks generously displayed their religious sensibility. "God," he wrote in the words of St. Peter, "is no respecter of persons" (Acts 10:34). He also read John Wesley's *Thoughts upon Slavery*, in which the English leader—also impressed by Quaker example—condemned slaveholding as "villainy" which violated "all the laws of Justice, Mercy, and Truth." And Asbury must have been deeply affected by the impressive conversion experience of one of his chief assistants, Freeborn Garrettson, who renounced his inheritance, emancipated his slaves, and began to preach against the system under which he had been raised to comfortable manhood.[18]

By 1780, Methodist preachers could begin to transform the views of Woolman, Garrettson, Wesley, and Asbury into definite rules. In that year a conference of preachers ordered circuit riders to free their slaves and advised all Methodists to follow their example. The reason given was that slavery was "contrary to the laws of God, man, and nature, and hurtful to society, contrary to the dictates of conscience and pure religion." In 1784 the Methodists went even further. Sharing with other Americans a sense of expectancy, as if the providential moment had arrived when a new order was to be

created in the New World, and hoping to create a new kind of pure
church from the wreckage of Anglicanism and the promise of
revival, Methodist preachers brashly attempted to do in one bold
stroke what Quakers had taken over a generation to achieve by
debate and communal pressure. They promised to excommunicate
all Methodists not freeing their slaves within two years. A noble
gesture, perhaps, and one reflecting a commendable view of blacks'
just claims upon the twice-born, but it also reflected the preachers'
overconfidence in the consistency of Methodists' repudiation of
the world and the power of moral exhortation to bring about social
revolution. Even so, the moral position was one shared by other
Evangelicals who prayed for "final abolition" (Presbyterians 1787)[19]
because, as Baptists said in 1789, slavery was "a violent deprivation
of the rights of nature and inconsistent with a republican
government."[20]

   The move against slaveholding was a brave extension of the
Evangelical ethos beyond the internal life of the believer into social
relationships. The thesis that Evangelicalism in its essential
character was concerned only with individual piety is not very
plausible, given the generation of debate over slavery from the
Revolution to the great western migration after the War of 1812.
Discussion began as soon as action was taken against slaveholding.
The Methodist regulation of 1784 almost shattered the infant
church, creating such dissention that within six months the act of
excommunication was rescinded in favor of the less confrontational
policy of education and moral suasion. Despite this setback,
antislavery Evangelicals continued to hope for the kind of pure
church envisioned by the most sanguine Methodists, who could
never quite slough off their admiration for Quakers. A few seemed
unable to escape the moral torment of the evil that their preachers
deplored. "When I consider," wrote one slaveholding farmer,
"that these people [Africans] of their forefathers were born as free
as my Self & that they are held in bondage by compulsion
only . . . , when I consider that they are human creatures Indeed
with Immortal Souls capable of Everlasting happiness or liable to
Everlasing misery as well as our Selves, . . . It fills my mind with
horror & detestation."[21] In Methodist quarterly meeting conferences, Presbyterian sessions, and Baptist church conferences the

debate went on, not in the measured eloquence of the slaveholding author of the Declaration of Independence, but in the angry and frustrating search for biblical texts, the bitter tears of fraternal controversy when the logic of words exceeded the bounds of Christian affection, the anguished passion of an illiterate preacher crying out: "O blood, blood ... America: blood and oppression will be thy overthrow!!"[22]

Why and how the Evangelical world view gave rise to such ferment are not easy questions. Many of the answers lie in the personal psychology of a few people whose creative and moral energies, unleashed by the mysterious trauma of conversion, settled upon slaveholding as symbolic of evil itself, even when equally pious neighbors failed to agree. But there are nevertheless important connections between Evangelicalism and anxiety about slavery, especially the commitment to an active life of stern self-discipline and personal holiness. A demonstration of one's conversion, this commitment in most Evangelical literature borders on a radical moral heroism which, had it been taken seriously, would have had social results. Individuals could not brood over moral failings and eternal obligations without including perforce their relationships with other people. They could not devise plans for individual self-improvement—such as Garrettson's freeing his slaves—without suggesting those plans to others who had been brought to the same mental state by conversion. Evangelicals had an almost fanatic faith in the power of a good example.

The black was thrust dramatically into the individual and collective meditation about the moral life because he was at once alike and unlike his white brethren. He was like them in his conversion; this was evident in the experience which blacks professed and which whites—according to almost every surviving local church record in the South—accepted as authentic signs of God's grace and blacks' humanity. This last matter is very important because the conversion experience, which whites believed had elevated all believers to a common level, could not be denied all its egalitarian implications for blacks, despite racial stereotypes, anxieties, and fears. Furthermore, the conjunction of the slaves' despised position and their perfervid response to Evangelical preaching made the apostolic promise into an impera-

tive that the "oppressed go free." To preachers who explained
themselves in almost Romantic terms as bringing release to the
captives, the connection was easy to make. All too soon would come
the distinction between spiritual and civil oppression and release,
but for one valiant moment blacks and a few whites appear to have
seen and heard the same thing.

The two people also shared, theoretically at least, a commitment
to moral responsibility, a posture symbolized by their common
conversion. As partisans of the view that all persons were morally
accountable for their actions, and as stern disciplinarians of themselves as well as others, white Evangelicals could not easily ignore
the moral dilemma into which Christian slaves were cast by a system
which could place Evangelical blacks under worldly masters.
Although it is doubtful that empathy for slaves was widespread
among white Evangelicals, the latter group was very much aware of
the destructive impact of slavery upon the bastion of Evangelical
morality, the family. In fact, it may have been the moral contradictions revealed so dramatically in attempts by local churches to
honor and give security to the Christian slave family that first led
Evangelicals to oppose slaveholding. The dilemmas which Evangelicals faced, however, did not allow them to waver in their belief
that slaves were and should be treated as morally responsible
human beings. This belief allowed a few Evangelicals to come to
the conclusion that any human authority which claimed—as did
slaveholders—to be absolute was illegitimate.

What was allowed by Evangelical theory, however, was not
necessarily demanded. Despite their similarities to white Evangelicals, blacks were also very much *unlike* their white coreligionists.
The cultural determinants of white ethnocentrism combined with
the blacks' skin color, broken English, deviant behavior, and exotic
appearance to reinforce distinctions between white and black. The
whites' belief that blacks' sexuality was far greater than their own
and that the license of such libidinous creatures had to be controlled
no doubt heightened whites' perception of African distinctiveness
and inferiority. White Evangelicals were especially aware of the all
too alluring wiles of voluptuousness, as we have seen; and they
easily perceived in the undisciplined, disorderly black man the
demon which possessed themselves. By projecting upon Africans

72 Chapter 2Chapter 2

their own internal disorder and then bringing blacks under discipline, they brought greater order to society, subduing the sensuality of both blacks and whites. In thus confronting the slaves' voluptuousness, they were forced to ask what made it possible. The presence of mulattoes as well as other evidence told them to scrutinize the master-slave relationship in order to deal with this grave problem.[23]

Natural as the unfolding of antislavery sentiment from Evangelicalism may appear, it took place in a ferment of ideas which gave the emancipationist vision a compelling forcefulness. It is virtually impossible to understand the swift spread of antislavery ideas even among Evangelicals without taking into account what Bernard Bailyn has called the "contagion of liberty." The debate and war with Great Britain produced in every rebellious province a few articulate persons who felt acutely the inconsistency of fighting against the slavery with which British power intended to shackle Americans while at the same time keeping Africans in the "vilest" form of bondage. As a result, Evangelicals as well as coalitions of more politically active groups began to make the War for Independence into a revolution. The first public attacks upon slavery made by formal Evangelical bodies are very instructive on this point, for they did not condemn slavery as un-Christian or sinful, but as "contrary to the laws of God, man, and nature," "a violent deprivation of the rights of nature and inconsistent with a republican government." Evangelicals did not, let it be noted, rest their appeal on the basis of Evangelical morality, but on the principles of the American Revolution: natural rights, God-given rights, the rights of man, and that government—*republican* government—which best safeguarded those rights. These were principles which Evangelicals shared with other Americans and not ideals which set them apart as Evangelicals in conflict with the world.

To be sure, Evangelicals also argued that slavery was contrary to the teaching of "pure religion." In page after page, sermon after sermon, rule after rule, southern Evangelicals proclaimed the "horrid evil," "the crying evil," the "enormous evil" of African slavery. Days of humiliation and prayer were announced, letters were written, pronouncements were trumpeted, petitions were

signed, and pamphlets sold or given away in an effort to drive the
cruel system from the land. In many ways the argument, with its four
basic themes, was very simple. The first was that slavery was unjust,
having deprived Africans of the same kind of liberty for which
white republicans had just fought. The crime against blacks was
especially to be deplored, since they had done nothing at all to
deserve such cruel exploitation. Innocent victims of immoral men,
they had been denied the rights of gaining property, assuming
moral responsibility, and protecting themselves from the masters'
power. If slaves were victimized, however, Evangelicals argued that
masters were no less damaged by owning slaves, for their position
encouraged sexual indulgence, arrogant claims to special privilege,
and legitimation of the idea that the strong might exploit the weak.
This corruption of both masters and slaves suffused the whole of
society by sapping "the foundations of moral and consequently
political virtue."[24] It weakened the faith of honest men in
governors, who hypocritically pretended to protect the rights of
some men even as they denied the rights of others by holding them
in bondage. More dramatic and obvious a danger than personal and
social corruption was the presence of a large servile population
which had no loyalty to the masters' state and which therefore was a
real danger to public order in time of war or civil unrest. Finally,
Evangelicals charged that slaveholding was contrary to the principles
of the Republic and the Christian religion. Taunting his fellow
Evangelicals about their tendency to solve minor moral problems
without addressing basic ethical issues, one preacher observed,
"We strain at gnats while camels choak us not."[25]

But even the Reverend James O'Kelly, who penned these words,
did not have a solution consistent with the clarity and uncom-
promising style of his public address. He, like other Evangelicals,
could be very confrontational in tone—some of O'Kelly's colleagues, complained the offended Devereaux Jarrett, were most
indecorous, comparing slaveholders to "horsethieves & Hog-
stealers."[26] Evangelicals labeled slaveholding as blasphemous,
cruel, heartless, unrepublican, impolitic, imprudent, immoral, and
inconsistent. But when policy was to be determined, most Evangelicals after the Methodist fiasco of 1784 hemmed and hawed.
Their inability to find a solution to the problem they deplored is

revealed in their cautious language. They suggested that as soon as "possible" and "consistent with the principles of good policy," authorities should "pursue the most prudent but effective method" to achieve an immediate emancipation through some sort of process. With regard to individuals' responsibilities, O'Kelly represented the essence of Christian understanding. If economic motives prevent your freeing your slaves immediately, he wrote, "acknowledge the wrong detention" and emancipate them in a "gradual manner" as befits "dear brethren in Christ."[27] In the meantime, antislavery Evangelicals encouraged masters to "forbear & suppress cruelty," and do "what is just and equal" for your servants, including granting them full liberty to attend preaching of the gospel.[28]

In brief, Evangelicals could never successfully identify slavehold-ing as sin itself. The importance of this omission is evident when we remember the Evangelical emphasis upon the necessity of a convic-tion of sin, which then led a person into psychic confusion, from which he was saved by conversion and reintegrated into society through the church. Words which called slavery a moral evil, and even defined it as sinful could by implication make slaveholding a sin. But the words were belied by a persistent reluctance to excommunicate slaveholders who knelt in prayer with their slaves. Moreover, the bold philosophy of human rights which had been appropriated by optimistic, prophetic, and admirable persons in their assault upon slavery continued to be problematic as a prescription for social action because it could be, as we shall see, easily pruned from the branches of a rapidly growing Evangelicalism as a secular graft foreign to the religion of Jesus Christ. The core of Evangelical doctrine, a conviction of sin, could never be successfully identified with emancipationism.

Opposition to antislavery activity from within Evangelicalism was pronounced throughout the South from the beginning. In fact, noisy and angry as emancipationists were sometimes inclined to be, they were not thought to be so great a threat as to force the development of a pervasive proslavery ideology. Slaveholders merely refused to be persuaded, pushed, or bullied. They defended slavery from assumptions of African inferiority and with arguments based upon the Bible, the rights of property, and the threat of servile insurrection. They stubbornly defied antislavery regulations, and their representatives in state legislatures passed laws expatriating freed slaves. In their local communities, where they were well known and respected, they could use local prejudices and interests rather than denominational directives to guide disciplinary procedures of the local churches. Slaveholders suffered their annoying opponents with relative equanimity until 1800, when fears of insurrection made them demand stricter slave codes. In response, new state laws restricted slaves' freedom of assembly even for religious purposes, and mobs enforced their own laws against suspected antislavery preachers. The burning of Methodist antislavery pamphlets in Charleston in 1800 was a symbol of the new more direct hostility emancipationists would face, and even though Methodists wanted to give antislavery pamphlets to South Carolinians in 1803, they soon resigned themselves to silence.

As any thoughtful Evangelical should have known, the world in its social context is a persistent foe of the free development of a radical ethic. Evangelical moral surveillance and self-discipline did indeed lead to emancipationist activity, but they could not create a long-lasting abolition movement where the social context could not support it. The social realities of slavery and the psychological realities of racial prejudice simply could not be counterbalanced by religious commitment—they could be affected but not destroyed. As it spread across the South, Evangelicalism became part of the personal experience of the people, but the personal experience of the people also became part of Evangelicalism.

A generation of preachers who confidently attacked slavery gave way to a younger group which was unwilling to continue what would later be called "counterproductive" measures. In 1818 the Presbyterian General Assembly declared slavery a moral dilemma, but discouraged emancipationists by calling their activities socially disruptive. Earlier, in 1816, the Methodist General Conference had already confessed defeat—"little can be done to abolish the practice so contrary to the principles of moral justice."[29] People were simply "too easily contented" with slavery to change the law. Southern Evangelical antislavery sentiment gradually became limited to the mountain areas of the South, where slaveholders were not so powerful nor blacks so numerous as in the low country.

Many Evangelicals fled slaveholding by joining their Quaker friends in the trek to the Northwest.

The weakness of the southern Evangelical antislavery movement was obvious. It could never acquire a broad social base from which to operate. The specious breadth of Methodist activity was really a function of ecclesiastical structure in which antislavery rules were made by preachers who, as circuit riders, were never so staunchly identified with local practices as were Baptist or Presbyterian clergymen. Preachers who had given up slaves for reasons of conscience knew that what they demanded could be done. And colleagues who had given up any pretense to property by joining the itineracy were less affected by worldly attachment than the laity. Rules worked out in the rarefied moral atmosphere of preachers' meetings were unworkable where Methodists owned slaves or hoped to. The cleavage between antislavery preachers and slaveholding laity was not so great in Baptist and Presbyterian churches, except in a few notable cases. By and large, congregational discussions about slaveholding in these two denominations dwindled out by the end of the eighteenth century, and if any scrutiny of slaveholding was undertaken, it was usually aroused by a charge of cruelty or other misconduct and not by a questioning of the master-slave relationship itself. Southern areas where the laity did persist in distinctly antislavery attitudes until the 1820s were those where attacks on slaveholders' power, lust, and apostasy could be most easily believed—where Evangelicals were less likely to own slaves. Only in those regions could slaveholding be identified with the world as easily as other forms of conformity in more radical days.

Part of the failure of antislavery Evangelicalism lay with its most ardent proponents. Their argument that the black's servile condition had degraded him could not completely dissuade them from accepting amelioration of the condition as an alternative to challenging it. This is to say that their environmentalism was tempered by their bias. Although a few independent souls clearly empathized with blacks, many assaulted slaveholders in ways that suggested a dislike and perhaps envy of the power, status, and property of their enemies, rather than a fellow feeling for blacks. And a few could be said to have approached the problem of slavery with a sterile, naive idealism shaped more by the beauty of a consistent morality than

an appreciation of social reality. Neither opponent of slavery was
equipped for a long fight, and none—not even the most purely
motivated—could overcome the limitations of their Evangelical
bias. Quakers, who were not so intent upon expanding their
numbers, and who could count on the loyalty of their membership
when they moved against slavery, had acted carefully and slowly to
establish a consensual renunciation of slaveholding. Not expecting
to gauge truth by multiplying conversions, they were content to
remain a small "righteous remnant." This view was alien to
Evangelicals, who saw the Spirit of God in their own expansion and
were therefore unwilling to place opposition to slavery above the
need to bring all manner of folk—masters as well as slaves—within
the community of faithful people. Thus encumbered with unrealistic expectations and contradictory values, antislavery Evangelicals were no match for their stubborn and well-entrenched
opposition.

Evangelicalism contained a more basic internal dilemma as we
have already seen. All Evangelicals, emancipators as well as slaveholders, agreed that the first priorty of a Christian was to save souls,
and that the seal of success in this endeavor was personal holiness or a
life of serving God in prayer and self-discipline. The bold, often
quixotic confrontation with slavery settled once and for all the
problem of whether or not the moral struggle of the Christian
would be carried on in the world of power and traditional
relationships or within the mind and psychology of the individual
believer. Already inclined to individualize the fight with evil,
southern Evangelicals were forced by slavery to settle for a personal
struggle to gain possible victories, rather than social warfare to
achieve impossible dreams. Richard Baxter, in his timeless guide to
piety, had anticipated the southerners' solution over a century
before they saw the problem. Addressing himself to the slaveholders' counterparts of the seventeenth century, he had suggested
that men "of wealth and authority" take responsibility for the
conversion of their "tenants"—here southerners would have read
"slaves." "See whether they worship God in their families, and
take opportunities to press them to their duties. Do not despise
them because they are poor or simple. Remember God is no
respecter of persons."[30]

The impact of slavery upon Evangelicalism was in this case clear.

It placed constraints on the freedom of individuals to explore the full extent of their moral responsibility, and in so doing limited their role in the historical process. They were given sovereignty only over their internal life; beyond that, their role, dictated by race, sex, and power, defined how their Evangelical commitment would be lived. Long before the Missouri Compromise or William Lloyd Garrison, Gettysburg, or Appomattox, the southern Evangelicals learned the meaning of defeat. The defeat of the valiant fight against slavery taught them the limitations of power and will. There were things they could not do, dreams they dare not dream. They had learned that perfectly moral life was not possible in history by the act of humanity, but only beyond time by the act of God. The only evil that people could fight was in their own souls, or perhaps more accurately, in their bodies, and their parents' or grandparents' attempts to project it into the social system by fighting slavery lacked humility and piety.

A skeptic might observe that the lesson of defeat and sense of helplessness was experienced only by Evangelical leaders, but not by the rank and file. To be sure, historians can only surmise the total impact of emancipationists' failure, but it should not be supposed that the debate over slaveholding took place apart from local congregations. Baptist associations received inquiries on slavery from local churches for over thirty years. Scattered local records for churches of the major Evangelical denominations suggest that the debate on slavery affected every local church in the South at some time before 1800. No matter on which side of the controversy one stood, the ultimate resolution taught the helplessness of the moral individual to alter basic social arrangements, the necessary defeat of an absolutist morality in a fallen world. The emancipationists who lost the fight would feel the sting of lost innocence more than the victors, but the latter had merely won their original point—moral people did not have the power to change history or social relationships as they had inherited them. The emancipationists had to learn "defeat" the hard way. Their antagonists could smugly justify their lack of social activism by pointing out that Evangelicalism did not require an assault upon social arrangements.

And of course those who had made their peace so easily with slavery were quite correct. The withdrawal of Evangelicals from antislavery activity was made possible by the inner logic of a

religious mood which elevated persons not by destroying the social
system, but by providing those who were demeaned and degraded
with an inner faith in themselves and in their destinies quite apart
from their social condition. The revolutionary quality of the early
Evangelical movement was not its assault upon power, for it made
none, but its weakening of the cultural, religious, and psychological
constraints upon people of relatively low estate by elevating them in
their own esteem and giving them the personal discipline to use
their lives as best they could in Christian service. The antislavery
impulse was a potentiality of Evangelicalism—one which seemed
greater in the republican afterglow of revolutionary passion, when
the best of the world could be joined with the best of Evangelicalism—but it was not a necessary, compelling conclusion of
Evangelicalism itself. The perception that worldly distinctions were
false could and did give Evangelicals the power of the Holy Spirit
but not the power to destroy those distinctions. The fact that
slaveholding could not be generally defined as sin was in part the
result of observing the conversion of slaveholders to Christianity
without their conversion to emancipationism. The fact that slaves as
well as slaveholders could be converted demonstrated to all Evangelicals—emancipationists as well as others—that God accepted
both in His mysterious love and mercy. The result of the slavery
controversies, therefore, was to restrict the field of Evangelicals'
moral responsibility—the ordering of "things that were wanting"
—to what could be done within the existing social structure.

And yet the impact of the radical vision remained. Although
renouncing reformers' moral bravado, reflective Evangelicals could
not slough off a sense of guilt in relation to blacks; they admitted
the slaves' special claims upon them for religious instruction and
supported the American Colonization Society. The society proposed expatriating freed blacks to Africa, and with this conservative
solution to the problem of slavery the Society attracted Evangelicals
who continued to believe that slavery was an evil, but who
despaired of freeing blacks in this country. Neither response
actually led to an appreciable number of manumissions, but the
persistent reminder of the discrepancy between the ideal and actual
conditions for black people helped to stir up emotions. Associated
with slaves in worship, whites were frequently subject to attacks of
remorseful frustration after personally witnessing the impact of

religion upon blacks. As a result, a few people were prompted to free slaves in their wills; others—usually women—poured out their despair in diaries. Moral anxiety about slavery could be silenced by ignoring or rescinding rules; it could even be repressed, but so long as Evangelicals preached sin, guilt, and freedom to blacks and whites together, it could never be completely destroyed.

3

"An Enlightened and Refined People"

Evangelizing the South took a long time—as long as it took to create the section's special identity. Economic and political processes which at last forced southerners to vindicate themselves through violence posed persistent problems in social organization and ideology throughout the antebellum period. In response to these problems and to the need to emboss the special qualities of southern life with hallowed righteousness, Evangelical theorists and organizers transformed their relatively limited role as spokesmen for specific religious groups into one more ambitious, demanding, and prestigious. They aspired to become preceptors for a whole society. To be sure, they continued to provide personal consolation and public expression for those who remained along the eastern sea-board, as well as for their more venturesome relatives who surged south and west in search of land, cotton, and power. The importance of the local churches, first demonstrated by Samuel Davies and Shubal Stearns, continued to be expressed in the pious distinction between the community of faithful people and the world. The power of this distinction continued to be supported by the churches' determination to set standards of respectability and to discipline the unruly. And widespread support for Evangelical values continued to rest upon the matrix of relations with other churches and organizations beyond the locality. But Evangelicals created more than personal security and communal solidarity. The organizations they developed to guarantee themselves and their children valued positions began to change from sectarian instruments into catholic institutions which became inextricable elements of the southern social system.

The process of institutional maturation was coincidental with an intensifying sectional consciousness. The result was to enable earnest publicists of the twice-born to believe that being southern and being Evangelical were really the same thing. The South, they boasted, was characterized by its piety, concern for persons, and profound sense of social responsibility. Evidence cited in support of this immodest but popular view was the ubiquity of Evangelical meetinghouses, publishing houses, academies, colleges, and missions to slaves. These institutions were to serve Evangelicals in two ways. First, they helped to define Evangelicals as a distinct group, quite apart from other religious bodies within the social system; when in coalition with these other groups, however, they would constitute a powerful "Christian public." Academies and colleges would provide Evangelicals with proper training for their youth, and periodicals and books were to help to shape policy within denominations. In addition, the laity and ministry were to be educated to meet the challenges of a more complex society in a way that reflected the greater glory of God and their own self-respect. The second purpose of these institutions, subtle in conception but often bold in performance, was to enhance the status, strengthen the power, and secure the role of churches in southern society. The Evangelicals' goal was to establish their position as moral preceptors of the South, so that academies and colleges founded as denominational agencies became almost immediately the means by which the South combated both secularism and Yankeeism, which were often confused as the same thing.

Evangelicalism in the nineteenth century had become a much different process from the relatively volatile, alienated, defiant, and charismatic movements of the previous century. The reason was at once simple and complex. In the antebellum generation, status and class were not so clearcut as they once had been. Power and wealth were more fluid, as population, agriculture, marketing, and transportation shifted in the rapid expansion of the 1820s and 1830s. The ministry, the family, education, Christian discipline, social responsibility, slavery—all these elements of the Evangelical ethos changed just as rapidly as did the society within which they had to be defined. The process of redefinition was shaped not only by societal transformation, but also by the change of social position which Evangelicals experienced—from a movement which provided bonds and identity for those otherwise deprived of them, to a social-cultural constituency whose symbols, style of self-control, and rules of social decorum became dominant in the social system. That is the reality behind the proud observation of a man not given to boasting that Evangelicals had become influential by the 1850s. Their ministry, he wrote, was "learned and polished; their Doctors of Divinity and professors numerous; and their membership enlightened and refined."[1]

The important transitional process which led to this pinnacle can be exemplified by examining some of the most essential aspects of the Evangelical ethos in the antebellum South. Accordingly, it is possible to see how refinement of ideas about the ministry, education, and the symbolic roles of Evangelical men and women represented changes within Evangelicalism and society, and how these changes affected social harmony among the religious of the South. In the subsequent chapter we will discover how model Evangelical men and women were supposed to transform society through the Mission to Slaves and the disciplined responsibility of the slaveholding ethic.

Chief architects and artisans of Evangelical institutions in the South were the self-confident, energetic, and ambitious young men who entered the ministry in the generation after the War of 1812. They thought of themselves as popular leaders of an expanding, self-conscious constituency through which they could exercise enormous influence. Theirs was almost a political vision, although they would have denied it, and the key to their power was "popularity." Samuel Davies had done much to remove the preacher from his traditional aloofness, but Shubal Stearns's missionaries and Francis Asbury's circuit riders made him a symbol of the people who were to be saved, as well as the conduit of salvation. So successful were these men in changing attitudes toward preachers that pastoral popularity had become almost as important as orthodoxy by the 1830s. The fact was scandalously unpleasant to conservatives, who valued restraint and scholarship over "popular talents," and who

viewed the capacity to arouse congregational enthusiasm a sure
sign of mediocrity. As one crusty Presbyterian snarled to a friend
about a pastoral candidate in 1819: "If he has a pretty face, and a
good voice, and abundance of graceful gestures, he will absolutely
run away with them."[2]

He could not run far, however, unless his authority were based
on something with a little greater staying power than a pretty face.
That indispensable quality resided in the preacher's ability to
symbolize in his person, words, and acts the values, faith, and
hopes of the people who made up his congregation. His was the
"gift," as Evangelicals called it, to make the life-death-resurrection
of Christ a contemporaneous event, and he did so with such vivid
and evocative imagery that many who heard him experienced the
meaning of the Christian religion through a familiar, reassuring,
psychic ritual: the conviction of pervasive sin, the nausea of just
condemnation, the joy of Christ's salvation. No wonder people
shouted or quietly gave thanks for deliverance; no high mass ever
more effectively presented the "risen Lord," nor priest more
dramatically reconstituted the community through a symbolic
reenactment of the myths of the Christian faith.

A projection of the people's religious and social needs, the
minister was at the same time someone special, around whom
developed an aura of power and perhaps even of mystery. But the
minister's power lay not merely in preaching, which invited the
epithet "Son of Thunder"; it also came from his being accepted as
guardian of the moral and intellectual life of the community. If he
were reflective and wise and the least bit imaginative, his ideas
could provision and amplify the minds of the faithful. Jeremiah
Bell Jeter, a distinguished Baptist clergyman, remembered repeat-
ing Sunday's sermon over and over again throughout the week
when, as a young man, he had obediently followed horse and plow
back and forth across the reluctant fields. It was a strange ritual
indeed for one who did not then aspire to be a minister; but he
savored every word the preacher had uttered, and fondly repeated
each metaphor and image "because," he later recalled, "it was the
most pleasant intellectual exercise within my reach."[3]

If popularity revealed a mystic identification of preacher and
people, it did not betoken the servility of one to the other, but the

responsibility of a talented few to convert, nurture, and guide the
many. To meet this grave responsibility, the preachers who succeeded Davies, Stearns, and Asbury gradually established formal
procedures for selecting and training new leaders. Evangelical
Presbyterians required very little innovation, following as they did
the course set by their northern brethren. They expected the pro-
spective minister to acquire a classical education at an academy
before apprenticing himself to read theology with an older, more
experienced clergyman. If he could attend college so much the
better, but such a luxury was rare. After this preparation, the
presbytery—the judicatory above the local level—examined the
candidate on theology, biblical scholarship, preaching, and personal piety before granting a license to preach. After a probationary
period, he was called to a specific church, where he was ordained.

A similar process was employed by Methodists, with that singular
exception—which demeaned them in the eyes of many Presbyterians—that they required no formal education beyond mere literacy.
If the candidate demonstrated clearly to the annual conference of
ministers that he had a talent for preaching and governing,
reasonable intelligence, ambition, and a call to preach, he was
accepted as a candidate and sent through the various stages of
Methodist leadership. Although these stages did not necessarily
provide Methodists with the classical education so prized by
Presbyterians, the process did train ministers in how to work with
people, conduct meetings, and preach. In the final stage of
training, the young man was apprenticed to an elder on a circuit
and learned from him how to assume responsibility for scattered
Methodist societies and how to create new ones.

Baptists were unencumbered by such elaborate structures. Their
local churches set apart orthodox youths of ability who were
convinced—and could convince others—that they had the call to
preach. Associations could suggest standards of education and
ability, but the ultimate decision on ordination lay with the local
church, so that its minister might be a simple reflection of the
urbanity, sophistication, and intelligence of his congregation. That
this situation invariably produced illiterate preachers was obviously
not the case, since Baptist ministers frequently were college graduates, and those who were not often surpassed in scholarship,

intellect, and wisdom those whose only evidence of intelligence was a diploma.

If the men selected by these processes had had time and opportunity to improve their talents, they could have overcome many of the disadvantages which afflicted them. But all too often their ability to fulfill ministerial duties and obligations was restricted by their having to earn a living in another occupation. The meager, token salaries earned by Methodist and Baptist preachers, and even the amounts received by Presbyterians, handsome by comparison, were simply insufficient to allow the clergy to commit all their time and energy to the work of the Lord—studying, visiting, counseling, preaching. Many Presbyterians became teachers, although a few also joined most of their Baptist and Methodist counterparts in farming. In the early years of Methodist expansion (1780–1815), itinerants were unmarried young men who rode circuit for a few years before "locating" or settling down in one area to marry and follow a trade or plow. The ministerial salary of sixty dollars per year was simply inadequate to feed a family. Often the key to financial security was a young woman who brought slaves, land, contacts, and prestige to her marriage with an impecunious preacher whose only visible assets were a talent for public discourse and management mixed with enough pious audacity and ambition to promise a respectable future.

When the circuit rider married and located, he committed himself to the same divided mind that characterized Presbyterian and Baptist farmer-preachers. This division could be speciously simple or subtly complex—either a choice of tasks for a hot summer's eve, or ambivalence about scholarship and learning and uncertainty about one's role in the church and society. At issue was whether the minister measured and defined himself according to the wishes, expectations, and demands of the local church or the standards of fellow ministers, whose sense of solidarity with him and his with them was based in large part upon how well he performed tasks and functions which they believed were important. Often unconcerned with scholarship and theological distinctions they could not understand, congregations might require only that their leader reflect their own status and class without unnecessary blandishment. By earning his way through a second occupation, the preacher could show his congregation that he was "one of

them," that he had neither scholarly pretensions nor parasitical
plans for relying upon holy religion for financial support. Baptist
leaders of the (N.C.) Kehukee Association complained in 1791 that
the congregations' memory of tax-supported Anglican priests' sid-
ing with the aristocracy made difficult any attempt to provide
Baptist preachers with an adequate salary. Too many people feared
that the money would break the relationship of trust existing
between preachers and their congregations; for, they recalled, paid
priests had once "regarded the *fleece* more than the *flock*.'"[4]

Such fears—which in many cases became accusations—did not
completely die out at any time during the nineteenth century. But
the compelling if slow tendency, driven on by the more aggressive
and better-educated Evangelicals, was to strengthen the bonds of
ministers to each other and to the ideal of a fulltime, professional
leadership. Merged with this goal and often indistinguishable from
it was the determination—consistent with their role as popular
leaders—to educate their coreligionists' children, regardless of what
vocation those children chose. To achieve this dual purpose,
churchmen began to establish academies where students could
receive a basic education in the ancient languages, English grammar, and mathematics. Presbyterian clerics often established schools
as part of their ministry, rendering rather artificial the distinction
between teaching and preaching as separate vocations. David Caldwell's school, founded in pre-Revolutionary North Carolina (1776),
Liberty Hall in the Valley of Virginia (1786), and Moses Waddell's
famous Willington Academy (1804) were but three of the many
small, valiant outposts of Evangelical learning in the early South. In
imitation of a fine example and as part of their own earnest but
fumbling attempts to assume "public" responsibility, Baptist and
Methodist ministers here and there tried to establish schools on
their farms or near their churches. Between 1784 and 1800,
Methodists, usually on their own initiative, tried to develop schools
in Maryland, Virginia, Kentucky, and the Carolinas. A few Baptists
other than Robert Semple of Virginia (1793) may have attempted
to build schools, but if they did they were unsuccessful. Only
Presbyterians seemed to have had wealth and clerical personnel
enough to build most of the academies founded before the War of
1812.

After the Battle of New Orleans redeemed an unfortunate war

and gave Americans a symbol for their newfound, undisciplined power, an elemental surge propelled American society into a new age of institution building. Evangelical leaders were among the most ardent, dedicated, persistent artificers, who exhorted, cajoled, pushed, and even tricked their coreligionists into creating new educational institutions to improve Evangelicals' position in southern society. Voluntary societies, first conceived in England and the Northeast, soon found in the agrarian wilderness of the South a constituency ready to be rallied into action on behalf of the Bible, Sunday schools, foreign missions, domestic evangelization, and education. Even so isolated and remote a place as Hillsborough, North Carolina, experienced between 1816 and 1822 what to the people there must have seemed a frenzy of activity; the Presbyterian church, the Protestant Episcopal church, the Methodist church, the Masonic lodge, the Bible society, the Missionary society, the Sunday school union, and an agricultural society were organized or reorganized, and a newspaper was established. As if to grant divine sanction to such goings-on, there was a great revival in 1821.[5]

Throughout the South this surge of interest helped to generate support for Evangelical educational institutions. Virginia Presbyterians had been perfecting their schools since Hampden-Sydney was founded in 1776 and had enhanced their reputation with Liberty Hall, which became Washington College in 1796. After the turn of the century, they attempted to counteract Princeton's influence in the South by establishing theological instruction at Hampden-Sydney. In 1827 and again in 1829, southern Presbyterians led the way in providing specialized education for clergymen by establishing Union and Columbia Theological seminaries in Virginia and South Carolina, but the force and zeal for Evangelical educational expansion was provided by Methodists and Baptists. Stung by past failures and the enviable example and irritating pride of educated Presbyterians, aggressive reformers began to assault the entrenched and holy bastions of ministerial illiteracy. Sensitive to charges that they would substitute educated arrogance for pious service, Methodist clergymen in the General Conference of 1816 admitted that although a college education was not "essential" for a "gospel ministry," its substitute, a *good* education, was "absolutely necessary."[6] Illiteracy and ignorance, argued reformers, would shame

ministers in the eyes of increasingly better educated congregations
and colleagues. The same arguments were made by Baptists, who
sought to intensify scattered and sporadic efforts to educate a few
promising young men for the ministry. The South Carolina Baptist
convention, founded in 1821 through the indefatigable efforts of
the Charleston Association's Richard Furman, had as one of its
primary goals the marshaling of Baptist support for education at
Rhode Island College, Columbian College (District of Columbia),
and peripatetic, tough little Furman academy (1827).

The cautious words of Methodists and the paper organization of
South Carolina Baptists represented a trend not so much in favor of
an educated ministry, as of general education itself, for Evangelicals
fought illiteracy and ignorance on behalf of all their people. By the
1820s, they were establishing interdenominational Sunday school
unions in many localities of Virginia and North Carolina simply to
teach children to read and write, since the state would not establish
a viable educational system. Some non-Evangelicals feared the
Sunday schools were merely a maneuver by clever Evangelicals to
seize the hearts and minds of the people, but they did precious
little to prevent the coup. Aggressive Evangelicals, most of them
Presbyterian, continued to expand their educational facilities, and
by the 1830s Methodists and Baptists were energetically establishing educational societies throughout the South in an attempt to
broaden the scope and constituency of Evangelical education. By
the 1840s it might fairly be said that precollege education in the
South was controlled by Evangelicals. Even academies which had no
connection with one of the major denominations promised parents
that their institutions taught and enforced a broad Evangelical
morality. And when in the 1840s and 1850s southern reformers
began to agitate for common school systems, a majority were
Evangelicals, and a plurality ministers.

Important as academies were, they did not represent Evangelical
aspirations and ambitions so well as the fragile "denominational"
colleges which began to spring up in the 1820s and 1830s.
Methodist educational entrepreneurs responded to their General
Conference's encouragement of "literary institutions" (1820) by
transforming a private academy in Augusta, Kentucky, into a
college in 1827 (chartered 1822). In 1830 they chartered Randolph-

Macon College of Virginia; in 1836, Emory College of Georgia; and in 1839 Emory and Henry College of western Virginia. In the latter year they also established the first putative woman's college in the South by assuming control of floundering Georgia Female College and christening it Wesleyan Female College. During the same period, Baptist educators were just as busy, establishing George-town (Kentucky, 1829), Wake Forest (North Carolina, 1838), Mercer (Georgia, 1837), Richmond (Virginia, 1840), Howard (Ala-bama, 1841), and Furman (South Carolina, 1850) colleges. Pres-byterians, who had already established two colleges in Virginia, joined the Evangelical collegiate impulse by chartering Oglethorpe (Georgia) and Davidson (North Carolina) in 1836 and 1838, respectively. By 1852 each of the three major Evangelical churches had colleges in nearly every southern state.

Although varying in detail with each individual college, the pattern of development usually dictated the creation of a special coalition. Among its primary members the educational cadre would include penniless but enthusiastic young clergymen—recently or-dained and often proudly clutching new college diplomas, rela-tively comfortable and generous benefactors, and local promoters, who thought a college would bring business and give tone if not learning to their hometowns. A small group of ministers usually made up the vanguard, whose task it was to persuade denomina-tional agencies such as Baptist state conventions, Methodist con-ferences, and Presbyterian synods and presbyteries to provide part of the funds and an agent to stump the countryside for more money. Agents emphasized to their coreligionists the college's potential contribution to the denomination. To people living in the locality where the college was to be established, they offered it as an object of community pride. And to believers of other faiths, they promised to avoid "rigid sectarianism," while promoting genuine Evangelical piety and learning as a leaven for the whole society. Each college was to be, as the president of Emory and Henry College said in 1838, "the great lever for the moral and intellectual regeneration of all this region of the country."[7]

As such, there was no room for sectarian exclusiveness, even if state law had allowed it. In Virginia, nondenominational status was encouraged by laws preventing the incorporation of colleges which

possessed theological professorships, religious tests, or the domination by one sect of the Board of Trustees. But these were small
difficulties indeed for Evangelicals, who knew that the new president, often an Evangelical minister, should choose a faculty
dedicated to the social group for whom the college could become a
symbol of commitment to the moral and intellectual regeneration
of a society and a concrete example of public responsibility.

That the social group was defined in denominational terms was
not surprising, although the chief reasons in so defining it were not
what suspicious anti-Evangelicals at the time cynically charged were
"narrow denominational motives." In fact, the motives of Evangelical collegiate entrepreneurs were anything but narrow, for these
men were determined to expand hitherto limited opportunities
for higher education. To parents whose lack of funds and abundant
suspicion of aristocratic state universities prevented them from
sending their sons to such institutions, Evangelical Christian colleges seemed a relatively inexpensive and safe alternative. The
colleges also protected the sensibilities of upwardly mobile people
who refused to subject their sons to the outrageously class-oriented
undergraduate life of state universities. Even more significant for
understanding the new aspirations, affluence, and public spirit of
Evangelicals was the development of their women's colleges. This
innovation—not given the scholarly attention it deserves—was a
natural elaboration of several factors: a majority of church members
were women, clergymen were accustomed to working with and
teaching women, and men who had no sons to honor with
monuments to their affluence and stewardship would gladly honor
their daughters. A few Evangelicals may also have had in mind the
training of new teachers. But more important still, the establishment of female seminaries, which were not content to remain
academies, betokened a major shift in the maturing role of women
among Evangelicals and therefore among southerners.

Despite the pretense and hunger for legitimation, there was for
the most part an admirable, creative impulse at work in the
establishment of Evangelical higher education. This was expressed
very well by William Hooper of North Carolina. A professor at the
state university and a former priest, Hooper had refused to
participate in the High Church campaign of Episcopal bishop John

Stark Ravenscroft and subsequently joined the Baptist church. Soon he was called to teach at Furman Institute and then to preside over Wake Forest college. As he anticipated leaving the smug security of indolent Chapel Hill for the challenges and uncertainties of a fledgling Baptist institution, he mused about his role and talents. He knew that he was not so accomplished as scholars in Europe or New England, but, he confessed to a friend, "in the sphere in which we shall be called to act, more moderate attainments will answer a good purpose and meet the wants of our denomination." Perhaps, he went on, we with our modest erudition "may raise our people & our ministry to a point from which our successors may raise them to still greater elevation."[8]

A second motive behind the Evangelicals' establishment of colleges, one put in focus by Hooper's remarks, was to educate the leaders and constituents of a sect or denomination. Publicists often emphasized the reflected glory in which all Baptists or Methodists or Disciples could share when their lay and ministerial leadership could demonstrate as well as any other church those educational attainments which betokened high social standing and perfect respectability. If appearances were important, however, they were secondary to the purpose of stamping out the ignorance and illiteracy of which all Evangelical ministers except Presbyterians had been accused—it was a matter of group pride. As Hooper intimated, the remedial work often required of Evangelical colleges kept many of them very near the level of academies, and the future ministers who graduated from them were not trained in theology, but received instead the tools of future self-education: elementary English grammar, history, mathematics, and science.

Another motive impelling Evangelicals into educational activities —and one which revealed their earnest striving for acceptance and influence as much as a devotion to education for its own sake—was the desire to build colleges as an expression of social maturity. They were to prove that Baptists, Methodists, Cumberland Presbyterians, and even Disciples of Christ had "arrived." The way in which Evangelicals talked about their colleges revealed a major shift from their eighteenth-century conception of themselves as a people set apart from a worldling aristocracy, establishing intimate, disciplined communities based on the celebration, conversion, and discipline of unruly but valuable persons. Then, the world had been immoral and threatening, and the small community of faithful people elevated to the center of one's consciousness. Responsible and pious Evangelicals would not have dared to admit concern about the acceptability of their actions to non-Evangelicals. Nor could they have confessed hungering for the respect of those who did not share their world view. And yet by the 1840s and 1850s this acceptability and respect is exactly what Evangelicals were concerned about, for they had come to think of themselves as not at war with society, and certainly not with traditional elites, but as constituent parts of the whole society with somber responsibilities to assume and a proud tradition of influence to uphold.

Indicative of this change was a circular which Alabama Baptists distributed in 1857 in an attempt to elicit denominational support for struggling—it was the universal adjective for such institutions— Howard College of Marion. Social change, argued the college agent, made great demands upon Baptists to maintain their "relative position" in society. Without a "well sustained College" to produce an "adequate ministry," which in turn would wield important influence in Alabama, the Baptists would "silently, surely, and continually decline." If the college were allowed to fail, Alabama Baptists would be "disgraced before mankind; and must hide from the view of posterity. A necessity is forced upon them, which they dare not evade, to take their part in public Collegiate education—at least of their own ministers, their own children, and the teeming juvenile populations connected with them."[9] Such responsibility, awesome as it was, was nevertheless welcomed by Evangelical publicists, who proudly argued over and over again that their colleges were unmistakable evidence that Evangelicals had "reached an influential position" in society, and that they could be counted among the most "refined" and "enlightened" people of the South. No wonder, therefore, that building colleges was so important to ambitious, aspiring young Evangelical clergymen. One of these, Basil Manly, Jr., revealed it all as he contemplated establishing a school for young ladies at Richmond, Virginia. He felt that if he, as a Baptist clergyman, failed in his endeavor, that failure would weaken the social position of the whole body of his coreligionists in relation not only to other denominations, but more especially to the "worldly people around us." "It would," he emphasized, "sink us almost as much in public opinion as the completion of the plan on the scale proposed would tend to elevate us and give us a firm hold in the community."[10]

Evangelicals built colleges to increase educational opportunities, improve the quality of their common life, and enhance their own prestige, but they had a strictly ideological motive as well. They wanted to make sure that the college education received by their children was shaped by Evangelical assumptions and goals. Fearful of a non- or anti-Christian ethos, which, along with an aristocratic bias, seemed to pervade state universities, Evangelicals were relieved when they could find ways to control their own colleges, in which their world view, far from being critically scrutinized, was acclaimed. Such safe harbor from the storms of Deism and Infidelity was not seen as the only virtue of colleges controlled by Evangelicals, who believed that they had something special to contribute to educational theory. The sense of reciprocity and unabashed utilitarian pay-off, which valued education as a means instead of an end, was universal, but nowhere more baldly stated than when the first president of Wofford College (Methodist, South Carolina), William Wightman, said in 1851: "Education . . . makes men *polished and powerful*, but Christian education alone, makes them good."[11] Or in the words of the Methodist *Quarterly Review* in 1847: "Unlearned Christians may be happy, but a mass of the irreligious learned will contain all the more fierce and destructive elements of the human character."[12] If education could "elevate" Evangelicals, they in turn could discipline education, putting it at the service of the Evangelical surge to tame and convert society.

Such statements and assumptions are not at all surprising within the Evangelical context. Men and women whose grandparents and parents had proceeded to emotional maturity through the process of conversion and sanctification could quite naturally understand higher education as a sophisticated extension of the traditional Evangelical formula. "Elevation" was not mere social mobility— although for many people it was surely that—but the conversion from illiteracy, ignorance, and powerlessness to learning, power, and self-respect. The sense of moral accountability and self-

discipline so important to sanctified Evangelicals was the basis for
the insistence by Evangelical publicists that only an education
shaped by conscious moral commitment would be useful and safe
for society. Education was itself value-free, Evangelicals believed,
which meant of course that it was capable of being used in the
service of any ideology. The aggressive and disciplined mind, which
educators thought ought to be produced in their colleges, could
become dangerous to society if not disciplined by Christian commitment. The anarchic abolitionist freethinkers of the Northeast
became a case in point for southern Evangelical educational
theorists in the 1850s, who believed the major problem with those
obstreperous and disorderly people was their rejection of orthodox
Evangelical values.

Evangelical orthodoxy or ideology taught in the southern colleges
therefore was not expressed in creeds or confessions which would
divide the faithful—and were therefore better left to the churches
—but was expressed instead in a world view which emphasized
social stability. The order which their predecessors had attempted
to enforce within small groups, antebellum Evangelical leaders
hoped to enforce upon the whole of southern society through
control of education. In expressing this hope, latter-day Evangelicals moved beyond the local institutions, in which personal
behavior could be easily affected, and into the areas where orderliness was less easily guaranteed but no less important. The move was
as vital to Evangelicals as it was natural, given the agressiveness of
their doctrine and the social mobility of their constituents. It meant
that the social cohesiveness which had kept Evangelicals together as
a group was being offered to society not in the sometimes hostile
tones of Evangelical preaching, which had once repudiated class
distinctions and threatened social order, but in the form of
respectable and enduring institutions which could use the Evangelical model of responsible and orderly behavior as the guide and
guarantor of social order. Evangelical aspirations had once been to
define the boundaries between the faithful and the world so that
the values of God's people would not be confused with those of the
ruling elites; but social and economic change had encouraged
Evangelicals to assimilate rather than repudiate the world.

Evangelicals came to want social order partially because they

would be the primary beneficiaries of it by the common acknowledgment of their role in achieving it. It was almost as if the
Kingdom of God had come without anyone's realizing it, for
Evangelicals themselves boasted of the wonderful change that had
taken place before their eyes by the 1850s. There was a special
satisfaction among the faithful when Christian chaplains assumed
their place at the University of Virginia, where once infidelity had
reigned supreme. As if to torment Thomas Jefferson's ghost all the
more, there was a great revival on campus in 1854. These acts—one
prudential and the other providential (as unanticipated collective
behavior was usually called)—were symbolic, and built something
much more significant than campus buildings. If Evangelicals had
not seized control of southern higher education, they were at least
the single most powerful influence upon it.

The metamorphosis of Evangelicalism, represented in the first
stages of ministerial professionalization and the creation of academies and colleges, was not experienced as a universally uniform
and irresistible process. It was all too often a lonely and difficult
fight waged by valiant individuals against seemingly overwhelming
odds of poverty, ignorance, pride, apathy, and suspicion—all of
which threatened to thwart the most optimistic of partisans. By
1850 only about one-fifth of the clergy could be said to have had
formal training.[13] And as if to confirm the exaggerated taunts and
glowering criticism of their enemies, Evangelical educators at first
had to face one unhappy and embarrassing fact. The bold words
and fine-sounding titles—"collegiate institution," "college," and
"university"—all too often described a few students huddled
around a rude stove in a drafty building trying to make sense out of
books, which they were often forced to read by the flickering light
of inefficient and dirty lanterns. Students were often very poorly
prepared for college-level work, a matter of less concern than it
might have been, since their teachers were equally unprepared to
teach college students.

Although achievements in education for both ministry and laity
never coincided with the goals of most Evangelical spokesmen, the
very fact that these goals represented the highest articulated
aspirations of major southern religious bodies is significant. The
trend of projecting Evangelical experience beyond the discipline

and piety of local churches into the social institutions of secondary and higher education had shaped the world view of only one generation of Evangelical leaders and publicists by Secession. But it was a generation much beholden to the Protestant ethic of hard work and the Evangelical belief that God's grace was nowhere more dramatically demonstrated than when He chose the foolish of the world to confound the wise. It was therefore a generation which believed that the little progress they had made would continue until they claimed the South for the Lord. Gradually the fledgling colleges began to produce graduates whose personal success and public visibility were celebrated in Evangelical periodicals and pulpits as proof of the progressive spirit of the denomination and the "Christian public." In a slow but impressive process, the "Doctors of Divinity," the "learned and polished" clergy, and the "enlightened" membership were becoming more than wishful thinking. If denominations did not decree into existence a network of colleges to symbolize and guarantee their internal union and external power, they were nevertheless the sometimes reluctant but happy heirs of efforts by some of their most energetic sons and daughters, who fought with characteristic Evangelical zeal to link their fierce Christian faith with the needs of an increasingly numerous and proud middle class.

Evangelical metamorphosis from alienation to influence affected areas other than education, and none more dramatically than southerners' conception of family and the proper roles of men and women. The evolution of Evangelical ideas about manhood, womanhood, and family life involved a subtle, complicated trans-formation of things—psychic responses, personal interaction, so-cialization, and normative patterns—which southern historians have yet to study in a systematic way. And yet this transformation was the basic stuff of an historical reality which profoundly affected southerners' views of themselves and those they loved. Lest this process be misunderstood, it should be emphasized that it was the creation of an *ideal* which, while shared by most Evangelical publicists and many of their constituents, failed to shape *all* southerners' behavior; indeed, the ideal was often in direct conflict with popular practice. And in some instances, the ideal itself harbored potentially contradictory elements. Thus the roles and ideals which Evangelicals developed became popular, in the sense that they were shared by a large minority of southerners or set rules of debate for others who were decidedly anti-Evangelical, or established claims of conscience upon those who could not escape them even though they wanted to.

From the very beginning of the movement, Evangelical preachers had offered as one of their major innovations the practice of "family religion." *"Many of the great people of the world,"* they said, *"entirely neglect it."*[14] Unfortunately, Evangelicals might have neglected it, too, but for the prodding, exhorting, and exemplary conduct of itinerant preachers, who made special efforts to generate family devotions. "We have made it to a point," Francis Asbury emphasized, "to pray in the families where we lodge, whether public or private, and generally when we stop for refreshment."[15] Church conferences, sessions, and quarterly meetings supported this practice. The movement, which demanded a profound, existential confrontation between the self and Ultimate Reality, and which could not accept as legitimate a church established by objective law rather than by subjective experience, was perforce required to provide for a way to anticipate and shape the important emotional crisis of conversion. In the Evangelical view, neither individual nor church was sufficient to prepare the potential convert to fight the world. Individuals had few if any resources of their own, and the church—even if Evangelical—did not have the pervasive influence and special psychic power possessed by the family. As the most basic of social institutions, where children learned how to deal with other individuals in face-to-face relationships and how to deal with society through the abstractions of state, church, and world, the family was the place where Evangelical Christianity would be perpetuated. It was in the domestic sphere, rather than the public and political arenas, that major Evangelical battles with the world would be carried on. After two generations (ca. 1800) of clerical exhortation, congregational discussion, and individual effort, southern Evangelicalism had not persuaded all adherents to pray thrice daily, read the scriptures at dawn and dusk, or consult with family members about the state of their souls, but the ideal had been established as one of the chief standards of

Evangelical commitment. Moreover, the practice of "family religion" was just widespread enough to give the ideal pragmatic legitimacy. In a sense, Evangelicals made the family the cadre of their movement. They wanted the economic, biological, affective, and socializing functions of the family to be simultaneously transformed by and supportive of the Evangelical quest for a disciplined, holy life. Every action from plowing to praying was capable of communicating something about God, Evangelicals believed, an assumption which, when combined with a commitment to family religion, made daily Evangelical surveillance through familial relationships quite logical. God, Samuel Davies pointed out, did not unite people in any social group without reference to their eternal salvation. Even by natural reason, he argued, it was easy to see that families were created to procreate, nurture, and care for human beings, functions facilitated by religion because it lent authority to the nurturing process, made personal interaction mutually supportive—suppressing "turbulent and self-tormenting" dispositions—and invested family relationships with a holiness that made them channels of God's grace. What nature implied, the Bible as the ultimate Evangelical authority clearly commanded through the example of Old Testament patriarchs and the precepts of New Testament apostles. Davies thought that families had a simple choice: "either to set up the worship of God immediately in your families or sin willfully against the knowledge of the truth."[16]

Most obvious among the purposes of family religion was its nurturing children so that when they came to adulthood they would be susceptible to conversion. The conventional distinction between revivalists' reliance upon an emotional crisis to effect conversion, as opposed to a developmental approach which nurtured children to grow up thinking of themselves as Christians, too easily ignores Evangelical insistence on teaching children to understand, desire, and expect conversion. Virginia Baptists in 1800 exemplified the Evangelical belief that family religion prepared children to become Christians. Daily reading from the Bible, the Portsmouth Association pointed out, would convey the knowledge necessary to understand the seriousness and importance of salvation. Daily exposition of the text would explain how the Bible could be applied to everyday situations. Daily exhortation "*with all long-suffering and doctrine*" would use "every possible argument," that all dependents might be "delivered from [sin], and translated into the kingdom of God's dear Son." Daily catechizing would provide the knowledge to understand the exhortation, and daily prayer would be the means of opening hearts to saving Grace.[17] All this was done not simply to reinforce the Christian commitment of parents, but to nurture children and servants, too; for as we shall see, Christian apologists for slavery would rest their argument on slavery's domestic character, its being an extension of family government, and therefore transformed by family religion.

Evangelical celebration of and commitment to family religion increased with every decade, as sermons, associational letters, and pastoral counseling were transformed by the publishing revolution of the 1830s into a long and persistent public campaign. There were, however, significant changes within the movement, which reveal something of the transformation of Evangelicalism. First, the place of the church conference or class meeting in enforcing Evangelical morality was gradually supplanted by the family. Discipline by congregational conferences diminished throughout the nineteenth-century South; local church records reveal ever fewer investigations into the private and family lives of members. By the 1850s there was a realization that something vital in the early Evangelical movement had been lost, as elderly Methodists, for example, began to complain about the demise of the class meeting, the accompanying loss of Christian discipline, and a weakened resolve to resist worldly allurement.[18] True, Christians and the world were still seen as being at odds with each other; and the institutional connection between public exhortation and private action was to remain the church and family. But the role of the church was diminished as excommunication and ostracism were gradually abandoned for the more subtle and probably more effective reliance on the training of children and the tempering of adults within the Christian family. And the Christian's citadel from which he sallied forth to do battle with the world became the family, or as many Evangelicals said, the "home"—"a sanctuary, a resting place, a shadow from the heats, turmoils, and conflicts of life, and an effectual barrier against ambition, envy, jealousy, and selfishness." And whereas for Christians the analogue of heaven had once been the church, it now became the home.[19]

This elevation of the home did not occur only in the South, nor was it the result only of Evangelical expansion. The phenomenon, complex and comprehensive as it was, was part of a general trend that transcended national boundaries. Though it was neither originated nor controlled by Evangelicals, this development was given its moral and religious legitimacy in the South by Evangelical theorists and preceptors, who in their books, pamphlets, and public exhortations were more active than any other group in explaining its meaning and urging its perfection. And as they elevated the home and its nurturing function to a central position in their world view, they presided over another change that was significant for Evangelicalism, the persons involved, and their society: the birth of the Evangelical woman.

When Evangelicals first began to preach the responsibilities of family religion, the father was the person they addressed. It was he who was to perfect his role as head of the household and command his family into their appropriate demeanor before God. To cite the Portsmouth Baptists once again: "If none of the family excepting the master thereof have any religion, it behooves him to extend his authority so far, as to make all under him submit, at least to the form of worship in the family."[20] There were no special words for the mother, the mistress of the household. Within a generation, however, the model of the ideal woman was beginning to take shape in Evangelical literature, and she was no longer absent from discussion about the family. Indeed, in much of the literature she had become the person primarily responsible for family religion because it was she who came to have the primary responsibility for religious nurture. This fact, combined with others, helped to create an ideal which gave women of the Old South a special role in the church and a public image quite unlike that of their grandmothers. Indeed, Evangelical preaching and theorizing about women called greater attention to them than any previous discussion about society, for in elaborating the ideal of the Christian home and the place of women within it, Evangelicals made the sphere of women a significant transitional concept which, whatever its conservative premises and intent, provided women with an important private and public life.

This transition is particularly important for understanding southern Evangelicalism because of the way in which the religion of Samuel Davies, Francis Asbury, and Shubal Stearns was absorbed and given new life by southern women. Early religious histories, church records, private letters, devotional diaries, and religious periodicals are suffused with the presence and importance of women in religious life. The phenomenon is not unique to the Old South, of course, for students of religion and society agree on its universality, even if they cannot agree on its cause. Too little research has been done on the theme of women and religion to make a definitive statement. Images about southern women and piety, projected by historical impressionism and literary imagination, remain tenuous. Scholars still await a convincing analytical paradigm of how religious concerns about sin, salvation, personal responsibility, and human destiny affected or expressed social and cultural realities of sexual differentiation. It is possible, however, to learn much about the social impact of Evangelicalism upon the South by focusing on the people who, as much as the preachers, made the movement possible, and used it—sometimes consciously, usually not—much as did their coreligionists of a different race, to fend off oppression, secure their personal and group identity, and assert themselves in new and sometimes surprising ways.

That women made southern Evangelicalism possible is evident from almost every surviving local church record as well as from the daily journals, personal letters, and sometimes sentimental memoirs of "tired and worn-out" clergymen. That women employed the Evangelical idiom to think about themselves and the meaning of their lives is revealed in their own memoirs, diaries, and letters. What is not revealed are such things as the ratio of women to men church members in the towns as opposed to the countryside, among the ruled as opposed to the rulers, and among the young as opposed to the old. That women comprised a majority of church members is as obvious as is the fact that they were not equal to men in terms of power, even though they provided indispensable support to the clergy. Almost every Methodist circuit rider and itinerant Baptist missionary who left an account of his work revealed an impressive reliance upon women for moral support as well as for basic physical comfort. Women—Francis Asbury was especially indebted to widows—frequently took on larger-than-life proportions to homeless, hungry, bedraggled, and sick itinerants, whom they housed, fed, and nursed as part of their contribution to the Kingdom of God. Moreover, they often transformed their homes into churches during the first two generations of Evangelical expansion, when itinerants were beholden to their hostesses for assembling the faithful to hear the monthly sermon.

That women were visible in southern churches is an historical truism. What such visibility meant is another matter entirely, a problem with no self-evident answer. The many, complex motivations which impelled men to join churches also affected women, but there were processes at work which were peculiar to women, necessary to the development of their "spheres"; these processes are suggested in part by assessing the negative response of numerous husbands to their wives' conversion. From the early days of the Evangelical movement, most men, even if remaining unconverted, probably attended worship with their wives. But others were not so cooperative, sometimes complaining about religious services which kept wives from their work, often making ministerial guests feel ill at ease, frequently interrupting or breaking up meetings, and on more than one occasion punishing the preacher for disrupting a happy home. Elder John Tanner bore the marks of one such confrontation. He once baptized a woman who had for a long time wanted to join the church, but whose husband—a "great persecutor," one clergyman called him—had persistently and stubbornly refused to allow it. Finally, during a revival, she gathered up her courage, related her experience of grace to the church, asked to be admitted into the community of faithful people, and was baptized. Her husband's fury was so intense that months later he deliberately intercepted Tanner on the way to meeting and shot him in the thigh with a horse pistol.[21]

Tanner's wound—which could be invested with Freudian significance—represented more than the anger of one man, and has to be understood in the context of opposition to Evangelicalism, an opposition which was apparent from the very first revivals of the movement. Preachers were "attacked" in various ways by civil authorities, local gentry, gangs of men and boys, and husbands. The pervasiveness of male opposition based on husbandly concern, as opposed to opposition based on considerations of taste, class, intellect, and personal comfort, is difficult to measure, but the former can be inferred as a distinct factor from itinerants' defensiveness after encounters with unbelieving male relatives of pious women as well as from such entries as this: "One was brought under deep distress, who some months back persecuted and kept back his wife."[22] The Reverend Jeremiah Norman was a circuit rider who frequently had trouble with husbands, one in particular who loudly interrupted the preacher's sermon by calling for his wife to fetch him a drink of water,[23] and others who simply taunted him, or scoffed, or offensively assumed the role of "pure heathen," despite their being married to "admirable" women, as Norman called them, of profound "Religious principles."[24] Scraps of evidence from church records also reveal conflict between husband and wife over religion. Sister Sarah Moss, like the wife of Elder Tanner's assailant, was determined to bear witness to her faith, although patience rather than confrontation was her style. Denied her husband's permission to join the Baptists upon conversion, she applied for church membership as soon as he died forty years later.[25] And if one is willing, through imaginative reenactment, to empathize with people locked into the mundane brutalities of past family life, he may guess at the frustrations and anger of the men and the mixed feelings of the women that arose when a committee from South Quay Baptist church investigated John Saunders's "abusing his wife."[26]

Since this kind of intervention in family life was not rare in Evangelical churches, and since conflict between religious wives and irreligious husbands seems to have been a definite phenomenon, it is possible to tease out of the reluctant sources one of the most subtle attractions of conversion. It provided women psychological and social space. The negative responses of people close to converts reveals the impact upon those converts of the sense of the New Birth. This is to say that conversion created a sense of release from the prior restraints of culture or class, role or stereotype. The release was from a sense of psychological dependence upon others—either

parents or spouses—and provided a sense of social distance from the
matrix of group relationships previously valued. The New Birth was
just what it was represented to be, a new entry into a new kind of
life. It was a renunciation of the old life; and the consequent
devaluation of that life was especially resented by worldly husbands
who did not share conversion and the conviction that the old life
was so bad and did not agree with the idea that their wives may
have suffered from it. Women's conversion could very easily be
interpreted as an independent action and a personal determination
to develop oneself through a new ideology, even against the wishes
of one's husband—or perhaps especially against the wishes of one's
husband. The intimate bonds of the religious community must
have provided some women with the care, sense of worth, and
companionship they did not receive from husbands.

In addition to the New Birth and the supportive role of the
church toward them, women could, without understanding the
interpersonal dynamics involved, employ the pastoral relationship
to create the sense of breathing space between them and the people
who lorded it over them. Wives and daughters could in all
innocence but with innate political shrewdness, cite Biblical passages and ministerial aphorisms to contradict or mitigate male
authority. When faced with dissenters or, worse, reformers in the
persons of their wives, men who were accustomed to laying down
the law to female dependents occasionally erupted into the kind of
rage that sent Elder John Tanner limping through life.

There is further significance to the assault on Tanner. Contributing to the alienation sensed by husbands was the subtle
attraction of women to the young men who led the Evangelical
movement. The repressed sensuality of a religion which emphasized love, care, and intimate companionship in Christ could easily
mix sacred and profane desire (assuming that they are indeed
different) into a volatile compound that provided women unaccus-
tomed to compassionate, impassioned, even passionate men, such
as the clergy seemed to be, with an emotional experience they could
not quite fathom, but which they knew excited and fulfilled them.
The interaction between women communicants and ministers is a
persistent problem in religious history; camp meetings were
thought by some suspicious people to be as licentious and sexually

dangerous as Evangelicals thought "promiscuous dancing" to be. The sensual overtones of women's responses to Evangelical preaching certainly impressed Mrs. Trollope,[27] but there were others less critical who were concerned about the problem. Generations of ministers were warned by their mentors to beware the hidden dynamics of even proper relations with the women of their churches. Every Methodist *Discipline* printed for the nineteenth-century South contained this warning to ministers: "Converse sparingly, and conduct yourself prudently with women. 1 Tim. v, 2."[28] But some advice was far more specific: "You are men, with the passions of men, exposed to the temptations of men, and in the name of God, we charge you to remember this matter."[29] Actual seduction, however, was never so common as emotional attachment and reliance, which seemed so innocent, but which nonetheless could inflict anxiety, as it did for one profoundly pious woman who wrote her young, aggressive former pastor an intense, emotional letter. "You will perhaps be surprised at these incoherent lines," she wrote, "but be assured that they flow from a heart that glows with love to the saviour of sinners, and to everyone who bears his image, and in a particular manner to those whose views and feeling correspond with its own, to you D[ear] brother as the Embasedor [sic] of peace, I feel a peculiar attachment." At the bottom of the letter she added: "Destroy this."[30]

More than social and psychological space was required for southern women in the late eighteenth- and early nineteenth-century South. Judging from the disciplinary trials of local churches, their position was not an ideal one, despite their presumed economic importance to the family. Students of women's history often portray women's status in preindustrial society, such as the late eighteenth-century South, as being higher than in industrial society because in preindustrial times their economic contributions were so important to the maintenance of the family. Later, as production changed, it is assumed that the husband's unique role as breadwinner elevated him above his wife, and the agrarian equality of the idyllic past gave way to invidious distinctions and the subjugation of women. The testimony of women in the South from the Revolution to the Civil War, however, raises serious doubts as to the Edenic quality of agrarian society, unless one keeps in mind that Adam's status was superior to Eve's.

Eve, however, had to be protected from the Adams of the world, and, alas, of the church, too. From congregational records of the 1780s through the 1820s, the stern Evangelical commitment to responsible behavior between the sexes is revealed over and over again, as is a special concern with protecting women from sexual abuse. Because of the subsequent "Victorian" suppression of female sexuality, scholars who have not studied church records closely may assume that Evangelical concern about proper sexual behavior was really an expression of the dominant males' desire to control and demean women through identifying them with the demon of sensuality. For the first fifty or sixty years of southern Evangelical expansion, this theory would be an ideological gloss unsubstantiated by evidence, although for the period after the 1830s, when the Evangelical ideal of womanhood began to be articulated into an ideology, it is an understandable hypothesis.

In the early days of the movement, however, it was the male predator who had to be suppressed. Three types of problems may be represented by three cases. The first case is that of Brother John Holms, an aspiring young preacher ·from Mill Swamp Baptist Church in Southside Virginia, who was charged with spreading tales about his wife and falsely representing himself to two women. Although the church record in such cases was usually written in a circumlocutory code, the story is fairly clear. Holms had attempted to have sexual intercourse with two women by promising to marry them, but his motives were scrambled, for after having compromised the women, he "exposed them" to the community. In the meantime, the women had apparently found out about each other and the wife he had calumniated. As a result, Holms was hailed before the conference of Mill Swamp church, found guilty, and declared "out of their Fellowship and from under their Watch & care." Black women could expect the same protection, for a few months later "Brother Sam, property of Mrs. Hardy" was charged with attempting "unlawful cohabitation" against the consent of a free black woman.[31]

The next two cases involve interracial issues. In the second case, William J. Newbourn, a white Baptist minister, was accused of attempting to have sexual relations with five slave women; he offered one a new dress, another twenty-five cents, but he failed in each foray. A church committee took the women's statements, as well as those of two male slaves and a white woman, and reported to a conference of five clergymen and a crowd of lay persons from four churches. The results were not so conclusive as was the swift justice meted out to Brother Holms. It is apparent that many, perhaps most, of the white people present believed the black women's testimony, but a majority would not excommunicate Newbourn. After a long debate, it was obvious that the conference had a guilty man whom only a minority wanted to punish. Finally "it was decided that the circumstantial proof was so strong against him, he should [illegible; written over and through]."[32] The third case involves a black woman's accusation of a man who was not a church member and therefore was not subject to action by the congregation. In a most disturbed manner, the woman confided to her pastor that her master regularly demanded that she submit to sexual intercourse with him. Frustrated by his inability to affect the situation directly, and perhaps made insensitive by class, sex, and race to the helplessness of the woman, the minister encouraged her to reason with her master, but she was raped again. Her master was not predisposed to discuss the matter with a female slave. The minister then suggested that she refuse to submit, on the basis of her Christian sensibilities and the sin and guilt with which her assailant had burdened her soul; but it was not her soul that interested the master. "Wasted and broken hearted," the woman endured her master's licentiousness until he died, after which the pastor brought her into his own home as his children's nurse.[33]

Within the cultural context, the minister's act was much more than a salving of conscience—it was a symbol of personal redemption. Placing a former concubine over one's children, where her moral influence was commonly acknowledged to be great, was an impressive act of faith in her, which would have elevated her in the eyes of the church and helped to heal her battered conscience. But such private actions, while they reveal the moral quality of many black-white relationships in slavery, reveal also the impotence and essential futility of such personal actions insofar as victims of oppression were concerned. The structural supports and protection offered women by the church were only so powerful as the oppressors, by virtue of their own religious commitment and moral integrity, allowed them to be. To this extent, therefore, Evangelical churches provided ideals and practices which, however flawed, offered haven to women as well as the "breathing space" of religious commitment and participation.

Much more important to women in the evolution of their sphere than any of the factors already discussed, however, was the fact that through Evangelical expansion women were brought together in a public body. The significance of such an obvious, simple fact could easily be overlooked, especially in a culture accustomed to assemblies of women. But in the sparsely populated, agrarian states of the South during the early national period, public assemblies were primarily male affairs, where men came to court, muster, market, and poll. If women attended on these occasions, it was as an extension of their relationship with men or because of extraordinary circumstances. Doubtless the social contact with other women on these occasions was very important, as much so as when families gathered to celebrate a wedding, preside over a birth, or bury the dead. But nothing in public life served to establish the importance of women as individuals with special, intense needs, anxieties, and hopes which had to be met. By filling this social vacuum, the revivals of Evangelical expansion added a new dimension to the social life of women.

For women, the crux of the matter was, not surprisingly, the conversion experience, the subsequent relation of that experience to the church, and ultimate acceptance as a member. In this process, the individual was indeed under judgment, but she was confronted by a friendly tribunal, to whom she explained her conviction of sin, her reliance upon Christ, and her hope for eternal salvation. This one act of public speaking—traumatic and hedged about by male authority as it was—became the symbol of newfound maturity and a claim upon the Church of Christ for respect and honor. She had stood up in meeting on her own, without the intercession of a male, and had expressed some of her most private thoughts, which were accepted by the community as significant and praiseworthy. That a majority of her fellow Christians were women like herself could not have failed to encourage her; that a few older women of the church were revered by men and women alike as exceptional Christians could not have been missed in her fervent search for maturity. And that women such as she were in a public assembly as essential participants—even as a majority of them—must have had some subtle, unconscious effect upon her conception of herself and especially on her self-esteem and self-confidence. The result of her joining other women in the church was not "liberation" or "equality," as we have come to use these terms, but the beginning of a slow process, which would move from the abstraction of emotion to the reality of exclusively female organizations through which women could participate in public affairs outside the family and locality. Before the end of the eighteenth century, women were organizing their own prayer groups, and after the revivals of 1802 were creating here and there local "female" missionary, education, and aid societies. By the 1830s, these organizations would become, with the churches, the focal point of social activities for women in the South.

That this structural development of formal associations for women should have occurred is not surprising, especially when considered in light of recent information on female friendship and companionship in nineteenth-century America. In an original and admirably incisive study, Carroll Smith-Rosenberg has described the emotional bonding of women to each other, a bonding which created "a specifically female world," a "world built around a generic and unself-conscious pattern of single-sex or homosocial networks." The explanation of these networks emphatically rejects the psychosexual bias which would distort them as homosexual relationships. The importance of these networks in a society developing distinct roles for women and men was to bond women to each other in mutual support, personal companionship, and social solidarity within women's sphere, which was, as Smith-Rosenberg emphasizes, the creation of women.[34] By projection of their shared experiences into associations, such as the churches and related organizations, women built a world which was theoretically acknowledged and valued by men, but which men could never penetrate. Evangelicalism, through bringing women together in churches, academies, seminaries, and societies and providing the framework within which to form this homosocial network and the language in which to explain it, made a profound impact upon southern women, the effects of which still persist in many parts of the twentieth-century South.

The trend that made churches the chief means of establishing a
public life for women was probably the most significant aspect of
the process which helped Evangelicalism to express the world view
of an "enlightened and refined people." The early Evangelical
movement had created a self-conscious people who rejected the
cultural and social hegemony of traditional elites, and by the 1830s
this new constituency was evolving in turn an even newer constituency—Evangelical women. The radical implications of early Evangelical rhetoric and behavior, which were clear to the point of
exaggeration for eighteenth-century gentry and civil authorities,
and which were quashed in the traumatic controversies over
slaveholding, were powerful enough to make Evangelical publicists
begin to think about women as having a special role to play in
society. Some of those implications were articulated in the manner
in which Evangelicals distinguished between themselves and the
world by focusing on the differences between worldly and converted women. They viewed the former as frivolous, flighty, and
careless, mere ornaments to their men, the thoughtless accoutrements of wealth and position. This last accusation was especially
important for understanding the thrust of Evangelicalism because
invidious distinctions between Evangelical women and others were
usually directed upward, against women of a superior social
position rather than against those of the same or lower class. When
women of a more modest social position were addressed, they were
warned against aping the style, dress, and behavior of the idle rich,
whose only claim to esteem, according to Evangelicals, was position
based on birth, rather than personal worth. To supplant the sinful
power of the aristocratic ideal of womanhood, Evangelicals began to
shape a model of behavior and ideals which was peculiarly the
possession of women and was based on their unique contribution to
the ideal community. This emphasis on, indeed *commitment* to
"women's sphere" therefore came out of the early Evangelical
perception of the cosmic conflict between the church and the
world. It was subsequently made possible by the participation of
great numbers of women in religious life, the important part they
played in the early movement, the homosocial world they developed, and the failure of men to perform their ideal role in
establishing family religion and the Christian home. The nurturing

function of women within the family came to take on ideological significance as Evangelical southern women became the ultimate model of Christian discipleship. Ministers repeated, sometimes to the point of obsession, the importance of feminine contributions to the common life in Christ, responding to the imposing presence of women at religious assemblies, and speaking out of their own romanticized but indelible experience with pious mothers and wives.

The ideal of southern Evangelical womanhood began to arrest public attention in the 1830s. Then and thereafter, Evangelical publicists, preachers, and women spent a great deal of time and energy in developing an abstraction which, if put in theological context, replaced the Holy Spirit as the bearer of God's grace with the "virtuous love of a pure woman." And because the home supplanted the church as the essential Christian community, and because the mother's role in nurturing the family in Christian love had become so important, it is not surprising that one of the chief qualities of the southern Evangelical woman should have become domesticity. Although it eventually became a boundary to be maintained, rather than a quality to be prized, the domestic ideal, women's indispensable and unique contribution to religion and morality in the household, offered them honor and respect equal to that of men. The rearing of children became not only an economic and social necessity, but also an ideological requirement, since Evangelical theory demanded that every person assert herself to the utmost in the relentless drive for Christian maturity. As the moral and mental preceptors of the family, pious mothers were in a position to shape the next generation of Evangelicals, as well as to provide theorists with one of the most important distinctions between themselves and worldlings. Repudiated was the presumed carelessness of worldly women, who were said to be lackadaisical about child care, mental discipline, and moral improvement. Affirmed was the superiority and strength of Evangelical women.

They were considered superior, that is, to everyone but their husbands, "the anointed lords of the creation."[35] This exception, the source of much scolding by ill-tempered clergymen, rested on a sentence in one of Paul's apostolic letters in which the sainted bachelor warned wives to "submit yourselves to your own husbands

as to the Lord." This command, made as it was to those responsible
for Christian nurture and the quality of family life, required
women to assume a Christlike role of suffering servant and to play
out the drama of salvation in the family. It required her to be
married in order to be valued as a contributor to the social good, to
have children, and to lose no opportunity in teaching them social
responsibility, religion, and appropriate demeanor. It required her
to support her husband without thought for her own selfish
interests, maintaining a demure, self-denying submissiveness even
to a husband who was unreasonable, inconsiderate, and immoral.
Her only means of reforming those "anointed lords of creation"
who had fallen further out of Paradise than most men was not
through confrontation—that would be too "self-glorifying"—but
through the indirect, subtle, insinuating influences of wifely
devotion. Evangelicals believed that even "men whose souls seem
to be brutalized by long habits of cruelty and crime" could be
reformed in this manner.[36] The domestic realm was not intended to
be Golgotha, but that sphere of activity in which the Evangelical
woman would be highly valued. In this area where Christlike
qualities were required, however, there was always the possibility of
a Christlike end.

To strengthen and temper them in exercising their domestic role,
Evangelical women, it was believed, were endowed with a capacious
piety—not that men were thought to be impious, but women were
thought somehow to be more intensely and consistently pious
because they were assumed to be more emotional and affectionate
than men. Evangelicals explained the fact that there were more
female than male church members by observing that women were
by nature more religious than men. That the reasoning was circular
did not diminish its appeal, and with infallible certitude it thrust
upon women the role of mediating religious affections. It was
almost as if men willingly conceded the moral superiority of women
in order to prevent active female participation in worldly affairs.
How thoroughly women of all classes and ages adapted to the ideal
expectations of their piety is of course impossible to say, but in the
devotional diaries of middle-class women is eloquent testimony
that many southern women took quite seriously their role as
religious preceptors. In writing down their innermost thoughts

about their personal relationships, daily cares, and attempts to come to terms with the world and with themselves, pious southern women displayed a knowledge of self which undoubtedly surpassed in profundity and sensitivity most of the sermons they heard. On pages in their private confessionals, they admitted their doubts and fears, worked through the meaning of personal disappointment and hardship, and found in the language of Evangelicalism the symbols required to resolve the problems of their suffering and ignorance and to express their happiness and pleasure in simply being alive.

The careful scrutiny of self required by the Evangelical faith is everywhere evident in these devotional diaries, and to an age suspicious of deferred gratification and relentless drive may seem to be an unnatural, if pathetic, attempt to deny, discipline, and drive the self to impossible limits. And yet there is a surprising absence of self-righteous cant and invidious distinction between the self and others, unless such a distinction is made to humble the writer herself in her act of confession. In her personal life, the pious southern woman of "low estate"—even if not so eloquent or educated as those who wrote diaries—must have appropriated the religious language available to her, as to her more articulate sisters, not as a problem of doctrine or dogma, but as a means of understanding all the encounters of life, whether losing her temper over a daughter's insubordination or discovering the limits of her own religious knowledge when confronted with the unsurpassed saintlinesss of a slave whose intense, elemental piety was an expression not so much of Galilee as of Africa.

Piety could very easily have become an insipid, limp, and paralyzing retreat into oneself but for the demands of Evangelical usefulness. This essential quality in the Evangelical ideal of woman-hood required something much more profound than a dour commitment not to enjoy life. It was a quality which distinguished her from the "thousands," described by novelist Augusta Evans, "who [were] graceful, pretty, witty, and pleasant companions for a promenade or a pic-nic." The problem with these young ladies, however, was that "their information [was] scanty; their judgment defective, their reasoning faculties dwarfed, their aspirations weak and frivolous."[37] They were, charged one young Evangelical clergy-

man, "trifling butterflies."[38] And an older man, a bishop, argued
that young women of the church were not called by Christ to
"dance well, dress finely, and be adorned and flattered by men of
empty heads and vicious hearts, without any reference to usefulness."[39] To achieve this usefulness, the serious Evangelical woman
was to be thoughtful, reflective, well-read in religious literature,
and "mistress of herself and her actions."[40] It is doubtful that early
Evangelicals intended women to infer from Evangelical usefulness
what eventually became independence of mind. At first, the
concept of usefulness meant that pious women would in demeanor
and affections establish themselves as persistent reminders to the
whole Christian community that life was to be based on eternal
principles, not ephemeral fashion, the passion of the moment, the
immediate gratification of undisciplined desire. That entry into the
Evangelical community was made through the transformation of
the nonrational conversion experience, and that women were
thought to be by nature more emotional than men helped to
reinforce the belief that women were more religious than men. If
Evangelicals had left the matter of conversion bereft of its perfec-
tionist connotations, the dichotomy between emotional women
and rational men could have been sustained even in the best of
Evangelical thought. For many thoughtless and unreflective people, of course, that was indeed where the matter rested, but not for
consistent and thoroughly versed Evangelicals. The emphasis on
usefulness, which when applied to men reinforced their pretensions
to rationality, was seen as the intellectual and psychological means
through which women could repudiate the canard of their "affectionate and emotional nature" and eventually demand and receive
the same education as their male coreligionists. Usefulness made
such claims upon the mental discipline of woman that it was not at
all surprising that by the 1850s she should have asserted her "right
as an immortal being, and duty as a responsible agent of society, to
unfold and improve, enlarge and refine *all* the powers of the mind,
and to enrich and embellish her intellect with all the treasures of
science and adornments of literature."[41]

The measure of usefulness for Evangelical women was the extent
to which they tried to make their religion normative for southern
society through personal example and good works. This quality,

benevolence, was a commitment to action. As one woman wrote to her brother, "My heart and hands & thought are ever employed, & this is what is called happiness—something to love, something to labor for, something to be accomplished, before I go hence & be no more."[42] It was this concept of southern Christian women that encouraged Angelina Grimke, the Charleston-born abolitionist, to plead with her "sisters in Christ" to scorn persecution and free their slaves.[43] In the context of time and place, hers was a romantic and unrealistic appeal, but by the time Grimke wrote her pamphlet (1836), Evangelical southern women had already established their peculiar and most important act of benevolence by becoming tribunes, teachers, and missionaries to slaves. Perhaps much antipathy to slavery seethed from disgust with its licentiousness, personified by mulattoes, and with its degradation, exemplified in ignorance, deceit, and suspicion; but this antipathy was channeled by Evangelical women—theoretically at least—into benevolent acts on behalf of slaves. One woman recalled with grief and pride the Christian maturity of her little daughter, who in the weeks before her death would "sit an hour or more at a time and repeat a verse of a hymn to the negroes and in that way she gained the respect and love of many poor blacks. The last hymn she selected and taught to several of them is a beautiful one, 'Did Christ o'er sinners weep, Ec.' "[44]

The Evangelical woman at work is best exemplified in the life of Anne R. Page, who personified the qualities, contradictions, limitations, and strength of the ideal. Born Anne Randolph Meade in 1781, she became Mrs. Matthew Page in 1799 when she married a wealthy planter of northern Virginia. Her father and mother were devout Evangelicals, as well as Episcopalians, and almost immediately after her wedding she was able to endure an intense emotional crisis only through the healing power of her religious inheritance. She emerged determined to order her life according to strict Evangelicalism rather than according to the new, "fashionable" life of her husband's friends and acquaintances. Accordingly, she began to write devotional essays in order to clarify in her own mind the nature and depth of her religious commitment. She would confess the most terrifying sense of self-alienation and shame, and would express regret at "friends meeting together and

never speaking to each other of Christ and his salvation."[45] To turn
her own life in a new direction, she began to assert boldly her
private beliefs for the edification of all who came within her sphere
of influence—strangers, friends, children, overseers, masters, and
slaves. It is not surprising, therefore, that she should have had such
an impact on her young brother, William Meade, who became
bishop of the Episcopal diocese of Virginia, one of the leading
Evangelicals of his denomination, and for whom she provided an
indispensable lieutenant in the form of her son-in-law, Charles
Wesley Andrews. Nor is it surprising, given her importunate zeal,
independence of mind, and strength of conviction, that she should
sometimes be too aggressive. "Teach me," she entreated God, "To
pray more for my friends when I feel anxious concerning them, and
talk less."[46]

Her obsession as an Evangelical, however, was to convert and free
her slaves. These goals were the result in part of her feeling of
indebtedness to blacks for the piety and strength of character which
had influenced her own, and in part her belief that slavery was
contrary to the principles of Christianity. The evils of slavery, she
wrote, "are linked by a chain which reaches into the dominion of
Satan."[47] How she came to this view and whether or not she
believed that the chain was forged in the fires of what she would
have called licentiousness is difficult to say. But it is clear that she
made her efforts for slaves the measure of her Christian commitment, as did many other southern women. She sternly condemned
the sexual exploitation of black women and tried to prevent it
whenever she could. She schooled her slaves in order to erase their
terrible ignorance, provided religious exercises to convert them
from "heathenish darkness," and tried to persuade them to
prepare for freedom in Africa. Her commitment to colonization in
Liberia was based on her belief that blacks were not safe from
persecution and exploitation as long as they remained in the United
States. At three different times, therefore, she sent most of her
slaves to Africa together with provisions for a year. Such a
commitment cost her a great deal of money and effort, but because
she was not an easy person to live with—"By nature irritable and
proud," she said of herself—and was, after all, their "owner," her
slaves did not always appreciate her position and the work she

demanded of them. It was one of the trials she had to endure, she told herself, and prayed to God to "enlighten" slaves so that they would "bear with patience the trial of being under the guidance of one, who only from necessity as they well know, is enduring, and that for their sakes, the task of urging them to such duties as will lead them to their temporal and eternal freedom."[48]

The interest of Evangelical women in acts of benevolence for slaves was mired in contradiction and irony, and reveals that the original Evangelical interest in slaves had been transformed not only by the internal contradictions of religious ideology, but also by the changing class orientation of Evangelicalism. After the failure of antislavery activity in the early Republic, Christian benevolence for the slave had been relegated to that realm of "nice but impractical acts" which the powerful concede to the powerless when the latter have only morality on their side. Thus women, powerless in most public acts, could be humored in their attempts to change the quality if not the fact of slave society. As persistent problems in the southern social system, the ignorance, heathenism, and "pathetic" lot of slaves could attract all the pent-up passion to do good which Evangelicalism required of its devotees and at the same time consign any ultimately equitable solution of the class/race problem to heaven, the end of history, the millennium, or any other state of existence in which ordinary rules of practicality and logic did not apply. The beauty of this maneuver was that southern apologists could boast that they were trying through their women to make slaves into acceptable human beings, but that the blacks' native incapacity and the hopeless, if admirable, religious fancy of impractical women made the project unrealistic from the start. The South could get moral credit for attempting an "impossible ethic," and at the same time could get political credit for ensuring its impossibility.

Another interesting characteristic of the ideal of religious benevolence was that it focused attention on the responsibilities of Christian women to their slaves in a society in which most men and women did not own slaves. Evangelical women could give money to slave missions, which they did; they could support colonization, which they did; they could be inspired to respond to the religious affections of blacks in worship services. But most of them could

never convert, educate, or free their slaves as did Mrs. Page because
most of them had no slaves. All of which is to underscore the
orientation of Evangelical publicists in the antebellum South to the
slaveowning middle and upper classes—"enlightened and refined
people." The example of Mrs. Page—who through her personal
wealth could actually do more to free slaves than most women—was
significant for thousands of women who could aspire to the ideal.
And yet, they, like Mrs. Page, could never receive from slaves the
one thing which might have rewarded their efforts in a difficult and
demanding cause—gratitude for having braved the slave system on
their behalf. If female Evangelicals did not receive this bounty from
the powerless, perhaps it was because they were to slaves so
obviously an extension of the powerful—the men—who lavishly
heaped upon their women accolades, honor, and respect. It was
difficult for Mrs. Page and her sisters in the faith to accept this
bitter truth, and it served to make them dissatisfied with their social
role, if not to understand it.

A generation of religious publicists had elevated the Evangelical
woman to supremacy in her sphere—the private life of her home,
husband, and children. But even as they proclaimed her queen,
they stripped away her power by reminding her to be submissive
and obedient to her husband, certainly not the sort of attitude
which got Elder John Tanner shot in 1777. Submissiveness and the
strength of mind encouraged by Evangelical seriousness were not
complementary; indeed, to many young southern women they were
contradictory, a problem which bedeviled sensitive Evangelicals of
both sexes for many years. Nowhere was the conflict between the
two more apparent than in the Evangelicals' determination to
educate their daughters as well as their sons. Evangelical academies
for young ladies were part of the southern landscape by 1830, and
by 1850 female colleges were becoming as important as were men's
colleges to the Evangelicals' conception of themselves as responsible
stewards of public order, social cohesiveness, and civic pride. The
problem, of course, was how to justify collegiate education for
women without expanding their "appropriate sphere" and destroying their refinement, sensibility, piety and purity. The solution lay
in constructing the appropriate curricula; and in debating this
point the contradiction between Evangelical usefulness and female

submissiveness was never more clear. Conservatives argued that women had minds so completely different from those of men that the curriculum should be designed for "the cultivation of the affections," rather than of the intellect. Teach young women to speak, write, read, and understand moral issues, they suggested, not to cipher, speculate, or analyze public issues. Warning that such nonsense was "absurd in dogma, false in premise, and illogical in conclusion,"[49] progressive Evangelicals argued that the curricula should be identical for both sexes. Less concerned with the implications of their stand and more eager to praise intellectual achievement in women than were conservatives, progressive Evangelicals nevertheless agreed with their antagonists that the purpose of educating women was to create respectable, informed, sensible, and intelligent preceptors to shape the next generation of Evangelicals.

Almost everywhere she turned, the southern Evangelical woman was confronted with standards which impeded her free development as an autonomous person. She was to be perpetually busy doing the Lord's work, but never completing it; she was to be intensely devoted to serving the servants, but never rewarded with gratitude; she was to be supreme in her sphere, but bounded by it. The early promise of personal salvation, never withdrawn, was eventually transformed into the expectations of propriety. Evangelical women—endowed by the ideal with a unique capacity to sense religious and moral truth—were expected to personify the church itself in refined manners and pious attitudes. They were to behave in an appropriate manner among appropriate people to achieve appropriate goals. That restraint, discipline, moral fervor, and a sense of personal worth should have become the means to "refinement" instead of salvation was not always and everywhere true for southern Evangelicals, but it was universal enough to betoken a major shift among the aspiring class of "enlightened and refined people."

Within the same world of image and expectation which projected the Evangelical woman into her sphere, there was also an image of the Evangelical man. Like his grandfather, he was expected to be different from worldlings; but the younger man discovered that the distinction was less easily made and maintained than it was in his grandfather's day. Outright alienation from what was becoming an

increasingly attractive world was less frequently adopted than was a
happy medium between the two worlds. Preparing for a visit to his
father's brother Charles in 1844, Basil Manly, Jr., a Baptist,
reminded himself that he would be "exposed to all the dangers of a
gay and fashionable life," and might be tempted to "relax" from
Evangelical "sober-mindedness." He would, he promised himself,
be "Cheerful—but not gay. Serious but not solemn. Cautious but
not overprecise." But he added in words his pious grandmother
would have approved: "I must also watch against idleness & waste
of time in unprofitable employments."[50] This reserve of Evangelical discipline continued to shape the ideal Christian man as well as
the woman, and it was not merely for Baptists. Episcopal communicants, for example, were sometimes required by their ministers
never to engage in frivolous entertainments (gambling, dancing,
theater-going) "inconsistent with a Christian profession," or to
practice any "known sin."[51] "What a treacherous thing the heart
is!" wrote one man in anguish; and he continued to wonder if ever
it would be possible for him to whip himself into Evangelical "Self-
forgetfulness."[52]

Despite the common effort to discipline self, Evangelical men
and women were seen, in the ideal realm of divine imperative, as
being complementary to each other and therefore different. To
make the Christian wife's domestic sphere possible, the Evangelical
man, through the exercise of restrained authority, was to love,
protect, and govern her. If women were emotional and weak, man
should be rational and strong; if she were submissive, he was to be
worthy of deference by being faithful, kind, considerate, and
restrained in the use of his authority. Male restraint, unlike female
submissiveness, relied less on the traditional structure of male-
female relationships than on the refined sensibilities of a converted
will. The Evangelical ideal of female domesticity was reinforced by
law and custom, which already made the woman subject to, or at
least an appendage of, her male relatives. The Evangelical ideal of
restrained authority, which characterized the converted man, had
no such reinforcement. Victimized women had to rely—as we have
seen—upon the resolve and sensitivity of reborn Christian men;
they presumably had no power or authority of their own, aside from
their piety.

Even in the realm of the holy life, the words applied to women and men reveal power on the side of men, deference on the side of women. Piety properly characterized the latter—the urgent, intense longing for union with the object of devotion. Religious duty was said to characterize the Evangelical man—responsible action in the exercise of power in a public world from which women were barred. Essential to enabling the Christian man to do his duty, absolutely necessary for the protection of the Evangelical home, and indispensable for commending converted men to honor and respect was self-control. He who provided the framework of authority within which the pious woman could be protected from the world was commanded to subdue his sensual "appetites," to avoid the licentiousness, lewdness, and "carnal intimacies" of the world.[53] The furies that afflicted William McKendree when the Evangelical movement was young,[54] and which made local church records sometimes read like the invention of a gossipmonger's fertile imagination, continued to bedevil Evangelicals throughout the nineteenth-century South. But the converted man was to fight against them, to "curb, restrict, check every appetite, passion and purpose" which comforted the body in preference to the soul.[55] This self-control and sense of religious duty, together with the emphasis on restrained authority, served to reinforce the tendencies already noted in Evangelicalism to emphasize personal solutions to problems created by social situations—hence the minister who solved the problem of his black parishioner's rape by eventually buying her and giving her an honored position in his household.[56]

Another aspect of the Evangelical image of the Christian man, and one which also complements his female counterparts' usefulness and benevolence, was his Christian dignity, or example. The exemplary conduct of pious women was the demeanor of those presumed weak; but that of the Christian man had a special force to it because it indicated that those who held power could also personify and therefore commend to society at large the morally refined life of a Christian gentleman. This sense of Christian exemplification not only demanded the kind of self-consciousness which could very easily lead to stubborn pride, it also tended to create the attitude of self-assurance which could support one who found himself alone in a crowd of worldlings. And if this view of one's responsibility in public encouraged self-righteousness, it was

nevertheless one of the ways Evangelical theorists had of merging
their own values of self-discipline and responsible action with those
of a culture which celebrated the romanticized, self-generating,
virile, and aggressive man.

Images and ideal models rarely find their way into everyday
human experience as actual behavior. Evangelical publicists, with
their knowledge of human sin, should have been the first to
acknowledge that fact, but they often failed to do so, despite their
persistent exhortations to conform, obey, repent, and be born
again. The contrast between ideal image and mundane reality
revealed a perpetual warfare between the world and Evangelicals,
but the conflict of images and realities was much more complex
than the old dichotomy. The southern lady may have been
characterized by piety, but Evangelical theorists wanted their
women to be more than a "belle" or an adornment; they
demanded serious commitment to Christ and His work. Evangelical
demands upon men also continued to be at odds with popular
images of masculinity, virility, and honor, shaped as they were by a
system of values that celebrated strength, personal pride, worldly
acclaim, and independence of regulation, whether by church or
law.[57] Moreover, there was dissatisfaction among women who
resented the dependent role into which they had been thrust by a
world of men who were not so bound by law and custom to
approximate an ideal which demanded the perfection of Christlike
qualities as were women. Discontented with both reality and ideal,
and perhaps encouraged by northern feminists and abolitionists,
women restlessly resisted the "anointed Lords of creation" in so
many ways that the latter expounded all the more intensely upon
the peculiar qualities of the southern lady and her proper subjection to men. The purpose was to maintain the hierarchy of southern
society, but its result was to blur some of the distinctions between
the Evangelical woman and the southern lady. Evangelical insistence upon usefulness and the southern ideal of pious women
would, after the Civil War, create a mood and provide an institution through which women could make a better place for themselves in southern society.[58]

In the meantime, as we shall see, Evangelical theorists tried to
resolve the conflicts between reality and ideal and between female

and male ideals by diverting attention to responsibilities devolving upon both sexes because of African slavery. But if southern Evangelicals were able to do anything toward resolving such conflicts, it was because their constituency could believe in the reality as well as the ideal of the southern Evangelical lady. The problem would continue to be, however, how much of the ideal to hope for and how much of the reality to reject.

The transformation of southern Evangelicalism from a movement with radical implications to a model of social propriety was not quite so simple a process as recounting it may suggest. Social interaction and development are never simple matters, for with them comes a sense of loss among people who feel deprived of the rewards of change.

In some ways, Evangelicalism never changed. Among its persistent qualities was that which elevated worshipers to the central position in preaching services—the "warm, pathetic style" of address with which preachers evoked a positive, emotional, response from their congregations. Preaching could vary from Methodists' revivalistic harangues to the careful, modulated cadences of Presbyterians and Episcopalians, but at either end of the spectrum the purpose of the discourse was the same: either to trigger the emotional crisis which converted new disciples, or to remind mature Christians of their own experience of Grace. Out of this recurring celebration was to come the recurring commitment to the life of holiness and self-discipline. An equally indispensable quality was the church's role in directing those efforts which most distinguished Evangelicals from other, more quietistic Christian groups—their persistent, sometimes annoying, always active resolve to proselytize. These qualities were modified naturally over the years between the Revolution and Civil War. In response to educational and social development, preachers in town and large country churches became less flamboyant and incantational in their delivery, perhaps more sophisticated in their perception of problems, but no less direct in addressing the pew, nor less emphatic about the need for religious conversion and commitment. Now and then a disgusted preacher might confide his distaste for "the frothy effervescence of a lamentable imbecility,"[59] but he would do so as a committed Evangelical, firmly convinced that religious affections were essential

to religious experience. The mission also remained important, and
if changed at all, was more intense, widespread, and important to
the spiritual heirs of Davies, Stearns, and Asbury than to the
founders themselves. Evangelicals discovered by the 1830s that they
had it within their power not only to push back the boundaries of
the world, but to tear them down as well.

Skeptical dissidents from within Evangelicalism itself thought
such optimism not only unrealistic and pretentious, but also
unscriptural. It was impossible, they believed, for frail if ambitious
men to create agencies equal to the task of converting society—only
God could do so, and in His own time and way. The colleges,
which were so important to denominational identity and Evangelical aspiration, and which were supposed to enable the newly born
in Christ to "convert" society, were charged by dissenters, especially among Baptists and Methodists, with being merely the
nurseries of a new aristocracy. Higher education in their view had
always been one of the accoutrements of the upper classes, and their
experience with college-educated ministers did nothing to change
their minds. Too often the graduate was proud of the gulf between
himself and the laity and simply refused to bridge it. Too often the
colleges seemed to be demanding money from the faithful without
providing tangible, positive results in a sound and sympathetic
clergy. "We want preachers—not metaphysicians," these dissidents seemed to be saying, "working men not dandies—self-
denying, distinterested men—not those who will quit the pulpit for
a better salary out of it or marry a fortune and do nothing."[60]
Colleges, dissidents believed, robbed them of a responsive leadership as well as an honored place in the church, but instead of being
sensitive to this predicament, Evangelicals and historians alike have
accused dissidents of making ignorance and illiteracy virtues in
celebration of a mindless anti-intellectualism. To expect people to
value things and ideas for which their social position has not
prepared them remains a persistent trait of the middle-class
mentality, a kind of intellectual imperialism which the dissidents
resented and attacked.

Equally offensive to many dissidents—especially among Baptists
—was the machinery which Evangelicals created to facilitate their
aggressive expansion. During the revivals of the latter eighteenth
century, synods, associations, and conferences directed missionary

activity, so expansion seemed to be the extension of local churches or societies. Even so, Baptist churches were often cautious and sometimes reluctant to grant associations independent power to dispatch and direct missionaries. And in the Methodist church, a serious quarrel over the power of Bishop Asbury to centralize ecclesiastical authority in his office and to assign Methodist ministers where he chose thrust the antislavery leader, James O'Kelly, out of the mother church and into the Republican Methodist church of southern Virginia and eastern North Carolina, in 1792. Nevertheless, most Evangelicals gradually became accustomed to the rapid pace of expansion and the more complicated structures it required. After 1800, short-lived missionary societies were founded to give southern Baptists the same kind of organizational flexibility which characterized the Methodist Episcopal church. In 1814 many Baptists joined their most distinguished minister, Richard Furman of Charleston, South Carolina, in welcoming the creation of a national triennial convention of Baptists, designed to support and supervise foreign and domestic missions. The convention set a precedent that inspired young Baptist ministers—many of them from the north and often boasting college degrees—to agitate throughout the South for state conventions to rally moral and financial support for education, missionary, Bible, and tract societies. These pious but importunate mendicants seemed to scurry everywhere, always with bold, romantic phrases about converting the world and elevating their coreligionists, and invariably with hat in hand to hold the collection.

"Money-hunters!" "Hypocrites!" charged dissidents, who resented what they termed the presumption, arrogance, and intrusion of these "outsiders."[61] Throughout the South, Baptists began to fight over whether or not the Evangelical mission should be carried on by autonomous local churches or by larger, more inclusive organizations created by and responsible to a convention of all Baptist churches in a state and possibly also to national boards based in the North. The character of the debate and debaters can best be understood by recounting how each side understood the matter. Partisans for benevolence and missionary societies identified themselves as progressive, informed, intelligent people whose agencies and conventions were the natural means of fulfilling the mission of the Christian church. It seemed to these activists that they were the only people in the South who could convert the world, quell social disorder, strengthen social bonds, and educate the next generation. They were also convinced that they had to overhaul the Baptist clergy by establishing colleges to set the high standards of excellence so important to them. Their opponents were described as bigoted, irrational, xenophobic, *"indolent, covetous, soul-destroying, God dishonoring."* Convention forces even succeeded in attaching to their opponents the label of "antimissionary Baptists."[62]

The issue, however, was not the missionary goal of the church. To be sure, many dissidents reaffirmed their theological ties with John Calvin and his emphasis upon God's sovereign power, stern justice, and saving grace, which reminded men of their passive role in the plan of salvation. But this was not so much a doctrinal dispute as a way of reminding Evangelicals that they were simply too optimistic about what their vaunted agencies and conventions could accomplish, and too careless of the scriptural warrant which granted the task of the mission to the church and to no other institution. And the church, dissidents emphasized to their coreligionists, was a local congregation—a community—of faithful people who had been bound together in Christ; it was not some abstraction which was the sum total of agencies, associations, and conventions. A second accusation leveled at Evangelicals was that they were moneygrubbing, ambitious, and power oriented, that they wanted to use the funds gathered from localities to create institutions which they—not the people who had given the money —would control and through which they would rise to prominence. And yet they could not be called to account by the church membership! To make the point all the more forcefully, dissidents emphasized the alien character of many Evangelical agitators: they were often Yankees, youngsters from other localities who had served a church briefly if at all, and ambitious men who saw an opportunity to gain prestige and position by creating institutions to serve the emergent middle classes in the South. Many dissident accusations were, if allowance is made for the heat of controversy, accurate reports.

Dissidents also attempted to present themselves as common folk exploited by people intent on improving their social position. Careful study of Evangelical and dissident leadership suggests that

the metaphor was slightly exaggerated, for at least in some localities, dissidents owned no less wealth in either land or slaves
than Evangelicals. And often the fight seemed to be primarily
between older ministers already established in local churches and
younger men whose more formal education and commitment to
high standards of excellence in training ministers caused them to
reject local attachments in favor of more abstract loyalties to
denomination, the South, the nation, the cause. In other words,
the fight was between parochial and cosmopolitan, community and
society, locality and nation. But the dissidents themselves did not
leave the matter there, for they persistently described themselves as
common folk fighting to withstand the tyranny of a greedy and irresponsible upper class. The constant demand for money to support
Evangelical institutions seemed to prove the case for many dispu-
tants, but the actions of Evangelical agents themselves seemed to
clinch the argument. Where do they beg? asked "a Clodhopper of
North Carolina," Who do they court and with whom do they stay?
"They like the houses of colonels [and] squires, and to have very
rich and fat tables and stables."[63]

The result of this controversy among Baptists was the founding
of the Primitive Baptist churches as a separate denomination
in North Carolina and parts of Tennessee, Kentucky, and
Virginia. In many cases, churches simply refused to affiliate
with any association or convention, preferring to maintain a
lonely but proud existence apart from the controversy and dis-
content of the world.

A similar controversy afflicted the Methodist Episcopal church.
The issue never became associated with missions, since the church
was itself a missionary organization, and its theology supported
missionary activity. But the issues of local autonomy versus centralized authority and of democratic versus oligarchic rule were
debated by Methodists with the same kind of passion which
Baptists expressed. But whereas Baptist dissidents had opposed the
Evangelical innovation of centralizing agencies, Methodist reformers proposed the innovation of decentralizing and democratizing
their church. Beginning their agitation in the 1820s, they founded
the Methodist Protestant church in 1830 on the basis of lay
representation in annual and general conferences, participation by
unordained local preachers in the annual conferences, and a

general recognition of the importance of congregations' wishes in making important ecclesiastical decisions. Unlike Baptist controversialists, Methodists were not divided between Evangelicals and non-Evangelicals—the Methodist Protestant church was just as interested in colleges, educated ministers, and missions as the mother church. Indeed, the prominence of Methodist business and professional men (as well as the agitation of women who wished to vote on church matters) in the reform movement indicates that an assertive middle class would not be subject forever to ministerial direction.

And yet the Methodist Protestants were able to make inroads upon episcopal Methodism because there was with the growth of Methodist academies, colleges, and missions to slaves a sizable group of people who felt left out. They criticized the affluence of their coreligionists, an affluence which led to their wearing more richly ornamented clothing than "old Methodists," and their building of churches in the 1830s and 1840s which were more elaborate than the old meeting houses in which Francis Asbury had preached as if they had been cathedrals. And then, as if to repudiate the whole Methodist past, the churches were fitted with pianos. It was not merely bad temper, bigotry, or envy which led a few Methodists to write tirades against "piano thumpers," "fiddling Christians," and "catgut scrapers."[64] They felt themselves being demeaned and pushed aside by changes that reminded them all too forcefully of their own poverty and powerlessness. As one man announced, he was too poor to send his children to college, but he would still be able to teach them piety, which was, he emphasized, much superior to presumptuous refinement.

In thinking about southern evangelicalism, it is impossible to ignore the Protestant Episcopal church, which nurtured a strong Evangelical party especially in Virginia and the Old Southwest. As we have seen, the Anglican church in the southern colonies was so weak that its disestablishment in the Revolutionary era was relatively simple. By 1812 only Maryland, Virginia, and South Carolina had bishops and, even there the state of the church was only a little less desperate than in the rest of the South, for only six Protestant Episcopal churches in a state were required to form a diocese and elect a bishop. During the 1820s and 1830s a few plucky presbyters and bishops began to revitalize the church in such a way as to restore one's hope in the resurrection of the dead. Prime movers in the Episcopal revival were the Evangelicals of Virginia, under the leadership of Bishops Richard Channing Moore and William Meade. These men and their associates rejected their High Church colleagues' emphasis on the divine appointment of the apostilic episcopacy, arguing that the office was an apostolic ordinance desirable, but not indispensable, to Christian faith. A mediating priesthood through whose office the believer approached the throne of grace was abhorrent to them because, they insisted, "Every Christian is a priest!" They also rejected the idea that tradition was equal to the scriptures in establishing the rule of faith, for in this, as in all disputes with the High Churchmen, they insisted that the Christian life was achieved not through the structure and functions of the church and its ministry but through conversion of the sinful believer in direct confrontation with God. Therefore, like their fellow Evangelicals in other denominations, they emphasized the sin of man, his utter reliance upon God's grace and mediation, his need of a conversion experience followed by a life of discipline and devotion in spreading the Gospel. Thus it was that Bishop Meade's sister, Mrs. Anne Page, could have been the perfect model of the Evangelical woman. Because they had to develop their position in a church broad enough to include both self-styled Protestants and Catholics, they developed a theology much more sophisticated than need be elaborated here, but like all good Evangelicals, they were pious, intensely self-disciplined, and active proselytizers.

The way in which Moore and Meade proceeded in Virginia demonstrates their attachment to Evangelical means and ends. Young priests began to hold revival meetings—they were called "associations"—in each other's parish, preaching, praying, and taking up collections for missionaries in other parts of the diocese. Gradually the fervor spread throughout the Virginia church, until by 1828 the convention of the diocese resembled nothing so much as a more stately version of a Methodist conference or camp meeting. Worldliness, warned Meade, was the chief enemy of undefiled and pure religion, dancing one of its most popular manifestations. His predecessor in the episcopacy, Richard Channing Moore, had already made clear his own disgust with "gaming and theatrical representations, in particular" which, he charged, "from their licentious tendency, ought not to be practised or frequented." Given this episcopal attitude, it is not surprising that one of the clergy should threaten to excommunicate two women for dancing on New Year's eve and require of communicants proof of a converted and sanctified heart. For Charles Wesley Andrews as for his bishops, the bishops of the Methodist Episcopal church, leading Presbyterian divines, and prominent Baptist preachers religion was a "principle which gains strength by exercise, by effort, by warfare."[65] Evangelical intensity, which had once been directed against the Church of England, had now become, especially in the South, the measure of religion—even for communicants of that church's successor. It was more than Shubal Stearns and Francis Asbury could have hoped for.

That the Protestant Episcopal church grew only as part of the broadening Evangelical movement is of course not true. High churchmen—especially in North Carolina, whose Bishop Silliman Ives submitted to the Church of Rome in 1852—were as ardent if not as successful as their Evangelical colleagues. But the compelling power of the Evangelical ideal was so great throughout the South that even the liturgical, understated church of the aristocracy was ✓ affected by it. This fact did not throw Baptist and Episcopal Evangelicals into each others' arms, nor did it forge an alliance among non-Evangelicals. Baptist non-Evangelicals were at the opposite end of the social structure from Episcopal non-Evangelicals, and they criticized their respective opponents from opposite viewpoints. To Baptist dissidents, the Evangelicals seemed too anxious to achieve power and prestige, too worldly perhaps, and certainly too eager to ascend the social ladder, instead of Jacob's ladder; High Churchmen saw Evangelicals as being almost "religious enthusiasts." Evangelical Episcopalians, on the other hand, did not always appreciate the rampant revivalism and emotionalism which seemed to characterize Baptists and Methodists, whose antics occasionally resembled nothing so much as a "religious carnival" or "circus."[66] And no amount of "experimental religion" could really make Evangelicals of the more popular churches feel at home with the liturgy and reserve of the Protestant Episcopal church. If differences remained, however, they did not diminish the hold of emotion, experience, piety, and expansion upon religious southerners.

If a broad umbrella of similar attitudes and values covered southern Evangelicals, it did not prevent periodic theological controversy. We have already surveyed some of the conflict which separated progressive Evangelical leaders from suspicious dissidents, conflicts which came and went in cycles of intensity no one has yet undertaken to explain. Nor have scholars explained the nature of those recurrent, sometimes heated, often playful theological exchanges across denominational lines, which paradoxically celebrated the unity of Evangelicalism and the concept of a "Christian public." Nor do we thoroughly understand the persistence of two seemingly contradictory trends which were probably part of the same social process: that which promised to establish common ground for all Evangelicals and that which demanded the reestablishment of boundaries among Evangelical denominations.

The first trend was primarily noninstitutional, an intellectual commitment to using the theological insights and ecclesiastical forms of each denominational tradition to realize the Evangelical ideal. This commitment meant for the leaders of various churches that, important as theological and ecclesiastical differences were for maintaining the various truths of the Protestant reformation, they should not stand in the way of spreading the basic values of intense piety, rigorous self-restraint, and the conversion of society. There were, however, two attempts to give this commitment institutional solidarity. The first was the camp meeting, which focused on means to provide the social basis of a psychological experience that could later be elaborated in specific, dogmatic formulations. But the camp meeting as an ecumenical device failed.

The second institution developed out of a movement among certain Evangelicals to reject those differences which, they believed, all too often had led to denominational wrangling. Characteristic of the volatile quality of most movements in their early stages, these self-styled Christians came from several sources, but primarily from a few sectarian offshoots of the Great Kentucky Revival of 1801 and the fertile mind of Alexander Campbell. Campbell proposed to restore the church to its primitive form, as described in the New Testament. In fact, the Disciples of Christ, as they styled themselves—called for a return to the New Testament as the rule of faith. The churches had deviated from the acknowledged standards of the faith, Disciples argued; they had placed too much emphasis

on emotion, or church polity, or authority beyond the local
church—even Baptist associations were suspect—and not enough
emphasis upon the coming of the millennium. In the end,
however, Campbell succeeded only in founding another denomination. His attacks on the traditional churches had alienated too many
people, a fact which made his call for Christian unity appear to be
hypocritical. Campbell, however, never attacked the values and
standards of Evangelicalism. His followers seem to have been
people who felt alienated from traditional Evangelical leadership,
but not from Evangelical goals.

Both institutional attempts at uniting all Evangelicals failed
because the social basis for formal unity was absent. Most Evangelicals still required the intellectual structure which explained clearly
what distinguished them from others with different views of
authority and man's knowledge of and relationship with God. They
also valued their peculiar historical experience, which justified their
original group identity and developed over time a claim to authenticity based as much on longevity and appeal to certain groups as
upon doctrinal explication. Evangelical standards of thought,
action, and social goals were broad enough to include millions of
people across denominational lines, specific enough to create
division from non-Evangelicals, but not concrete enough to provide
the kind of psychological assurance, mental frame of reference, and
authentication of authority which denominational structure still
provided.

This meant, of course, that as society changed and new groups
developed out of the beneficiaries, nonparticipants, and victims of
such changes, Evangelical goals and actions would be under
constant surveillance. Leading denominational Evangelicals who
were inclined to ignore or discountenance the need for specific
ideological and structural supports could find themselves in a good
bit of trouble should their leadership and commitment to broad
Evangelical goals, as opposed to denominational purity, be called
into question by men who sensed resentment among large numbers
of their coreligionists. Nowhere was this more dramatically demonstrated than in the Landmark controversies among southern Baptist
churches in the era of the Civil War. Complicated and rather drawn
out, the Landmark disputes began in 1854 when James G. Graves,
a young, ambitious Vermont Yankee who edited a southern Baptist

paper in Tennessee, began to print articles, tracts, and books denying that pedobaptists were members of Christian churches. Only those bodies which practiced complete immersion of consenting adults were churches, wrote Graves in an outpouring of vitriol against Methodists, Presbyterians, Episcopalians, and all other religious "societies" which pretended to be Christian. A master controversialist, Graves was in turn eloquent and witty, devious and pedantic, pretentious and ridiculous. In his naive drive to establish the historical as well as doctrinal and biblical authenticity of his church, he insisted that even those who immersed the faithful had to have had direct contact with an apostolic line of Baptist churches through most of the heretical sects of the ancient church—including Gnostics and Donatists—back to John the Baptist, which was not, as some may assume, an attempt to do the Disciples of Christ one better. Of the Landmarks which distinguished Baptists, Graves argued, the most important was immersion. Faithfulness to this primary tenet required repudiation of all cooperation with nonchurches—worship with pedobaptists, exchange of pulpits, or participation in nondenominational projects. Graves and his protagonists argued that Baptist leaders had been so intent upon the war with the Devil that they had not seen the dangers of allying themselves with non-Christians. Although he offended many Baptists with his sometimes unfair, always abrasive tactics, he attracted many supporters in the antebellum South. Evangelicals of all denominations had to be sensitive to similar appeals which could undermine the concept of a "Christian public" and test the brotherly love of Evangelicals when differences in doctrine, procedure, and authority took precedence with people to whom distinctive characteristics were more important than latitudinarian principles.[67]

Less threatening to Evangelicals were those churches which did not necessarily repudiate Evangelical values, but whose tradition, practice, or ethnic identity set them apart from Evangelicals. The Lutheran and German Reformed churches of the South, for example, were based largely upon the German population in the great valley of Virginia and the Carolinas. The Moravians of North Carolina were also almost entirely the descendents of German quietists, whose stern devotional life and rigorous self-discipline were very much akin to the Evangelical ideal, but whose missionary ideal was not so aggressive. Quakers were, strictly speaking, not an ethnic group, but they, like the German churches, had developed a quietistic way of life, with a mission to their own children rather than to the larger society. These people shared many of the same attitudes expressed by Evangelicals about the quality of the Christian life, but preferred to keep the rest of society at bay, maintaining as best they could distinct boundaries between themselves and the majority of people around them. Like their Evangelical neighbors, however, they found with each passing generation that the distinctions became less clear.

The conflicts erupting from the search for landmarks, refinement, or identity reveal the extent of Evangelical influence in the antebellum South. The field of tension between southern lady and Evangelical woman which sometimes disappeared in a conflation of ideals suggests the way in which Evangelical images and structures could become important even for the unconverted. The old dichotomy between church and world, however honored in rhetoric, theological controversy, or tradition was becoming less clear as Evangelical leaders and publicists—especially the innovators—created institutions and provided ideas as useful to the world as to the twice-born. And as this dichotomy diminished, conflict within Evangelicalism revealed social divisions not always dictated by class, but always affected by it. The eighteenth-century denunciation of a "bloated," unconverted aristocracy was taken up again by such people as Primitive Baptists who were suspicious of the aggressive, optimistic innovators of a younger generation. It is slightly misleading to call the innovators Evangelicals simply because they were able to control the flow of Evangelicalism in channels which they selected. Dissidents from encroaching refinement, organizational sophistication, and persistent orientation to upper- and middle-class models of piety and service personified by Anne Randolph Meade Page were Evangelicals, too. At least they said they were, and raised serious questions about the consistency and piety of those who seemed bent on rejecting traditional Evangelical humility, independence, and anti-aristocratic bias. Class division and social conflict were, in other words, expressed in the cadences, images, and moods of the Evangelical ethos.

4

"We Who Own Slaves Honor God's Law"

"We who own slaves," wrote James Furman, "honor God's law in the exercise of our authority."[1] These words were not a defiant response to abolitionist rhetoric or a statement about the divine origins of black slavery. They were words of admonition in a letter from a South Carolina Baptist clergyman to a fellow slaveholder suspected of perverseness in his treatment of a male servant. Furman's message was that we masters may not treat slaves according to our own will because our authority—as all authority—is really delegated by God, and in exercising it we have a solemn responsibility to convey that fact to servants and thus elevate our relationship with them to a "high moral plane." In writing the letter, Furman naturally assumed that he would not be condemned as an abolitionist meddler, for his statement was not the command of an outsider so much as a confessional prayer acknowledging *our* common responsibilities as masters. His was a brief exposition of the Evangelical slaveholding ethic.

When Evangelicals had been routed in their battles with slavery, they were forced to redefine the scope and shape of personal responsibility. They continued to bring slaves into Christian fellowship, arguing that civil and social condition affected neither the need for salvation nor the responsibility to provide it. Indeed, Evangelicals seemed to assume that their having abjured the attack upon slavery in order to convert slaves gave them a special claim upon the conscience of the South. The institution which best exemplified the southern Evangelical ethic became, therefore, the

Mission to Slaves. And it was in the Mission, too, that Evangelicals best stated their claim to the trust, respect, and leadership of southerners in making an orderly and benevolent social system.

As a specific movement detached from the daily work of the churches, the Mission did not begin until the 1830s. Before that turbulent decade, Methodists had been especially determined to convert blacks. In fact, the Methodist Episcopal church in most southern cities was a black society with a few white members who held power and protected worshipers from hostile authorities. Baptists, too, had large numbers of black members, some of whom formed their own churches and joined associations in their own right, rather than existing as auxiliaries to the churches of their masters. By 1830 there were at the most 140,000 blacks in the South who were members of an Evangelical church; this left about two million black people without formal affiliation, although many were the children or spouses of members. By even the most optimistic calculation, Evangelicals, who of all Christians boasted most stridently of their commitment to missions, had failed to take significant action to convert blacks. Most white Evangelicals—laity and clergy alike—were willing to bring blacks into local churches, where their beliefs and activities could be monitored, but they were not very eager to undertake costly, conceivably subversive action to provide blacks with the ideas, values, and structures which had been so instrumental in the white middle class's own rise to respectability. It is not surprising, therefore, that as late as 1820 a group of South Carolina Methodists should have failed in their attempt to form a missionary society for the conversion of slaves.

Yet by 1830, and in increasing intensity throughout the decade, the Mission became a popular cause. The reasons are at once complicated and simple. The Denmark Vesey conspiracy of 1822 in Charleston, South Carolina, and the Nat Turner insurrection in Southampton County, Virginia, in 1831—both led by intelligent, forceful, and charismatic religious teachers—demonstrated that black religious leaders would rise to power with or without the sufferance of white men. The first event, followed as it was by a restlessness among Carolina blacks which terrified the fainthearted and worried the wise, helped partisans of the Mission to attract support, for they now attacked the foolhardiness, not to say idiocy, of trying to maintain social tranquility while keeping in servitude people whose ideas, values, and behavior were alien to those of whites. Finally in 1829 in response to this line of reasoning, Methodist and Episcopal planters in the South Carolina low country invited the South Carolina Conference of the Methodist Episcopal church to send missionaries to their slaves. It was a small beginning and preceded by two years the thunderbolt which shook southerners' confidence even more in their ability to control blacks, for Nat Turners's bloody vengeance delivered dead as well as fretful whites.

Throughout the South spread rumors of insurrection and death, reinforced by the discovery of a new antislavery periodical. It was William Lloyd Garrison's *Liberator*, and it came from the same city (Boston) whence had come just a few months before a notorious and insurrectionary pamphlet written by David Walker, a southern free black emigré, who warned whites that neither his people nor God would continue to suffer slavery.[2] Frightened and angry, white southerners tightened their control upon the black population, forbade the education of slaves as antisocial and dangerous, and curtailed independent religious activity on the part of slaves. In the flurry of debate which accompanied these acts, Evangelical publicists saw an opportunity to expand the Mission despite the ill-tempered complaint that blacks had already been pampered too much. To increase religious instruction, warned a few hysterical alarmists, would be to whet the Africans' appetite for further education and eventual emancipation; but many powerful people had an open mind on the matter. The social situation could not dictate the Mission as a solution to the crisis in southern society, but it could make possible discussion in which reformist Evangelicals could gain a fair hearing.

To understand its publicists is to appreciate the complex roots of the Mission. First of all, there were churchmen who were already veterans of religious work with the slaves. Some, like William Capers of South Carolina, had as young men been caught up in the exhilarating if naive assault on slaveholding which Methodists had undertaken with more zeal than understanding at the turn of the century. Capers had been so impressed by antislavery ideas that he had turned his farm over to slaves whom he had inherited in the hope that they would learn to become independent and free people. Their failure to do so and Carolinians' hostility to emancipationists persuaded Capers to divert his activities to pastoral work with blacks and eventual directorship of Methodist missions. Other missionary enthusiasts shared with William Meade of Virginia a brief apprenticeship with the American Colonization Society; they believed that blacks could live free and useful lives only in Africa, far away from the white man's prejudice.[2]

A second, slightly younger group shared with Capers and Meade an uneasy dissatisfaction with the slave system and the way in which it brutalized people. Charles Colcock Jones, for example, the man who eventually became chief theorist for the Mission had, while a young seminarian in the North, condemned slavery as "A violation of all the Laws of God and man at once. A complete annihilation of justice. An inhuman abuse of power, and an assumption of the responsibility of fixing the life and destiny of immortal beings, fearful in the extreme."[3] When he returned to the South he did not leave such feelings behind, but it would be simpleminded indeed to argue that persons sharing his opinions wanted to use the Mission to destroy slavery—that was neither their stated nor subconscious goal. Instead, they proposed to change blacks' behavior and beliefs so that they would share the same world view as white Evangelicals. Once that herculean task was accomplished, they believed the debate over slavery would take on a character much different from that afflicting antebellum America while slaves were still in a heathenish and degraded condition. The evils of the slave system had shocked these publicists. They had to admit somewhat shamefacedly that criticisms made by northern reformers were true; but their predecessors' failure to sustain antislavery activities and the almost hysterical southern sensitivity to an open discussion of slavery limited their options. The only option available, they believed, was to attempt to change the nature of slavery by bringing self-discipline to blacks.

In addition to men and women of troubled conscience was a third group of Evangelicals who had never really given much thought to the evils of slavery or to the condition of slaves until northern abolitionists had begun to berate their position, or lack of it, after 1831. And then—in order to make their critics out as liars—they turned to the Mission as concrete proof of the South's benevolence to black people. Thus support for the Mission was a volatile compound of anxiety, shame, guilt, humane concern, rationalization, and self-interest, and all of these feelings were brought to bear as Evangelicals developed their program.

To speak of "the Mission" is to attribute more concreteness and uniformity to the phenomenon than it possessed. It was an elusive, if noble, ideal, the kind to which one hopes reality will one day correspond, but which he knows in the innermost recesses of his mind will never take form. It envisaged a mass ecumenical effort based on local auxiliaries and regional societies that would send missionaries to areas where there was a large black population without adequate churches. Men, women, and children of each denomination would contribute time and money to educate the slaves; masters themselves would become teachers and preachers, guided by detailed and carefully designed catechisms. The reality of the Mission, however, was that it could never capture the imagination of southern Evangelicals in numbers sufficient to achieve its goal. It was like the reform movements of the North. A few dedicated individuals organized local societies to support systematic religious instruction of slaves; Presbyterian synods and presbyteries would now and then find a missionary they could trust, and Baptists would do the same. Moreover, local pastors were sometimes able to increase the number of black people among their communicants, so that without a vast organization or even efficient coordination of efforts between various groups, more slaves were gradually brought under care of the churches. Methodists' efforts were the best organized of any, but even though their General Conference made Capers secretary of a new Southern Department of Missionary Work in 1840, they relied primarily upon the annual conferences to do the work. As a symbol of hope, therefore, the Mission attracted a few hard-working people, who collectively became much more than the sum total of their efforts.

Although the Mission could be spoken of as a single entity, it actually was *three* missions, each so important for understanding southern Evangelicalism as to require special attention. First and foremost was the "mission to society." It would be foolish indeed to think that southern Evangelicals always had distinct goals in mind when speaking of the Mission, but they could all agree that it would make the South a safer place in which to live. The basic problem facing society, they argued, was that with each succeeding generation, the division of the South into two, basically inimical cultures became greater. The predominant white culture was primarily responsible for that cleavage, it was argued, and masters were more responsible than anyone else because of the way they treated their slaves—as laborers to be managed and driven, as digits in a profit or loss column to be balanced, or as brutes to be chained. In personal relations with slaves, masters all too often acted disrespectfully because they were so easily and blindly frustrated by the slaves' ignorance and "vicious habits." If missionaries could agree that slaves were ignorant, dishonest, lazy, immoral, and degraded, they also could agree that such depictions of slave life were irrelevant. To leave blacks in such a condition, charged Charles C. Jones, revealed irrational prejudice and stupid arrogance. "Having reduced them to ignorance," he observed, "and by our neglect of duty confirmed them in vice, we now quarrel with their stupidity and obduracy."[4]

The argument went on to say that whites had allowed blacks to perpetuate their own religion, ways of selecting leaders, and patterns of behavior, all of which were based upon their African background and fashioned out of their experience as slaves. And all of which created "heathens" in the midst of a "civilized" people who had done very little indeed to break up ever-increasing black solidarity or "brotherhood." Such a process could not only provide a basis for more effective rebellions, but—even more dangerous because more likely—could provide a basis for the undermining of the values of the predominant class. Blacks often raised the children of their white masters and by their licentious example could lure white children away from the Evangelical goals their parents wanted for them. A superstitious "mammy" with her songs and tales for white children to marvel at was, in the Evangelical view, almost as dangerous as an angry rebel with a gun.

Missionary partisans offered to heal the breach between the two peoples by making blacks learn and pass on their masters' values to their own children. It was a momentous task, but it could be done if masters could be persuaded first to change their attitudes and behavior in relation to slaves. The mission to society, therefore, merged into a "mission to masters." The measures to be taken were suggested by an ingenious combination of common sense and Evangelical guile. To bridge the chasm between blacks and whites, Evangelical theorists argued, masters first had to take an interest in slaves as persons—a reasonable expectation, really, because the effective control of any work force avoided physical coercion and relied instead upon a sense of mutual support and trust. Masters had to begin the necessary transformation by taking into consideration the slaves' feelings, personal pride, and individual integrity. More specifically, they were told to take an interest in the family life and personal cares of their slaves, and see to it that when discipline was required it was unquestionably fair, a measure designed to reassure everyone concerned that they could count on orderly, rational, predictable government. More than one missionary publicist even suggested that masters give slaves garden plots of their own to help develop industry, thrift, and honesty.

Once this aspect of slave management—taking an interest in slaves as people—was begun, the next became even more important, if more difficult. The master was to indoctrinate his slaves with the idea that they were a "people under obligation" to do their "duty." The goal seems almost ludicrous to an age which understands duty as an extension of responsibilities assumed by mature citizens who receive benefits from the social system. But missionary theorists believed that the problem was ideological instead of social and could be solved by appropriate education. Intelligent Evangelicals were especially annoyed with the cloying, pretentious, insensitive—some would have said idiotic—harangues to slaves to obey masters because they knew that slaves were not so stupid as to believe the sincerity of such drivel. Indeed, many missionaries thought it would drive slaves from the church. As far as these Evangelicals were concerned, developing a sense of obligation among slaves required something more than carping continually about "obedience." Masters had to demonstrate that they were themselves under obligation to God by protecting and honoring the slaves' families and persons, and by including their servants within their own family circles. Blacks, said one Presbyterian divine in 1843, "should conscientiously be regarded as members of the family, for whose spiritual no less than their temporal welfare the master is obliged to have concern." If the Bible allows you to own

slaves, I. S. K. Axson told masters, it also teaches you how as
"spiritual beings you must treat them."[5]

In this mood, missionary enthusiasts were obviously urging non-
Christian masters to convert. They hoped that the masters' conversion would have such an effect upon blacks that the latter would
themselves try to change the adversary relationship of the two races.
The conversion would demonstrate to pious blacks the sincerity of
the new measures which slaveholders were expected to institute.
Sincerity could not be feigned, missionaries warned whites; blacks
would respond only to authentic transformation in attitudes because they were so well acquainted with their masters' moods and
self-interest. An enthusiastic publicist who was himself a slaveholder cautioned: "When you call upon [your servants] to fulfill
their duties they will expect you to set the example by a fulfillment
of *your own*."[6] Mission advocates believed that masters could,
theoretically, achieve a better world by desiring it, for their desire
would create the same commitment in their slaves. Whether or not
the idea was true, or whether or not many Evangelicals actually
believed their own propaganda, there was enough passion behind
the belief to motivate a few missionaries to seek a redemptive
society.

The most basic aspect of the Mission was its message to slaves.
Although not all whites ordered priorities in exactly the same way,
it is quite obvious that a major purpose of the Mission was to
convince slaves that whites had the slaves' best interests at heart. To
achieve this impossible goal, Evangelical leaders hoped to strengthen
and support the black family. To begin with, Charles Jones wrote in
1847, whites had to treat black people as adults with "responsibilities to bear ... duties to fulfill."[7] How better to do that than
to strengthen the role of father and mother in the slave family and
encourage the father to discipline his children, the mother to teach
morality, and both to lead them in prayer. This control, together
with the master's commitment to keep the family together and to
enforce morality, was, in the Mission's view, indispensable for
resolving the adversary relations between white and black.

The second goal of the Mission to slaves was to preach the gospel.
According to Evangelicals, this was the first priority of the movement. But the Mission was so closely identified with the purpose of

healing the breach between white and black that the gospel of love
could sometimes be mistaken as a means instead of an end; the
conversion of slaves became the means of saving the South. The
process of conversion was based primarily upon teaching. The
blacks—missionary theorists believed that a majority of blacks (1.6
million) were in the impressionable under-24 age bracket—were
first to be taught the concepts of Evangelical Christianity before
they could have enough information and sensibility to understand
the preaching which would lead them to conversion. Presbyterians
were much more insistent upon thorough "understanding" than
were Methodists and Baptists who—although they too emphasized
instruction before conversion—were inclined to believe the authenticity of blacks' religious experiences, if accompanied by sincere
repentance and an honest commitment to live an upright life. The
Evangelical message to blacks was much the same as to whites, a fact
which sometimes improved the general quality of sermons, for as
one white communicant confided to a friend, his minister was
much easier to understand now that he had learned to preach clear
and simple sermons to slaves.[8]

How blacks responded to this gospel will be discussed in the final
chapter, but it is important to keep in mind what whites thought
they were telling slaves. They believed that they were helping
servants to understand themselves better, to learn why society was
structured as it was, and to feel that they, as servants, were
important to God as individuals, despite their "station in life."
Missionaries also believed that they were explaining to slaves what
prevented blacks' receiving the love of God, and what they could
do about it. In the Evangelical view, original sin required the
shaping of society into duties and responsibilities appropriate to
each person's station; those who in this context did His bidding, He
would repay with a clear conscience and a happy life. Each person
(black) was expected to do his duty whether or not others (whites)
did theirs because God would judge for Himself breaches of His
law. In His plan of salvation, therefore, God did not expect His
children, black or white, to wrangle with each other over right or
wrong, justice or mercy. Rather, He desired His people to wrestle
with the demons within themselves. The adversary who had to be
conquered was not the black man or the white man but the sinful,
disorderly, disobedient *self*.

For Evangelicals, the beginning of this struggle, and the event
which legitimated it, was that moment when the whole universe
seemed both to condemn and to affirm the self—the conversion
experience. In this, Methodists and Baptists were much more
willing than Presbyterians to accept blacks' interpretation of the
vision of God. In fact, a few missionaries wrote and talked as if
Methodist and Baptist practices were just as bad as those which
came from Africa. But in the final analysis, the process of Evangelical
conviction, conversion, and self-discipline was to be the same for
both races. The final result was supposed to be a general agreement
between the races on what was to be valued (hard work, self-discipline, piety) and on what authorities were to teach and guarantee
those values (the church and Christian family). That the church was
in the hands of whites, and that the message was filtered through
the gauze of whites' moral perceptions seemed only natural, since
whites were as they understood such matters, the very personification of Christian civilization.

To achieve and secure missionary goals, local societies were
expected to initiate missions or to redirect activity of extant
churches to include more black people. The most important means
in achieving this end were the conversion of black leadership,
education of the young, and imposition of ecclesiastical discipline.
Since missionary publicists knew that black leadership would
develop with or without white approval, they were determined that
it should develop with Evangelical guidance. Methodists and
Baptists had been allowing blacks to preach since the eighteenth-
century revivals because slaves were so much more responsive to
people like themselves than to the alien whites. Later missionaries
continued, even encouraged, the practice, provided it took place
under whites' supervision so that black ministers could be counted
on to preach the same Gospel to slaves as white ministers preached
to masters. In terms of morality there was indeed much agreement
between black and white; in terms of the final outcome of history
there was, to say the least, a difference in perspective.

After converting black leadership, the next priority was to teach
young slaves the world view and values of Evangelical Christianity.
Adults were already set in their heathen or pagan beliefs, publicists
admitted, so that the hope for society lay in teaching younger
blacks. The primary means was oral instruction, since most slaves

(89 percent) could neither read nor write, and most southern states forbade teaching them such revolutionary tools. With these limitations in mind, missionaries wrote catechisms to guide teachers in a question/answer procedure that had worked so well in early New England, and which was now tested successfully among illiterate blacks:

Q: Tell me some of God's goodness to you.
A: He gives us father and mother, meat and drink, and clothes to wear; and when we are sick he makes us well.
Q: Is it not great goodness in God to make us live in a Gospel land, and to give us His holy word?
A: Yes.

Blacks soon learned what white teachers wanted them to say, and missionary reporters were often romantically ecstatic about their progress. But sentiment was shaped by strict accountability: each church or missionary station had inquiry meetings or some sort of ecclesiastical court to entertain charges of misconduct in relation to family discipline, morality, and sobriety. In this process as in all others, missionary leadership was guided by the principle that "persons under authority should feel they are so."[9]

It has been as difficult for historians to take the Mission seriously as it was for northern abolitionists, who condemned it as a vast plot to perfect the slave system. And of course, at one level the Mission was precisely that—a promise to masters that society would be much safer if masters and slaves were both converted to Evangelicalism. The Mission was probably more successful with blacks than whites, since no superior social authority could reward masters for conversion. The Mission very carefully outlined in a new, concerted fashion what whites expected of slaves' behavior, and the result was presumably not so much an internalization of whites' values on the part of blacks, as the imparting of knowledge of how blacks should behave in order to fend off whites' wrath. At the same time, however, blacks who were fortunate enough to have a dedicated missionary enthusiast for a master might truly discover an improvement in their status within the plantation community, their own rule within the family strengthened, their claims upon the Gospel sustained.

Church records tell repeatedly the story of orderly disciplinary procedures being maintainted for both races. Christian discipline

enforced by the church was one of the most important functions
which the Mission was to expand throughout the South, for there
was an important tradition of black-white relations being supervised by local congregations. In August of 1780, for example, at
South Quay church in Southside Virginia, there were "Charges
brought against Lawrence's Nero by his master of disobedience &
harsh language to him; in consequence of which he is laid under
Censure." Not to be outdone, Nero brought countercharges of
"misconduct" against his master, and Lawrence, too, was "laid
under Censure." Six years later master and slave were still squab-
bling, and charges brought by the white man against Nero were
dismissed. Finally Nero was excommunicated for threatening to run
away from Lawrence and take his fellow slaves with him.[10]

Such interaction continued throughout the antebellum era, and
although few cases ended in the blacks' vindication, most cases of
discipline initiated discussion and the exchange of viewpoints. A
cause for much debate was the issue of theft. For example, in the
Salem Baptist Church of Marlborough County, South Carolina,
during the 1850s, masters brought charges against slaves for
stealing such things as hams from the plantation's smokehouse.
Blacks denied that taking provisions was theft, arguing that
since the persons in question were servants on the plantation when
the act took place, and since they had, through their own labor,
contributed to the preparation of the hams, they had merely taken
what was justly theirs. Blacks lost their case, but the importance of
such proceedings is not that white persons could have their own way
with blacks, but that masters admitted both races were accountable
to a higher authority. The master did not take matters into his own
hands, as the civil law allowed; he submitted the case to the church,
where both sides of the issue were considered. Blacks and whites
both agreed that the rules of the church were important for
mediating relations between races.[11] Merely one example, the
process was nevertheless indicative of the way many blacks and
whites had been placed under obligation to each other, and the
procedure by which slaves could claim acknowledgment by masters
of their respect and dignity as morally accountable human beings.
In such cases, blacks learned that whites sensed their own accountability, a knowledge which must have lent blacks some pleasure at

white discomfort and perhaps hope that someday God would judge whites even as whites now judged them.

In this interaction, however, was evident the failure of the Mission. All but a few masters failed to adopt the self-denying, self-disciplined relationship with slaves that would have made plantations into idyllic Christian communities or extended family units envisioned by the Mission. The dichotomy between the races —which civil law demanded by giving master almost total power over slaves—could simply not be resolved by the voluntary action of a few Christian masters. Cautious slaveholders too often believed that religious education of blacks would lead to education in such dangerous abstractions as natural rights, equality, and justice, and as a result, many remained suspicious of the great crusade. Consequently, the Mission could never begin to achieve the whites' respect for blacks which publicists had promised; race prejudice was just as strong at the end of the missionary movement as at the beginning. To be sure, missionaries learned much about blacks and often came to respect them, frequently to feel more at home with them than their masters. But even if sensitive and well-meaning white ministers took upon themselves the anguish of black parishioners, their personal catharsis never really solved their basic failure to "reach" blacks. The reason was clear. As long as whites had the means to dictate the rules of discussion between the two peoples and to dismiss the slaves' moral perspective as more self-serving than their own, the community of faithful people could never achieve social harmony. A few whites and blacks reached across the abyss in a profoundly moving way, and their example became the sentimental image which diverted attention from less pleasant reality.

When everything is taken into account, neither whites nor blacks ever acted as missionary theorists promised they would. True, those theorists never promised perfection, but problems of missionaries with stubborn masters and recalcitrant slaves seem to have reinforced whites' belief in the persistence of black degradation and ignorance, no matter how many slaves were converted. Because a perfect state of black submissiveness never developed and because blacks persisted in exotic beliefs and behavior, many whites used the "failure" of the Mission as proof of black inferiority and the impractical, romantic, irrational idealism of white philanthropy.

The problem lay in the missionary mentality. Devoted missionaries often had an exaggerated view of what their mission could
accomplish, and they promised too much without making clear the
preconditions of success. Their less profound, sometimes simpleminded followers usually ignored most of what theorists said and
seemed to expect social problems to be solved by getting people
unlike themselves to "shape up" and show a little self-respect and
dignity. The propaganda for the Mission backfired by promising
too much. Early descriptions of the slaves' degradation, employed
to arouse support for the mission in the 1830s, were still shaping
white attitudes in the 1860s; after a generation of trying to transform Africans into "civilized" people like their pious masters, the
ingrates were still stubbornly "heathen" and unregenerate.
Whites' experience with "licentious and thieving" slaves in local
church trials throughout the South reinforced the masters' low
opinion of black people in general. They would not behave
properly; they had not been, in the words of the hymn, "washed
whiter than snow." The failure of the Mission to make blacks
behave as whites wanted them to served to fortify the prevalent
southern view that abolitionists were madmen for demanding that
blacks be set free at once. If slaves could not be made to adopt
Evangelical discipline and learn to behave like civilized folk under
white control in local churches, it would be dangerous indeed to
tamper with the only system which guaranteed a stable, secure
social order.

Missionary leaders never really came to terms with the faulty
perception of their followers, for the Mission was as much an
assertion of Evangelical power and prestige as an honest effort to
make southern society into an integrated whole where everyone
shared the same values and behavior patterns. Although it salved
consciences and offered earnest young men and women an opportunity to serve "suffering humanity," the Mission represented
better than any other action of southern Evangelicals their departure from the morally halcyon days of the eighteenth century. Then
they had stood steadfast against the power structure of society and
preached a personal salvation which undermined patterns of deference and styles of leadership. Their grandchildren in the nineteenth
century preached a new revival which also converted thousands of
people, many of whom were slaves, but the message was not so

much to repent and cast off ungodly deference to wordlings and wordliness as to repent and submit to those who ruled the world. The radicals had become the guardians.

The metamorphosis did not diminish moral ardor, but it did redirect it. To square the cautious and respectable present with the valiant and unruly past is a Procrustean task for ideologues who have assumed the power which their predecessors fought. For white Evangelical leaders, the task was especially painful, suffused as it was with feelings of ambivalence, frustration, guilt, and anxiety. The Mission could not compensate for the fact that all southern Evangelical groups had once harbored antislavery enthusiasts, the memory of whom worried slaveholders, who did not want soft-headed idealists tampering with their slaves. Evangelicals' problems were compounded by their own memory, which was not merely a corporate acknowledgment that misbegotten romantics had once preached emancipation, but a very personal recollection that they themselves had once condemned slavery as inhuman and un-Christian. Thus afflicted, southern Evangelicals solved their most basic social and moral dilemma by developing with the Mission a slaveholding ethic.

Rather than the product of one man, group, or generation, the white South's unique contribution to Christian social ethics was the result of a long dialectic between forces at work within southern society—indeed within white southerners themselves—as well as those forces emanating from the conflicting politics and economic interests of the Republic. For the sake of clarity, it is possible to divide the process into three stages. The first resulted from Evangelical antislavery agitation during and after the Revolution. Although few if any theoretical defenses of slavery were produced during this time, southerners did establish a precedent of circumspection when discussing social problems. With this posture came deference to civil authority in defining social relationships, and commitment to converting blacks to Christianity.

This retrenchment was in direct contrast to the happy contentiousness of an earlier age, and betokened that most disdained of all moral resolutions—compromise; but it was nonetheless a compromise made possible by the value system of Evangelicalism itself. We have seen how Evangelical self-scrutiny and discipline could lead to an attack upon slavery, but we have also observed the importance of personal experience as a sign of conversion. Movement in the social pecking order was not seen as a necessary result of conversion, although the experience was meant to certify that to God all believers were of equal worth. Converts of low status who compared themselves to those of higher rank were elevated in their own esteem and in the esteem of others in their religious group who shared their social position. Only in rare cases, however, would conversion lift persons of lower status to equality in the minds of social superiors. Thus the impact of early Evanglicalism upon blacks was to provide a means legitimated by those in authority to enhance blacks' own self-esteem, but it could not demand that their white, social superiors admit blacks' equality as human beings. To apply the same principle to other persons, Evangelicalism could strengthen the self-esteem and inner life of women, but it could not require men to upset the order of Nature and Revelation by giving women rights which belonged more properly to men, who were the innocent victims of Eve's indiscretion.

This limitation within the process of elaborating one's personal religious experience was reinforced by the fact that manumission was never successfully identified as one of the marks of authentic conversion. When converted slaveholders balked at obeying anti-slavery rules or admonitions, they could justify themselves by calling attention to the undeniable, personally experienced presence of God's grace in their own lives. And if they demonstrated as great an interest in their slaves' religious lives as in their own, they could convince all but the most stubborn and irascible "fanatics" of their piety and therefore of the righteousness of their actions. Such reasoning was based on the premise that all verifiably converted Christians were "good" people whose personal qualities and attitudes—rather than such impersonal abstractions as "justice" or "equality"—should be the measure of human actions. "Good" people lent their "goodness" to the positions they held in society.

The first stage in the process of creating a slaveholding ethic, therefore, was to strip the act of slaveholding itself of immoral connotations. This accomplishment did not occur everywhere in the

South at the same time, nor was it uniformly acquiesced in by all Evangelicals. For example, in North Carolina during the late 1850s, the blatantly abolitionist Wesleyan Methodist church enjoyed surprising missionary success, and all along the ridge of the southern highlands Evangelicals warily expressed mental reservations about the morality of slaveholding. The prevalent, common-sense moral philosophy of southern Evangelicalism, however, embraced as truisms the defenses of slaveholding first encountered by antislavery preachers in the 1790s. Southern Evangelicals held that God had sanctioned slavery among the ancient Hebrews and had permitted it among primitive Christians; slavery was the appropriate government for a degraded and inferior race; slavery was an inheritance from the past upon which was based the wealth of the future and the prosperity of an upwardly mobile people. Moreover, slavery was a burden to the white man, but one which had to be suffered in order to protect society from moral decay, anarchy, and insurrection. A corollary to these bromidic rationalizations was that the institution of slavery was so ingrained in the structure of society and so protected by civil law that it was beyond the reach of individual, converted Evangelicals. All that previous agitation had achieved was dissension, misunderstanding, and suspicion.

Hidden within the conventional wisdom, however, was a persistent, gnawing doubt expressed in the admission that slavery was a "burden," perhaps even an "evil." If the role or fact of being a slaveholder entailed no guilt, the piety of the master had still, even into the 1830s, not redeemed the institution. Southern clergymen were still embarrassed to defend servitude, lacing their letters, columns, and books almost ritualistically with such phrases as "I am no advocate for *slavery*," or "The Bible does not by any means *Justify* slavery. It only serves to explain African slavery in this country."[12] And the ritual, for all its self-delusion, moral obtuseness, and mindless repetition betrayed an inner agitation and persistent moral "cramp" which made more than one Evangelical slaveholder damn "the curse of slavery!" and hope against hope that something could be done to fight it and its consequences: the "grossness, the prejudices, the littleness, the selfishness which taints to corruption the atmosphere of public life" in the South.[13]

Such feelings as these made possible the Mission to Slaves and the movement to colonize blacks outside the United States. In support of colonization, eager young clergymen bravely denounced the evils of slavery in the traditional Revolutionary rhetoric of freedom and liberty, and promised with thoughtless and sentimental vagueness a day when "this government may with propriety declare herself the friend of universal emancipation; When all America shall lift an united Voice over the abodes of slavery and wretchedness, and proclaim an eternal jubilee."[14] These were bold words indeed, and they expressed a genuine discomfort about slavery, but they were as significant for what they ignored as for what they emphasized. Celebrating the Revolutionary ideal of "liberty" and counting upon the slow process of moral influence to ease slavery effortlessly out of existence, southern Evangelical publicists ignored black peoples' claims for justice by making the "burden" of slavery essentially a problem for white people, and also by endorsing through reluctant admission or tacit consent the principle that so long as slaves remained in the South they could not be freed. The form in which Evangelical writers expressed themselves on slavery and slaveholding belied their traditional optimistic emphasis on the regenerative power of a will freed by conversion to serve God, unfettered by the careless considerations of the world. The image projected instead was that of a people weighed down by historical forces over which they had little control. Perhaps the future offered hope, but the present baffled them.

Having made freedom for blacks a transoceanic, transhistorical goal, and having officially absolved slaveholders of moral responsibility, southern Evangelicals were ill prepared for the explosion of abolitionism in the 1830s. From the cauldron of social and intellectual ferment in the North, kept bubbling by an increasingly volatile dialectic between authority and its opposition, was poured out what seemed to southern Evangelicals to be the wrath of the Devil himself. For in their most simple and basic descriptions of the problem of slavery and its solution, these "modern" abolitionists directly and unequivocally contradicted southern Evangelicals' frail but fundamental resolution of the "slavery question." They denounced with alarming passion and subversive disregard for southern "delicacy," the *sin* of slaveholding. And they repudiated the sentimental theory that the gradual almost imperceptible impact of enlightened and refined thought would eventually allow whites to slough off the burden of slavery. Instead they demanded "immediate emancipation without expatriation."

The effects of this new formula for dealing with slavery were at first inconsequential. Few people joined the movement; the discussion of slavery in the North, where it was all but abolished, had a forbidding, abstract quality to it; and the attack on northern race prejudice limited the appeal of abolitionism. Yet throughout the 1830s, the movement grew despite mob attacks on its members, ecclesiastical censure, and rampant denunciation. By 1840 the issue of slavery—not slaveholding—had entered politics; by 1845 it had split the two largest Evangelical denominations, Methodists and Baptists, into North and South, free and slave.

The process which wrenched Evangelicals apart was the second stage in the development of a slaveholding ethic. Without appreciating its significance, southern Evangelicals all but ignored the publication in 1832 of William Lloyd Garrison's *Thoughts on African Colonization*. Written in response to blacks' denunciation of plans to deport them, Garrison's pamphlet condemned the injustice, immorality, and impracticality of a plan designed to alleviate the guilt of sentimental whites, rather that to change the status of blacks. Damaging the appeal of colonization to northern reformers, Garrison's pamphlet was only the first of thousands which employed the metaphors, values, and symbols of Evangelicalism to condemn the sin of slaveholding and preach the duty of emancipation. Young ministers throughout the North began to ask ecclesiastical agencies to censure and excommunicate slaveholders— acts which would, they hoped, isolate recalcitrant masters from the moral support of northerners and those southerners whose personal salvation was more important to them than their slave property. To make their points as clearly and forcefully as possible, antislavery reformers identified the sin of slaveholding with other sins about which there was no public hesitation in condemning: fornication, adultery, theft, kidnapping, procuring, and murder. There is, charged one enthusiastic abolitionist, more virtue in the brothels of New York City than in the entire Methodist Episcopal church.[15]

At first, southern Evangelicals watched with approval as their northern friends tried to fend off abolitionists with appeals to reason, national unity, and Christian charity. Southerners applauded attempts to muffle controversy; they celebrated northerners' sometimes lyrical panegyrics of the Mission; and some of them must have felt rather smug as allies begged for an appreciation of southerners' "peculiar circumstances." But almost imperceptibly at first, and in clearer accents with each disagreeable confrontation, southerners began to hear something they did not like. Northerners conceded that slavery was indeed an unfortunate burden, a moral evil, and something which everyone hoped would one day disappear. Even though southerners had said some of the very same things themselves, they did not like the tone of moderates, who seemed to be telling abolitionists to calm down and be patient because all Christian men and women—including Evangelical slaveholders—could agree that slavery was wrong. The words "wrong," "moral evil," and even "unfortunate burden," when coming from northerners instead of southerners, seemed to betoken a condescending attitude, a shadow of doubt about the morality of slaveholding—a belief that the taint of original sin was more deeply embedded in the South than in the North. "They pity us," wrote the Reverend James Henley Thornwell of South Carolina, "they lament our lot—admit that our case is bad, desperately bad—but then we are not so much to be blamed. They curse us in their sympathies."[16]

In response, southern Evangelical publicists struggled in an intense, sometimes hysterical, often confessional manner to show that the act of owning slaves did not determine a person's innocence or guilt before God. This much they had decided among themselves before the abolitionist attack, but now they were forced into developing arguments which carried this privately held truism into an issue for public debate and beyond that to a position which was the logical outcome of their belief in the transforming power of personal piety, that is, to provide a patina of morality for slavery itself. As a transitional stage in the development of a slaveholding ethic, the immediate response was quantitatively different from the previous stage before abolitionists had used the printing revolution of the 1830s to flood the country with hundreds of thousands of antislavery pamphlets and broadsides. There was now more need than every to vindicate themselves.

There was a qualitiative difference, too, for in addressing northern sympathizers as well as abolitionists and their own consciences, southern Evangelical leaders were faced with a dilemma. They needed to absolve themselves of moral responsibility for slavery, but if the process unleashed by this need were taken too far, Evangelicals would place themselves in the ludicrous position of arguing on the one hand that men could make all the significant moral decisions which affected their lives, and on the other that they were not responsible for slavery because they had not had a hand in fashioning it. The dilemma ran even deeper the longer they argued the matter, for if slaveholding did not entail guilt, why had they argued so heatedly that they were not "responsible" for it? The question was posed just beneath the surface of public consciousness, and it hounded them. If they had tried to vindicate themselves by claiming victimization by history—therefore God— they would have had to renounce belief in the ability of humanity to make free moral decisions, a belief indispensable for distinguishing between the righteous and the damned. Part of Evangelicals' self-consciousness was that if *they* had made the free decision to join the righteous in conversion, other people could do so just as well. When abolitionists turned this formula against southerners, demanding they do the "impossible" by destroying slavery in a great act of the will—repentance of the sin of slaveholding—Evangelicals were forced to face the implications of their parents' and grandparents' retreat from an antislavery posture. The first attempts to do so were understandably awkward because they were guided by the unexceptional effort to absolve themselves of guilt, throwing out arguments in a confusion that revealed their author's defensiveness, anxiety, and uncertainty.

A major theme which erupted almost immediately was that slavery was part of the institutional structure of southern society, and as such was a matter which could be debated only in terms of public policy, political expediency, and social stability. Participation in the slave system as either master or slave was a matter of no concern to the church, except as each fulfilled duties and obligations which were his as the result of membership in the body of true believers and the commitment to follow the explicit teachings of the Bible. Recounting attacks upon slavery in the Revolutionary era as a disastrous deviation from this principle, southern Evangelicals intoned in a kind of litany: Slaveholding is a civil institution; *and we will not interfere*. The character of civil institutions is governed by politics; *and we will not interfere*. Politics are beyond the scope of the church; *and we will not interfere*.

Supplemental to this rationale was one which abrogated southerners' responsibility by virtue of the fact that they had inherited the slave system; it had been foisted on their unsuspecting ancestors by money-grubbing Yankees and Britons. Thus shackled, southern Evangelicals had done their best to make moral decisions for the benefit of the poor and unfortunate Africans by converting them to Christianity. The process had only just begun because of the degradation of the aliens, but southerners had assumed moral supervision of their charges only to be abused by the children and grandchildren of the people who had sold the Africans in the first place! It did not seem fair.

As if to sustain the belief that the proslavery argument betokened a back-to-the-Bible crusade, the beleaguered southerners rested their case on Holy Writ. The Declaration of Independence and theory based on a social compact might very well subvert slavery, but people who justified and ordered their lives according to the Bible knew that God had sanctioned slavery in the Old Testament among the patriarchs and Hebrews, and had recognized its existence while enforcing its obligations in the New Testament. The argument rested on the belief that only those things were sinful which broke a law given by God directly, as in the case of the ten commandments, or indirectly, as in the exemplary lives of the patriarchs. The stone tablets of Sinai did not explicitly condemn slavery, southerners pointed out; indeed, by forbidding the faithful to covet their neighbors' manservants or maidservants—slaves— God had recognized and therefore sanctioned the existence of servitude. The debate over such matters could easily become a sophistic and pedantic wrangling if northerners with good instincts, if not scholarship, challenged the translation of the Greek *doulos* into "slave" and argued instead that it should be "servant." The point at issue, however, did not always represent an esoteric debate about translation, for abolitionists argued that the kind of bonded servitude recognized in the Old Testament passed out of existence as a result of faith in God, and that the whole tendency of the New Testament was to undermine and eventually repudiate slavery. So say you heretics—who talk of "influence," "tendency," and the "spirit of Christianity"—responded southerners, but we who read the Bible for what it says and not for what we want it to say discover explicitly and distinctly that God has sanctioned slavery. Else why would He through the Apostle Paul have sent the slave Onesimus back to Philemon? Not only so, argued one famous Methodist clergyman, Augustus Baldwin Longstreet, but Philemon was a minister, a *slaveholding* minister.[17]

Biblical exegesis among northern as well as southern Evangelicals was a familiar way for points at issue to be reconciled. But the first biblical "proslavery" arguments had a limited purpose. They were not intended—save perhaps in a few cases—to justify southern slavery as it existed at the time of writing; they were not defenses of the southern system without self-criticism or some implied hope of social reform and improvement. Rather they were a way for southern Evangelicals to escape the things which tormented them— their own antislavery past, the equalitarian principles of the Declaration of Independence, the suspicion of northern allies and southerners who owned no slaves, and the painful darts cast by abolitionists. The latter had denounced slaveholding in *all* circumstances as a sin; and slaveholders' denial of historical and moral responsibility for creating and maintaining a "civil," inherited institution was linked with the "biblical argument" presumably to establish doubt about the applicability of such rash generalizations. There was a pathetic almost frantic quality about the drive to get northern Evangelicals to agree that in *some circumstances* slaveholding might possibly entail no guilt, for southern Evangelicals were determined to wrest from their tormentors and strangely bewildered allies a moral "escape" clause. Abolitionists refused to agree to so devious and self-serving a formula, warning northern moderates that to do so was not simply to compromise with sin—that was merely a rhetorical flourish—but to give up the attempt to determine who was responsible for perpetuating slavery and therefore for ending it. Furthermore, intoned the radicals,

once admitting that *circumstances* could vindicate slaveholding,
"every villain in the Church or out of it, would plead that this is his
case exactly."[18]

Conceding what seemed to be a reasonable if slightly irrelevant
point, southern Evangelicals proceeded to prove abolitionists correct.
They asked that northern churchmen concede also that the circumstances surrounding slaveholding in the South absolved all Christians there of guilt; they wanted a blanket endorsement of southern
Christianity, and they wanted northerners to agree that slavery was
an amoral context within which moral decisions could transform
relationships established by law into moral relationships based on
the conversion experience of the master. Slavery as a "civil"
institution is not, they decreed, "a moral evil," and turned to their
northern allies for the expected "amen"; but for the most part
there was only a very irritating silence. Northern antiabolitionist
Evangelicals were not prepared to deny that slavery was a moral evil
because they believed that that was exactly what it was, and they
were annoyed with southerners who expected them to say anything
else.

By the 1840s what had once appeared to be an abstract moral
argument between reformers and reactionaries had become a
process which threatened to divide the Union. Political parties were
straining, with diminishing success, to resolve conflicts between
southern and northern constituencies. Social change created frustration and anxiety in the North, lest the national government
continue what seemed to many northerners to be an increasingly
anachronistic policy of responding more to the "sensitivity" of
southern slaveholders than to the needs of northern freeholders and
industrialists. Political demands from northerners afflicted by
suspicion of the "slave power" in Washington naturally alarmed
southerners, and people began to talk of disunion and conflict. The
plight of Evangelicals when viewed against this background takes
on greater significance than a debate in moral philosophy because,
as political leaders observed, if religious people who valued forgiveness, reconciliation, and love could not resolve their differences,
what hope for compromise was there for politicians—most of whom
were lawyers—whose philosophy of social action was based on an
adversary view of issues. Had religion been all that shaped Evangel-

icalism, the problem would have been academic. But the truth was that the conflict within the two largest Evangelical denominations, Baptist and Methodist, revealed just how deep were the divisions between the two sections.

The confrontation came in 1844 and 1845 when the Methodist Episcopal church split in two, and Baptists created their own Southern Convention. In the Methodists' case there was an embarrassing antislavery tradition rooted firmly in the founding of the church, but by 1836 southern Methodists had persuaded their northern brethren to join them in disclaiming any "right, wish, or intention to interfere in the civil and political relation between master and slave."[19] As abolitionist agitation tore northern annual conferences apart, suspicious southerners finally found an issue which would prove once and for all just where their condescending northern friends stood: whether or not a Methodist bishop could own slaves. Although the issue exploded at the General Conference of 1844, it had been discussed with increasing intensity and frustration by southerners throughout the previous decade because of northerners' refusal to consider slaveholders for the episcopacy. Since bishops theoretically were merely itinerant ministers with supervisory responsibilities, they were affected by the rule which forbade traveling preachers of the Methodist Episcopal church to own slaves where circumstances allowed emancipation without expatriation. Applied in conferences on the border between slaveholding and free territory, the rule was a dead letter in most of the South, where law made it extremely difficult, but not impossible, to free blacks without forcing them to leave the state. Thus ministers who were stationed in a slaveholding area could become masters, exempted by circumstances from ecclesiastical censure. Bishops, however, theoretically supervised work in both North and South and were not required to live in one section or the other, although as a practical matter their work was usually limited to one section.

The rule on slaveholding ministers was a perfect symbol of the Methodists' predicament, for it combined the antislavery past and the slaveholding present, the requirement of free moral action and the acknowledgment of its impossibility, the theory of moral rigor and its major exception. And Bishop James Osgood Andrew of

Georgia became the perfect personification of southern Methodists'
view of themselves and their responsibilities. Andrew was almost
the prototype of the scrupulously moral slaveholder, for although
he had inherited two slaves, he offered to free one, a young black
woman, and send her to Liberia or the North, since Georgia law
forbade freed slaves to remain in the state. She refused the offer.
The second slave was a young boy who was to be freed and sent
North as soon as he was old enough to fend for himself. When
Andrew married his second wife, a slaveholder, he executed a deed
of trust securing her continued ownership of the slaves, thus
relieving himself as best he could of the responsibility of being a
slaveholder. When all these facts became known in 1844, abolitionists demanded his resignation from the episcopacy. At first maintaining a modest silence, northern moderates hoped Andrew
would resign in order to keep peace in the church. Angered by what
he considered "an impertinent interference" in his private life, but
ever loyal to his office and the church he had served so well,
Andrew decided to resign. Southern delegates to the General
Conference persuaded him to change his mind, for they saw in his
case an excellent opportunity to resolve once and for all the issue of
whether or not northern nonabolitionist Evangelicals really respected southern piety as much as they claimed.

   Southern Baptists sought a similar confrontation. Plagued by
abolitionist invective, they, like their Methodist confreres, were
disturbed by what they considered to be a devious and condescending manner on the part of northern moderates. Determined to
expose the hypocrisy of their friends, southerners finally hit upon
the issue of whether or not Baptist missionaries could own slaves.
Baptists' disputations paralleled those of Methodists in time,
psychology, and result. As the episcopacy was the symbol of
Methodist unity, so the missionary enterprise was the symbol of
Baptist solidarity. Each local Baptist church was autonomous; there
was no national church to coordinate the activities and expansion of
the denomination. To solve some of the problems resulting from
the absence of minimal ecclesiastical machinery, a group of Baptists
from throughout the country organized a triennial convention in
1814 to supervise the development of foreign missions; three years
later they added a board of home missions. Members of the

convention were individual Baptist churches, state conventions, regional associations, or even private individuals who contributed money to support the missionary program of the Baptist churches.

Northern and southern Baptists worked very well together until abolitionists demanded that slaveholders be thrown out of Baptist churches—a course of action for which neither denominational machinery nor disposition existed. Abolitionists also demanded that churches, individuals, associations, and conventions which continued to have fellowship with slaveholders be thrown out of the triennial convention. Gingerly and diplomatically, northern anti-abolitionists tried to deflect confrontational tactics of both abolitionists and southerners. Abolitionists wanted the board of the convention to state emphatically that being a slaveholder disqualified a person from being a Baptist missionary; southerners wanted just as clear a statement to the opposite effect; and moderates succeeded in avoiding the issue until 1844. In that year Alabama Baptist leaders—some of whom were native Yankees—learned of clandestine antislavery sentiment in high places. The corresponding secretary of the American Baptist Home Missionary Society had been trying to get a Baptist missionary—Jesse Busyhead, Chief Justice of the Supreme Court of the Cherokee Nation—to resign his post because he was a slaveholder. Busyhead died before the matter was resolved, but the Alabamans were apoplectic with rage. To the Board of Managers of the Baptist General Convention they demanded an "explicit avowal" that slaveholders were equal with nonslaveholders in qualifying for appointment as missionaries.

Southern Methodists and Baptists finally received the rebuff which they had labored so diligently to achieve. During the spring of 1844, northern Methodists carried a vote in General Conference to relieve Andrew of his episcopal duties until he had purged himself of the "impediment" of slaveholding, and in December of the same year the Baptist Acting Board of Foreign Missions admitted that they could not in conscience appoint a person as missionary who insisted on retaining slaves. "We can never," they wrote, "be a party to any arrangement which could imply approbation of slavery." Southern Evangelicals' response to both actions was a strange mixture of outrage and relief, for they now saw themselves freed from the hypocrisy of pretended friends as well as from the threat of avowed enemies. In May, 1845, Methodists met in Louisville, Kentucky, to form the Methodist Episcopal Church, South; and the Baptists gathered in Augusta, Georgia, to form the Southern Baptist Convention.[20]

Southern Presbyterians—smallest of the major Evangelical groups—did not repudiate institutional ties with the North until 1861. They did not have to do so because the expulsion of New School Presbyterians from the mother church in 1837 had in effect excommunicated most Presbyterian abolitionists as well. After 1801 the Presbyterian church outside of New England had become a union of Congregationalists and Presbyterians who joined forces to fight Satan on the frontier. But the theology of Congregationalists who entered the union tended to be what became known as the New School, whereas the traditional Presbyterians were as conservative as their designation, Old School, suggests. The division focused on a theological debate about the nature of man and his responsibility in the historical process. The issue was posed by the problem of how a person moved (or *was* moved) from an unsaved (unregenerate) to a saved (regenerate) state. Inherent was the question as to whether or not Adam's guilt was imputed to mankind, thereby destroying all vestiges of Edenic innocence with which to respond positively to God's action in conversion. Conservatives (1798, 1811, 1816) maintained man's total corruption by the imputation of Adam's guilt to all humanity, and denied any positive activity on the part of a potential Christian in conversion. Consistent with this view was an attitude of passivity, even resignation, when it came to thinking about the individual's relation to institutions and social status.

The opponents of this rather dour view came out of a tradition which emphasized the ability of humans to respond positively to God's activity. Adam's guilt was not imputed to humanity, the New School argued; people were guilty only for their own sins. Despite the fact that they still believed that humanity had lost the inclination to do good through Adam's fall, they were part of a trend which developed into an emphasis on human activity in conversion and in the subsequent search for perfection. Consistent with this view was an activist mood, a faith in human ability to alter the historical process for the better. Conflicts between the two views became more frequent in the 1830s, exacerbated by Old School resentment at qualifications of Calvinist orthodoxy emanating from New England colleges and seminaries. When the abolitionist movement erupted in the early thirties, theological debate, institutional background, and charges of heresy had already weakened the Presbyterian church. Southern Presbyterians had remained aloof from the debate as a group; but in order to stave off abolitionists who were identified with the New School, and seeing in the conservative theory of history a view compatible with their need to maintain extant institutions against the raging sin of mankind, they agreed to side with conservatives to drive the New School from the Presbyterian church. Thus Presbyterians had already cut ties with northerners who refused to approve slavery when Methodists and Baptists divided in 1844. Southern Evangelicals were now free to develop a clear, consistent, mature slaveholding ethic.[21]

Contributing to the final development of this ethic was a body of thought which helped southern Evangelicals to interpret their experiences in a forceful, positive fashion. That they needed such a boost is clear, for they had had to explain a long and sometimes embarrassing retreat from previously held positions, and finally to justify themselves in a defensive battle of denial and self-vindication. Part of what they were looking for came from the ideology of northern Federalism.

Not merely a political party which had been drummed out of American politics amid charges of treason and monarchism, Federalists were theorists of a conservative Republican order who valued historical continuity, social stability, and acquiescence to authority above innovation, swift social change, and democratic assaults upon irresponsible power. They were just the sort of people whom eighteenth-century southern Evangelicals would have offended, despite their agreement on the indispensable role of religion in maintaining social bonds. Gradually losing control of national and state governments to Jeffersonians, Federalists continued to exercise a limited but important influence in institutions beyond the grasp of electoral politics—the colleges and churches of New England and the Middle Atlantic states. During the 1830s, when southern Evangelicals were building their own colleges and expanding their churches, they relied upon these northern bastions of Federalism for some of their most valued leadership. Indeed, without Feder-

alist-educated Yankees there would have been few if any southern
Evangelical colleges founded in the generation before 1861; it is not
surprising, therefore, that Evangelicals who developed a slaveholding ethic should have been influenced by Federalist ideas.

Attributing influence is far from attributing causality. Federalists
did not supply southern Evangelicals with a proslavery argument or
even with the predisposition to develop one. Many Federalists
helped to abolish slavery in the North before 1801, a few continued
the attack upon the southern system into the 1820s, and many saw
their sons and daughters enter the abolitionist crusade of the 1830s.
This record notwithstanding, Federalists also supplied southerners
with two important intellectual tools for putting together a slaveholding ethic. The first was a body of thought which made room for
the principle of social inequality and hierarchy in Republican
ideology; the second was a conspiratorial theory of history. Both
ideas grew out of Federalist responses to the French Revolution.

During the 1790s, in response to radical developments within
France and an intensifying anxiety about social changes at home,
New England Federalists had seen the French Jacobins' policy as the
archtype of democratic goals in the United States. The fact that
partisans for Thomas Jefferson were less offended by French actions
than Federalists, that the Virginian, like Robespierre, was a Deist,
that Jeffersonians flaunted the tricolor in public—all carried a
lesson for thoughtful Federalists. The dangers of liberty, fraternity,
and equality were obviously not perceived by many Americans, and
Federalists, like the good preachers and teachers they were, thought
they ought to warn their fellow countrymen. Accordingly they
argued that Republican institutions were safe only so long as the
mob—the mass of people—was controlled by institutions which
taught submission to authority, self-restraint, and resignation to
social inequality. French Jacobins had mischievously preached the
doctrine of equality to a people who could not appreciate the
necessity for self-restraint and social discipline, and the result of
their wicked irresponsibility was violence and tyranny. Confronted
by abolitionists in the 1830s, northern conservatives saw yet another
attempt to subvert the Republic with the dangerous, enticing call
for equality unleashed by the French Revolution. They responded
by marshaling Federalist social theory to stave off the new Jacobins.

Abolition, charged Calvin Colton in the cadences and mood of anti-French writers of an earlier generation, is a *sedition*![22] With Colton, other northern antiabolitionists attempted to fend off abolitionism as a conspiratorial subversion, a distortion of Republican theory which weighed it down with the demonic promise of equality unbalanced by restraint and public virtue.[23]

Southern Evangelicals had had experience with antislavery radicals, but they had not been able to develop a balanced proslavery ideology merging a hierarchical social order with Republican values. Even the sage who wrote that all men were created equal could not devise a theory to defend slavery. He could prevent its spread to the Old Northwest, he could cut off its lifeline to Africa, he could shudder at the wrath of a just God, but he could not come to theoretical terms with Republican slavery. Even in the 1820s young southern orators lifted the Jeffersonian banner high and celebrated liberty for all people some day, somehow, somewhere. It was all very vague. But if one studied in the North at Yankee colleges, or in the South under Yankee-trained moral philosophers, he might have discovered the Federalists' solution to the southern problem, a solution which called for constructing a theory based on the need for social order—especially in a Republic—admitting that men were not created equal, but emphasizing that those atop the social hierarchy were responsible for protecting and supporting those at the bottom in return for service. That this solution came to southern Evangelicals from northern Federalism has yet to be proved, but it is certainly suggested by a recent study.[24] In an analysis of 55 major proslavery tracts written by clergymen between 1831 and 1840, it was discovered that 37 were written by persons born in the north. Even more significant is the discovery that in a sample of 123 clergymen who wrote major proslavery tracts, 71 studied in northern colleges and 52 in the South. Of the total, 28 studied at Yale and Princeton, where Federalist social philosophy was entrenched, and two-fifths of those educated in the South studied at institutions influenced by northern, Federalist-oriented colleges. On the basis of this and other evidence, it is possible to entertain the hypothesis that Federalist impact upon the southern Evangelical slaveholding ethic was direct and impressive.

This is not to say that Federalist ideas alone shaped southern

Evangelicals' thoughts on slavery, for they most certainly did not;
there were other factors as well. One was the Evangelical predisposition to distinguish clearly between the pious and the worldly.
In the development of any ideology there is a natural redefinition
and strengthening of boundaries between true believers and threatening infidels. Already committed to such a distinction, southern
Evangelical publicists invested it with new meaning by removing
the world to the North, identifying infidelity with Yankee fanaticism and piety with southern sensibility. Another factor, and one
which would complement Federalist thought very nicely, was the
Evangelical emphasis on order. The early southern movement had
been an ordering process for both individuals and groups. The
flagellant drive for perfection, which was the key to Evangelical self-
discipline, provided the mood through which social control by the
pious and their allies came to be more highly prized than the
democratic and unruly expressiveness of the conversion experience.

In a category different from ideologically defined factors were
those which reflected the position which Evangelicals held in the
social system. One of them—the accelerating drive for honor and
prestige—has already been explored at length. Nowhere was this
tendency better exemplified than in the development of a slaveholding ethic among the most populous southern churches in a
society where most people did not own slaves. And the factor which
gave force to this and all the others was belief in the inferiority of
black people. The sentiment was not peculiar either to Evangelicals
or southerners, but it must always be kept in mind, especially when
trying to understand why nonslaveholders would be susceptible to a
slaveholding ethic. So pervasive was the belief in black inferiority
that many Evangelical tracts on slavery never really took the trouble
to prove it, and instead merely assumed that it was one of those
social and moral axioms which competed with the law of gravity for
credibility. It was like gravity, too, in that one challenged the axiom
only if he were ignorant, stupid, insane, or bent upon suicide.

From this storehouse of historical experience and ideas, southern
Evangelicals crafted a slaveholding ethic. Never agreeing on a
definitive statement, they developed several themes which expressed their solution to the problem of slavery. The first was the
one most obviously affected by Federalist thought and most at odds

with the values and actions of eighteenth-century Evangelicals, since it rejected outright the "infidel" doctrines of equality and natural rights. Latter-day Evangelicals substituted a theory defining slavery as part of a social hierarchy which reflected the reality of human inequality, and which was maintained by a feeling of mutual obligation between superiors and inferiors. It is an undeniable fact, observed southern Evangelicals, that some people are more intelligent, talented, and moral than others, and this inequality could be ignored only at grave peril to civilization. The problem with theories of equality was that they flattered people of low estate and limited capacities into believing that they possessed sufficient knowledge and talent to rule, when their irrational aspiration alone was clear indication that they had neither. The appropriate attitude of people at all levels of society was submission to the authority of persons in ranks superior to their own, so the only legitimate motive force for social change was not the confrontational demand for justice from the bottom rung of society upward, but benevolent instruction and guidance proceeding in the opposite direction.

The logic of this view is seen clearly in the contrasting myths through which Evangelicals and the people they sometimes called "anarchoabolitionists" explained the origin and purpose of the social order. Abolitionists argued that all humans in a natural state had certain "inalienable rights" to which each person had claim equal to that of every other person regardless of race, sex, or capacity. To secure these rights, among which was personal freedom, they banded together in society and instituted government. Slavery was evil because it had deprived men of those very rights which they had banded together to protect.

Against this myth Evangelicals posed their own—the doctrine of the fall. In a state of nature, humanity rebelled against God, attempting to substitute its own will for His. The result was that humanity lost its original perfection and if left alone to its own devices would have destroyed itself in the chaos of licentiousness and violence. To prevent the destruction of His creation, therefore, God restrained humanity by establishing social systems and governments. Since the purpose of both was to restrain the raging effects of original sin, and since people were born with unequal capacities, societies naturally developed levels which were distinguished by how much external restraint and guidance were required to compensate for a lack of self-restraint. The higher the rank, the greater the power of self-restraint, and therefore the greater the right to exercise authority; the lower the rank, the lesser the likelihood of self-discipline, and therefore the lesser freedom to exercise authority. Human rights therefore were conditioned by social rank, or as one Evangelical wrote, "All men have an equal and perfect right to the *status* in which they were born with all its established rights and privileges, and also to whatever they can legally and meritoriously acquire."[25] But merit and law were shaped by a stratified social system where the best people ruled, a providential arrangement which could be tampered with only at great peril.[26] Slavery was one aspect of this government, keeping certain classes from hurting themselves and upsetting the balance and peace of society.

How far the logic of this view could be extended without eliciting cries of outrage or even murmurs of dissent is not at all clear. There is very little evidence that Evangelicals agreed upon just who comprised which social ranks, for almost by necessity they blurred distinctions among white men, while at the same time celebrating the principle of inequality. When departing from murky generalizations into specific argument, Evangelical publicists explained structured social inequalities as being analogous to those of the Christian family. Children could not govern themselves, much less one another or their parents, and were therefore under the restraint and guidance of their elders until prepared to exercise authority through education in self-restraint and the art of governing. Superior to the children but subordinate to the patriarch was the mother and wife, whose special sphere in Evangelical thought was presumably an honorable one, even if inferior to that of her husband, father, and sons. Here were two excellent examples of the principle of social subordination, instances which could be ignored only by a "fool or madman."

So eager were male Evangelical theorists to establish the principle of human inequality that they insulted and demeaned a majority of their own constituency with the same dull, oblivious insensitivity which they usually reserved for talking about black people. In tract upon tract, male writers emphasized the subordination of women as built into the very nature of human society by God Himself, citing scripture to that effect and rewarding the submissiveness of woman with elaborate praise to her grace, "passive fortitude," and "enduring love." It is a matter of record (Genesis 2:23, for example), argued some of the more simpleminded preachers, that man was created in the image of God, but that woman was derivative of man, being created for his benefit and placed under his authority. Indeed, some publicists were so sure of the inferiority of women that they justified the principle of inequality by comparing the position of slaves with that of wives. "Do you say," asked one clergyman, "the slave is held to *involuntary service*? So is the wife. Her relation to her husband, in the immense majority of cases, is made for her, and not by her." Turning to the wives, he reminded them that they, like slaves, were "under service," "bound to obey" their husbands in all things, and to submit passively to the will of God, the ultimate Patriarch. Continuing, he was triumphant: "Do you say the slave is *sold and bought*? So is the wife the world over."[27] This man, as so many others, responded to attacks upon social inequalities by shrugging his shoulders as if hearing madmen rail against the tide. In lumping together white criminals, lunatics, minors, and women as subordinate dependents, neither he nor his colleagues would have had any trouble at all in justifying the enforced subordination of another race.

If conventional gradations of dependency provided raw material for a theory of inequality, Evangelicals had very little difficulty in avoiding its implications for white people by diverting attention to the enslavement of Africans. Flagging arguments for inequality could be strengthened by calling attention to the institution for which they had been designed in the first place. Evangelicals explained that slavery was the only safe way white southerners had found to govern Africans. Corollary to the theme of inequality had been the unchallenged axiom that each level of social dependency had institutions and rules appropriate to its "moral and social condition." The result was that women and minors were restrained by marriage and family, children by schools, criminals by penitentiaries, and lunatics by asylums. Slavery was like these institutions because, although important as a way of organizing labor, it was essentially more important as a way of restraining inferiors "dwelling in the midst of a highly civilized people."[28]

If African inferiority were a universal assumption among whites, the nature of that inferiority was murky. At one pole in the hazy spectrum of perception was the conviction that blacks were innately inferior to whites because they were a race distinct from humanity, a condition which could never be changed. Supposed anatomical and physiological peculiarities were catalogued in an expanding literature which assigned blacks, among other things, thick skulls, cramped cranial areas, animalistic features, and flesh preferred over that of whites by sharks and feline predators. By nature too, black people were believed to be less intelligent and sensitive to pain than whites, but more sensual and licentious. Their original culture, unaffected by contacts with civilization, demonstrated what blacks were really like, for in their homeland, Africans sacrificed others of their kind upon "abominable altars," ate still others, and "worshipped the devil, practiced witchcrafts and sorcery, disregarded the marriage rites, murdered, swore false, practiced all kinds of dissimulation."[29]

In explanation of the chasm between white and black, some Evangelicals turned to their dog-eared Bibles to elaborate upon earlier scriptural defenses of slaveholding. They based the blacks' inferiority upon the will of God which, they claimed in tortured exegesis, was revealed either in the curse of Noah or the punishment of Cain. If one were really imaginative, he could find the origins of black people in the unnatural coupling of the accursed and exiled Cain with a female from among "pre-Adamites," who had been created before humanity. For the more traditional bibliophile there was a sufficient explanation in the curse of the drunken Noah upon the descendants of his son, Ham (Africans), because of an invasion of the patriarch's privacy. And a few expositors argued—just to complete the circle no doubt—that Ham had actually married into the race of Cain, thus making blacks twice cursed. That anyone was converted by such explanations is doubtful, for they were merely a way of lending legitimacy to views already shaped by personal experience, psychic need, and social interaction.

At the other pole of the spectrum of discussion on inferiority was the belief that blacks were not innately inferior to whites. They were simply culturally defective barbarians who had to be civilized. This argument was far more sophisticated than the gross and

Chapter 4

hateful racism which attacked and vilified black people because it was a thoughtful attempt to stabilize the volatile compound of antislavery past, proslavery ideology, personal ambivalence, and political necessity, and to reconcile two empirically based but contradictory beliefs: African inferiority and the transforming power of Christian piety. Whereas the racist emphasis upon innate inferiority led in the direction of symbolizing black people as beasts, the ethnocentric emphasis which proudly contrasted the achievements of white culture to those of blacks led to blacks' being characterized as children. The significance of the dichotomy is readily apparent when we realize that the former view required a complete moral disjunction between black and white, projecting the one beyond the benevolence of the other by assuming a perpetual state of war between them. This conflict made impossible any empathy through which mature human relationships could be established or a claim made upon whites for even a rudimentary, flawed sensitivity to the feelings, talents, ideas, and dignity of black people. Conceiving of Africans as inferior in culture did not betoken an emancipationist impulse any more than it did pathological hatred. Ethnocentrists echoed racists in speaking of African culture as inferior to European and attributing to blacks an inheritance of licentiousness, emotionalism, superstition, and ignorance.

An occasional similarity of rhetoric, however, did not imply a reconciliation of the two views. The racist dogma as promulgated by a few Evangelicals was part of a larger trend in the nation as a whole; but it was also, George Fredrickson has argued so persuasively, the means through which southern political theorists and politicians avoided class conflict. By emphasizing the racist contention that all white men were equal only so long as blacks were enslaved, they enlisted racist fears in support of the political and social system. Slaveholders could be secure in their property and social position within the electoral democracy of the Old South only by convincing the majority that owning slaves was a public service. The theory which thus developed focused upon the threat to all white men should slaves be freed, and although a pragmatic ethic could conceivably be inferred from the political-racist proslavery argument, it was not a matter of much concern. The slavery which racists justified was a strict government of blacks designed primarily to restrain their savage instincts, protect whites from African bestiality, and to do the work which would promote southern prosperity.

If such a view was, as Fredrickson has written, "the dominant public ideology of the South," it was not dominant among Evangelical theorists. This fact served to highlight the difference between a proslavery ideology and a slaveholding ethic. The former emphasized the structure of slaveholding society and was designed to explain how the system worked and why it should be maintained; it took no account at all of the moral character of black people and whatever rights they might be expected to have. The latter—the slaveholding ethic—emphasized the moral responsibilities of both master and slave and was concerned with securing benefits to both. The former was characterized by singleness of purpose and arrogant assurance, while the latter was characterized by ambivalence and a sense of guilt.

Slavery in this view was ideally adapted to the "moral and social condition" of blacks because on the one hand it provided them with the external restraint necessary to curb their licentiousness and emotionalism, while on the other, it provided a cultural apprenticeship in family life, self-discipline, responsibility, and Christian commitment. But education in civilization could not take place, ethnocentric Evangelicals argued, if masters brutalized their slaves through a martial regimen which established relations between the two upon raw power, coercion, and fear. Such idiocy would simply push Africans beyond the civilizing influence of white people, and reinforce the adversary relationship which cultural differences had already made too common. Slavery would be stable, most Evangelical theorists agreed, only when it was seen as a moral relationship in which whites demonstrated a real concern for blacks' well-being, established common ground between the master and slave, and appealed to the latter's best instincts instead of making him "stand in fear."

The best way to guarantee an optimum moral relationship between master and slave was through perfecting the "domestic" character of slavery. Rule over Africans was not exercised directly by the state, southern Evangelicals pointed out, but by individual families. Unlike northerners, who thrust black people as far from themselves as possible and relegated them to degradation and despair by cutting off intimate contact with them, southern Evangelicals emphasized that they had drawn blacks closer to themselves. In doing so they had provided the physical and psychological security so indispensable in preparing blacks for moral responsibility.

But when would the goal be reached? The question was rarely answered, even though ethnocentric Evangelicals had, by attributing African inferiority to history and culture, clearly implied that blacks could eventually be raised to a cultural level with themselves. Indeed, Evangelicals often congratulated southerners upon the fantastic improvement blacks had enjoyed since their arrival in the New World, implying that improvement would continue into the future. If so, slavery was not perpetual, an inference which abolitionists thought condemned southern Evangelicals of hypocrisy and which southern racists thought condemned them of abolitionism. Evangelicals had lived with contradiction and ambivalence for a long time, and if inferences were made about Africans' achieving cultural parity with whites, white Evangelicals could simply say that they thought it possible in the abstract, but most unlikely in the South. If slaves were perceived as children instead of beasts, they were children who would never grow up.

Another theme which helped to structure the slaveholding ethic was that slavery and Christianity were not only compatible, but actually symbiotic. Slaveholding was seen as not merely a permissible act, but as a positive, Christian responsibility. This view was of course directly contradictory to the earlier plaint that slavery was a political institution with which the church had nothing to do and has the taint not only of hypocritical inconsistency but also of self-delusion. Even so, the ease with which Evangelicals identified slavery and Christianity revealed a deviation from Evangelical principles no greater than that of abolitionists, and flowed quite naturally from the experience of three generations of southerners. Indeed, so complete was the merging of bondage and religion in southern Evangelicals' thought that by 1861 the traditional conflict between the pious and the world was projected by a few enthusiasts into the political arena, where South and North became locked not only in a struggle for power, but for the very future of Christian civilization.

In support of this belief, southerners marshaled all their religious resources, especially Evangelical deference to the Bible. It was the repository of all wisdom, the arbiter of all disputes, the very revelation of the mind and will of God Himself. In it southern Evangelicals had found irrefutable evidence that God had sanctioned slavery, whereas abolitionists had drawn their principles from "the abstrusest of all speculations upon the vexed question of human rights" and supported these with "forced inferences" and "strained" exposition. The tendencies thus established early in the debate over slavery had with each passing year indicated the inexorable declension of abolitionists from the Christian faith, as they made reason their God, sentimental speculation their mediator, the Declaration of Independence their ten commandments, and human equality their romantic counterpart to the doctrine of original sin. Southern Evangelicals had on the other hand defended the faith and presided over a rebirth of piety resulting in large part from the discovery that the Bible justified southern institutions and also provided a stable guide to everyday living which people could count on to mean exactly what it said.

Although a clear meaning in Holy Writ has always proved a false conclusion from questionable premises, the belief in such a proposition has always had a beguiling attractiveness, especially to people who need an inerrant authority. And in all fairness to the biblical exegesis of beleagured southerners, it must be admitted that the Bible literally does not condemn slavery and that there are passages in it—especially in the epistles of Paul—which recognize its existence in Roman society without negative comment. That these passages were written by people who believed in the imminent return of the Christ and the consequent transformation of the whole natural and social order would have been ignored even if such principles had been understood by southern Evangelicals. They needed the security of specific, literal, written warrant from unquestioned authority to justify themselves. The new critical analysis of biblical texts just seeping into the United States from Europe was even more anathema to southern Christians than the inferential analysis of abolitionists. Acceptance of such dangerous ideas in the North was indicative of the impiety there and reinforced southern Evangelicals in their commitment to the rigid, uncritical dogma that the Bible was in every sense and situation an infallible guide. The application of this principle could sometimes be both pathetically ludicrous and ingenious. For example, if the words of Genesis 16:9—"Return to thy mistress and submit thyself under her hands"—and Paul's letter to Philemon were to be believed, the Bible obviously sanctioned the Fugitive Slave Law of 1850. That thousands of Christians could thus be prepared for what became a thoughtless bibliolatry is not surprising when the South's most sophisticated Evangelical theorist, James Henley Thornwell of South Carolina, should have argued that the church had nothing to do but to explain the Word of God; it had no "opinions," no "attitudes," no "speculation," but only the right to say, with the Bible in mind: *"Thus it is written!"*[30]

Southern piety presumably also benefited from the peculiar tendency of slavery to evoke and enforce a sense of Christian obligation and duty. Servitude made a Christian ethic more possible in the South than the North. Emphasis upon *obligation* and *duty* as exactly the right words to characterize moral sensibility was not at all surprising, for it connoted a sense of accountability to superior authority for obeying rules which were always binding, regardless of the actions of others. Whether enforced externally by law or internally by self-discipline, these rules were all that stood between the self and society on the one hand and sin and chaos on the other. That a Christian ethic which understood moral responsibility in this fashion should have developed in a slaveholding society is consistent with the needs of that society, but the process is also a logical extension of the Evangelical drive for personal restraint and self-discipline. The orderliness of Evangelicalism merged nicely with that demanded by the infidel theory of human rights; affirmed was the submissiveness of inferiors to superiors, obedience to authority, and perpetual exertion in the personal struggle to prevail over passion and sin. This view did violence neither to slavery nor to Evangelicalism, although it could be argued, and was by abolitionists, that such Christianity was severely limited by southern culture.

But neither Christianity nor slavery, observed southern Evangel-

icals, left the matter with the individual alone. Unlike the impersonal, riotious North, the South through its churches and slavery
obliged citizens to do their duty. The argument often took a
remarkably pragmatic turn. One Baptist clergyman, for example,
argued that slavery was the only institution which could require
racist whites to assume their responsibilities with regard to blacks.
Believing blacks incapable of withstanding the destructive impact
of a racist society by themselves, he insisted that granting to white
people property rights in slave labor was the only way to marshal
their self-interest in support of blacks and thereby to guarantee a
righteous society.

Besides enforcing a sense of moral responsibility and instilling
allegiance to the Bible, slavery and Christianity also complemented
each other in imposing social order. It was no rhetorical accident
that white southern Evangelicals labeled their most outspoken
opponents as "anarchoabolitionists"; for anarchy and emancipation were identified deep in the troubled psyches of most whites.
The black "child" of "domestic slavery" could become the beast
of racist theorists once the externally imposed order of servitude
were destroyed. The fear of chaos, always apparent in Evangelical
thought, was compounded by the deeply imbedded fear that blacks
beyond white control were libertines in morality and anarchists in
politics, just as the French had discovered their own "mob" to be
during their Revolution. Robespierre's Red Terror merged, in
psychic function at least, with the Haitian Rebellion of Toussaint
L'Ouverture which sent terrorized emigrés fleeing to America at the
end of the eighteenth century with hysterical reports of atrocities
and destruction. And Nat Turner's rebellion in Southampton
County, Virginia, fanned the smouldering fears of white southerners when they found that they could not really distinguish between
the contented and loyal slave of their public statements and the
ravaging beast of their most tortured private fantasies. Thus slavery
and Christianity combined to fend off any subversion of southern
institutions, southern will, southern order, whether by infidelity,
speculation, Red Republicanism, or forced emancipation. The drive
to perpetuate slavery became the social expression of a traditional
tenet of Evangelicals' private morality.

Within the context of desire for order, the Mission to Slaves comes starkly into focus, for it became the ultimate proof that slavery and the Gospel were compatible. Sometime in the 1850s the Mission ceased to be an extension of the old antislavery tradition and became instead the ultimate expression of the slaveholding ethic, the perfect statement of true Christian love and care in a slaveholding society.

The Mission, the inerrant Bible, the morality of duty and obligation all indicated the sometimes desperate search for order as the underlying tendency of white Evangelicalism in the Old South. Indeed, slavery had become the objective, social expression of Evangelicals' obsession with imposing order on a sin-ridden, anomic existence. Inner tensions increased within the devout as they surveyed the worldly chaos about them through pain inflicted by the repressed and terrifying chaos within themselves, and the result was to give discussion of slavery on the part of religious folk a moral tone which has rarely been appreciated. All too often, romantic liberals and guilt-ridden southerners have been so offended by Christian "proslavery" arguments, and at the same time pleased with the hypocrisy and immorality with which they could accuse the pious, that they have ignored the fact that these arguments were the logical extension of the Evangelical demand for discipline and restraint.

Slavery became the objectification of the human dilemma. The black man became the personification of sin itself, especially in his original or emancipated states: licentious, degraded, disorderly. His presence, conversion experience, spirituals, and religious sensibilities provided each white church with a continuous morality play; and the structure of slavery, sustained by the discipline of law and church, represented in an objective way the processes which created the perfect Christian. The presence of the black man in a European culture affected by Evangelical values did not necessarily mean emancipation, as so many historians have argued with regard to abolitionism, for they have ignored what white southerners were never allowed to forget—that after conversion came the pursuit of discipline and perfect obedience. If white southern Evangelicals found that they could not follow the impossible demands of the Gospel as they understood it, it is not surprising that they should have embossed with unassailable morality that one institution

which could provide a means for enforcing the Gospel upon others
and therefore upon themselves. The moral failure within oneself
could be mitigated by having attempted to realize the Evangelical
goal outside one's own tortured soul in the objective world.

Having said this much, however, it is necessary to recall as with
almost everything southern that there was a theme running through
the slaveholding ethic which seems contradictory to the others. In
fact, the theme was necessary to make proslavery discussions by
southerners into an ethical system, rather than an elaborate vindication: it was the frank admission that slavery was indeed flawed and
that slaveholders had a responsibility to correct the evils of slavery.
There was, in brief, a reformist theme at the very core of the
slaveholding ethic. "The right of the master," wrote the Reverend
Richard Fuller of South Carolina, "places him under the deepest
corresponding obligations to promote the interest, temporal and
eternal, of his slaves."[31] Or as James Furman had written to the
person suspected of abusing a servant: "We who hold slaves, honor
God's law in the exercise of our authority." The fond if futile hope
of reformist sentiment was to shape southern slavery into a
humane, smoothly operating institution in which human relations
were regarded so highly that both races would support it.

At the heart of the matter was the division between racists, who
thought of blacks as savage brutes, and ethnocentrists, who thought
of them as human beings. Most Evangelical theorists argued the
latter point and were never so vehement as when they repudiated
the hypothesis of the American school of ethnology that blacks were
a distinct and inferior race of subhumans. The resulting debate has
presented historians with something of a problem because it is not
clear whether clergymen were more concerned about a scientific
threat to scriptural authority and Christian belief or the attempt to
demean blacks. Some have viewed the shocked cries of "Infidelity!" as proof of the former, but George Fredrickson has pointed
out that for a great many people the distinction between biblical
and scientific theories of blacks' inferiority was irrelevant, so long
as inferiority were proved; and the Bible could itself support a
theory of separate creation for blacks.[32] Charges of infidelity
associated with scientific themes had punctuated Evangelical po-
lemics since the 1790s, and because they had been used before to

carry arguments rather than to define them, there is no reason to believe that their function had changed in the 1850s.

Evangelical theorists whose primary concern was for the Mission and the care of black people thought that the hypothesis of the American school was demonic because it supported the petulant reluctance of brutal masters to grant slaves that most important recognition of their humanity, their conversion to Christianity. Masters, argued the eloquent Fuller, owe slaves everything due to an "intelligent, social, immortal being."[33] And Charles C. Jones, the missionary patriarch, never ceased to insist that slaves were really people, much like the more civilized whites had been centuries ago, who responded favorably to dignified, respectful, equitable treatment the same as anyone else. In fact, Jones himself never really relinquished the views of his early manhood that blacks were what whites had made them and that it was therefore the responsibility of whites to undo the damage they had done. The essential requirement of the slaveholding ethic, therefore, was not good physical treatment alone—good food, clothing, shelter, and health care—but recognition of the slaves' humanity. The psychological damage of slavery, which had once been clear to a few sensitive Evangelicals—Jones brooded over it for years—could never be successfully identified with the institution itself. The result was that many reformist inclinations, while real in the sense that they eventually led to agitation for change during the Civil War, have the appearance of unreality, resting more on the sentimentality for which southern Evangelicals had condemned abolitionists than upon the logic of their own best convictions.

And yet a few people insisted on reforming the system, to make slavery into the benevolent institution they said it was. During the war they petitioned here and there to allow black preachers greater freedom of movement, and a few partisans tried to inspire passage of laws to enhance the Mission. One of the most universally pursued reforms was that which would have protected black women from rape and their families from dispersion. The rape of the mind, too, was to cease—or at least to diminish—for Evangelicals even went so far as to request that slaves be allowed a rudimentary education.[34] All these matters had been part of the slaveholding ethic before the war and were then, of course, a matter of voluntary compliance by masters to the privately perceived will of God. Almost every extended discussion of slavery written by an Evangelical included a section on the duties of masters, and a few pieces on that topic alone had been timidly submitted to what was at best an indifferent public. The reforming theme of the slaveholding ethic was an acknowledgment that white southerners had not done their duty by blacks, and the war itself became in the minds of many clergymen Divine judgment upon southerners for that very reason. But the ethics of duty and the need for order could never really come to terms with the issue of what was "due" black people as they themselves understood it.

Even without reform, Evangelicals thought the South more Christian than the North. In 1856 one Baptist clergyman even published quantitative proof of the fact. The census of 1850, he reported, revealed that the population of New England and the free population of the five original slave states were almost equal in numbers, and yet 4607 New England churches could accommodate only 1,900,000 people, whereas 8081 churches in the southern sample could squeeze in 2,900,000 worshipers. The true nature of New England Christianity and southern piety, he slyly observed, was indicated in two other statistics: the value of New England church property was well over 19 million dollars, whereas the churches of the southern sample were valued at only 11 million dollars; and even more significant, there were 487 Unitarian churches in New England and only eight in the south. "Pride" in worldly possessions and heresy so characteristic of the North were modestly posed against the "godly humility" and orthodoxy of the South. How strange, he mused, that such a state of affairs had come to exist by 1850, when New England had originally been founded by pious Puritans and the South by worldly Cavaliers; but such was the irony of southern history.[35]

The Mission and the slaveholding ethic were the most significant statements of white Evangelicalism in the Old South. As such they symbolized the best acts and reflections of people who attempted to make sense of Evangelicals' obsession with order and slavery, and also to elicit commitment to a belief system which reconciled the reformist implications of the past with the social realities of the present. To accomplish this task, Evangelical theorists addressed several groups. First of all, they were talking to themselves, trying to rationalize contradiction, suppress irrational sentiment, and resolve internal tensions. Many southern Evangelicals who wrote on slavery were uncomfortable with the institution. The Reverend Basil Manly, Jr., was one of these men. After reading an antislavery tract in 1847, he confided to his father that he longed for the "cessation of slavery for the south & negroes & for our selves" and hoped that God would soon give us "a way of escape from it."[36] Three years later he was delivering lectures defending the system. Just a year before his first lecture, his father observed to him that slavery would obviously have to die out, since its usefulness for blacks as well as exploitative "capitalists" would diminish with time.[37] Both men were slaveholders; both defended slavery; both harbored doubts; and both had to suppress them, just as did so many of their colleagues. Ambivalence and guilt, although present, did not torture them, for as articulate and creative Evangelicals they had learned to live in a state of perpetual suspension between Cross and Crown. That was the way life was; and writing about the Mission and slavery helped to ease the tension in a redemptive way.

The therapeutic exercise of writing out ideas obviously helped Evangelicals to believe they were accounting to God, but it had the even happier effect of answering to more immediate and less forgiving an authority—the slaveholding classes. Evangelical writing on slavery was a practical exercise in public relations, for it calmed masters' fears about southern churchmen's contacts with northern antislavery colleagues and their own emancipationist forebears; it assured masters that the churches looked upon them as special stewards of the Christian ethic, and in doing so offered to ease their awful responsibilities through educating their slaves. All that slaveholders had to grant in return was a little more prestige to the clergy, and perhaps their own presence at church services. And yet a more subtle reward was anticipated. In accepting the offer of vindication inherent in the slaveholding ethic, the southern leadership seemed to be rewarding Evangelicals by acclaiming their values as *southern* values. That this achievement was tenuous was true; and after the Civil War the taste for such acclaim would be translated into the surge for prohibition and a new triumph for the Evangelical values of orderliness and restraint.

People with doubts about slavery were also in the mind of
Evangelical publicists, who revealed in almost everything they said
on the subject that there were southerners as well as Yankees who
had to be educated. Many were not slaveholders and some could
not read, so that sermons and public lectures were required to
explain in language unencumbered by nice distinctions and ethical
theorizing just what was at stake in slavery. And if George
Fredrickson is right, the distinction between racist and ethnocentrist
has to be surrendered at this point, for the clear message at this
level of communication was that slavery was necessary to restrain
inferior blacks and maintain the brotherhood of white people. As
Basil Manly, Jr., said in one lecture: Slavery "abolishes invidious
distinctions" among white people, creating an "aristocracy of
color" and throwing more people "into the higher class than in any
other nation."[38]

Not completely convinced, nonslaveholders might grumble
about the aristocratic clergy's insincerity, and claim that the Mission
was designed for slaveholders' interests instead of their own. No
one took special consideration for *them*! Racism and lack of
leadership would usually prevent such people from confronting
clergy or masters, and entice them to divert their anger to the
hapless slaves; but this was not always the case. James Furman was
forced to resign his pastorate with the Bushy Creek Baptist Church
near Greenville, South Carolina, in October of 1863 because of what
amounted to a classic case in class conflict. His education, charged
his critics, had made him proud and aloof, and his preaching was
not fervent enough. Indeed, his sermons were lectures intended to
inform, rather than evocative celebrations of salvation. The identification of congregation and preacher which had made Furman's
father, Richard, popular as a young clergyman during the Revolution, had escaped the son, who became an adversary to his own
church. With Yankees threatening Greenville, Furman had expected his congregation to stand with him against the invader, as
his father's constituency had stood with the older man against the
British. But they did not. Instead, they remembered that James had
been an ardent secessionist and was therefore "instrumental in
bringing on the country the evils of the war which now rages on our
soil."[39] A pastoral relationship was impossible to maintain.

Persons other than nonslaveholders also had to be addressed. There is evidence to suggest that women were likely to be thought untrustworthy on the subject of slavery. They were, after all, assumed to be less practical than men. Moreover, the special work which Evangelicalism had assigned to women could have made them sympathetic to slaves; and the presence of mulattoes in the black population was proof of the licentiousness unleashed by slavery, a sin which threatened all Evangelicals and especially women, according to the prevailing ideology. And particularly in Evangelical churches were those affectionate, irrational, pious, and serious creatures likely to mistake the lessons of the antislavery past; worse, they, like abolitionist radicals, might even begin to identify the evils of slavery with their own subordination. Since one can never be too careful in these matters, it is not surprising that the many allusions to the submissiveness of women should sometimes have made that condition as much a goal to be achieved as a means to prove the principle of inequality.[40] Sympathy with slaves and anger with hysterical men did not make women into a disruptive force in the South, but the fear of such a turn did occasionally disturb men. The abolitionist Grimké sisters were southerners, after all, and it was known that southern women were actually hiding *Uncle Tom's Cabin* in their sewing baskets!

By the secession crisis, white Evangelical leaders had cast their whole history and destiny into the world which their grandfathers had fled. The act was no more than northern Christians had done, nor than their successors would do; it had an inner logic to it, even if the social milieu had not dictated it. The ideology of Evangelical slavery, the self-righteousness of Evangelical exclusiveness, the smugness of Evangelical piety did not make southerners any less generous as individuals nor more self-deluded than northerners. But the amalgam of social structure, self-esteem, and personal vindication forged a religious commitment to a vision of social order, restraint, and duty which still persists in much white southern religion. Parallel to this mood, and sometimes in conflict with it was—as there is to this day—a style which could sometimes transform attacks upon the world into a radical perception. And even more important, there was also a model of Evangelicalism alternative to that expressed by whites in the form of black Christianity.

5

"The Trumpet Sounds within-a My Soul"

Just as whites converted God to their society, so blacks coverted Him to theirs. Although the two peoples shared words, images, rituals, and worship, their religious experience and ultimate hopes differed as radically as their social positions. And yet, precisely because of that common public worship and because neither people could free itself of the other, the two religious modes of southern Evangelicalism—black and white—cannot be understood apart from each other. Especially is this true for whites, whose religion was so fettered by racism and social rank as to deprive it of the dynamic and celebratory mood which salvation in Christ theoretically should have conferred. Perhaps both peoples shared that mood for one brief historical moment when whites attacked slavery, but blacks possessed it as their own when white believers excluded them from the promise of freedom and equal companionship in Christ.

Southern Evangelicalism could never really constitute a balanced Christian ideology apart from the values and beliefs of blacks because without them there was no successful identification of believers with a Christ at once crucified and victorious. Because of their place in society, white Evangelicals were too conscious of their own respectability and too crippled by their ethnocentrism or racism to sense the agony and alienation of the cross and therefore to understand the Gospel as a truly liberating force. True, they sometimes exhibited such feelings in sporadic manumissions and sentimental stories about pious old men and women who, significantly enough, were always black—but even in these instances, most whites never achieved the religious maturity of their black fellow Christians. Southern blacks had a perspective on white religion as well as a way of expressing their own which gave southern Evangelicalism a profound sensibility. Enslaved, they sang of freedom; defeated, they awaited victory; powerless, they exercised the power of the "righteous remnant." Only through the prism of their experience can southern religion be seen in its full historical significance. Ironically, it was not the master class which sang of ultimate vindication by God in power:

> My Lord calls me; He calls me by the thunder.
> The trumpet sounds within-a my soul;
> I ain't got long to stay here.

Unexceptionable generalizations are as difficult to make about antebellum southern blacks' religion as about white Evangelicalism. But the limits of the present analysis help to ease if not to resolve the anxiety triggered by such difficulties. It should be remembered that we are trying to suggest themes, structures, and ideas of the southern Evangelical tradition which enabled people to come to terms with their social existence. Keeping this in mind will not diminish the problematic character of what follows, but it may help to sharpen issues. That blacks' religion may be discussed appropriately within the rubric of defining society through religious experience, symbols, and institutions is obvious from the agreement among scholars, publicists, and slaves themselves that blacks by their culture and social condition were much more likely than whites to cast their entire cosmos in religious terms. But there must be a stubborn reluctance to confuse black religion and Evangelicalism. White Evangelicalism was the principal means through which Christian ways of ordering experience, expressing self, and defining community were conveyed to blacks, but their social position and culture transformed the gift. The religious ethos which southern blacks projected into society was rich and powerful precisely because it was something which blacks had fashioned for themselves and in doing so had revealed a new way of expressing Christianity.

One thing more needs to be said by way of introduction. Discussion of the religion of antebellum southern blacks has all too often been freighted with awkward and misleading impressions

which have distorted the slaves' actual accomplishments. We are
presumably past dismissing the culture of antebellum southern
blacks for the "buffoonery, the lack of dignity and moral power
which characterizes much of the legend of plantation religion in our
own South." To have relied upon the unreflective, legendary
"yarns" of the same mentality that created the slaveholding ethic is
a flawed procedure at best, but one which dictates the conclusion of
an influential and provocative essay on slavery that "the range of
spiritual aspirations" which such religion "offered the Negro
cannot for a moment be compared with its counterpart in white
culture." Blacks would have been served far better by history, so
the argument goes, if a "national church" had been committed to
the strategy of "bringing the slave into the Christian fold" and
insisting that "he be offered a spiritual life marked by dignity" as
well as solid "instruction in Christian morality."[1]

Now of course this hypothetical strategy was precisely what white
churchmen thought they were following. If they failed, it was
because whites would not act as they were supposed to, and blacks
would not accept the rules as conveyed to them. A "national
church" which could have made both races behave differently from
the way in which they did would have required almost totalitarian
powers and was therefore not likely to have developed in America.
If such an institution had existed, its power would have been in the
ability to coerce rather than to elicit a sense of personal liberty.
Note the words above which describe the ideal situation: the slave is
the object of action and not the actor, as if he were to slough off his
enslavement, ancestry, traditional ways of viewing the world, and
sense of selfhood in order to think the oppressor's thoughts after
him. Then, and presumably only then, could the slave have
expressed "spiritual aspirations" which were a legitimate "counterpart" to white culture. The description of action in which the
slave is expected to remain passive while receiving a discrete body of
ideas and attitudes which exist apart from social and cultural
conditions reveals one of the most mischievous and flawed assumptions which scholars make. The very idea that there is a "spiritual
life," a "Christian fold," and a "Christian morality," each of
which exists apart from cultural and social heritage and context and
which can be communicated without such trappings is naive. More
important, it is utterly inconsistent with the experience of white

Evangelicals and black Christians, not to mention almost two thousand years of Christian history. The idea that the slaves' spiritual life, church, and Christian morality would be the same as whites', indeed, even that it *should* be the same, is the kind of value judgment which has warped so much American historical writing. The biblical observation that truths are held in "earthen vessels" carries an admonition which scholars should respect, even if white Evangelical missionaries did not.

Before revivals launched the southern Evangelical movement, African conversion to Christianity was a haphazard and sporadic affair. Most references to early Christian blacks are fleeting or murky. That after forty years in the New World Africans were consenting to baptism for themselves and their children is evident from the Virginia law of 1667 which stated that the act of baptizing slaves did not change their social condition. Despite the implications of this law for enticing white Christians to break down religious and cultural barriers between masters and slaves, they were never transformed from inference into action—at least on a significant scale. The Church of England, which had difficulty enough keeping track of its sometimes reluctant and usually isolated communicants, made little concerted effort to bring black people under its care. True, the Society for the Propagation of the Gospel in Foreign Parts after 1701 made erratic forays against African "heathenism," catechizing and preaching as time, circumstances, and personal inclination would allow, but the most obvious result of this kind of activity was to make ecclesiastical authorities agonize over what they had not done, rather than to boast of meager accomplishments.

Throughout the colonization process, a few Africans braved the taunts of their fellows to convert. House and body servants closest to pious masters probably came under pastoral care far sooner than those who lived and worked at a greater distance from white people; but how frequently conversion took place and how many people it affected is simply unknown. We do know, however, from colonial laws that African belief systems—Islam as well as those less familiar to whites—persisted among the slaves, and we also know from later sources that black people were deeply impressed with

newcomers from Africa. Presumably they would also have been
curious about African religion, which priests and holy men from
the mother continent embodied in the South well into the nineteenth century. But the interaction within the slave quarters between
Christian converts and the African religious is largely a matter of
speculation. It is safe to assume that the process of Christianization,
begun in the early colonial period, had brought most blacks into
some kind of contact with Christianity but without any compulsion
or enticement to convert. The Church's requirements of catechizing
and change in behavior patterns before acceptance into the body of
believers demanded a conscious rejection of one's African inheritance for the cultural trappings of the English-speaking peoples
without the supports of language and conceptual frameworks upon
which behavior and the catechism were based. It was an onerous
enough chore to make the transformation if one could read and
write English, but for those who could not do so the task required
almost too much. Most Africans would not have thought it
worthwhile to become more like the Europeans only to be refused
European liberty.[2]

Then came the southern Evangelical movement. Its message was
even more revolutionary for blacks than it had been for whites who,
at an accelerating pace during the last quarter of the eighteenth
century, had recast their sense of self-esteem, communal bondedness, and social position in terms of evangelical piety and expansion. To whites, the revivals offered direct contact with a God
whom philosophers had cast into aloof obscurity; they also offered a
direct, personal knowledge, through the transfigurating experience
of the New Birth, of a God whom natural theologians had said
could be known only indirectly by Reason. In other words, for
whites the revivals reordered a familiar world and made them more
important within it. To blacks, however, the revivals offered a new
world in which remnants of the old world of African inheritance
and American gloss made the New Birth possible to accept and
understand, but no less new and radical.

There is now as there was then a basic paradox in the conversion
experience because of the continuous elements in social and
cultural life which make it possible, and the discontinuous elements which make it a meaningful transformation. Historians once

considered continuous cultural patterns between Africa and English America to have been rare and of little significance, charging that the shocks of enslavement, transportation, and isolation from fellow tribesmen effectively stripped blacks of almost all their cultural heritage. Recently, however, historians have begun to pay much more attention to the impressive evidence of persistent cultural patterns and artifacts brought from Africa to the New World. One of the most important links between African culture and black Christianity has been the absence of a sacred/secular dichotomy in traditional thought. Although pious whites would in their own lives be unable or perhaps unwilling to make such a distinction, they knew that it existed for most people in their culture. This difference between Europeans and blacks may account in part for the whites' insistence that blacks were "naturally more religious" than whites. Blacks also differed from their masters in the ease with which their cultural systems could incorporate new images, symbols, or gods. Thus the total world view which blacks had inherited made it relatively easy to receive new religious insights into their own system if these were perceived as meaningful. The major problem, as white missionaries learned, was that there had been no apparent way to convey successfully the meaningfulness of their religion; at least not until the Evangelical movement erupted with the explosive power of the conversion experience.

A universal phenomenon of revivals in England, Wales, Ireland, New England, and colonies to the south, the conversion experience with its various forms of hysteria, ecstasy, and psychological transformation seemed to the Africans to be very much like the vitality of their own religion. Evangelical "experience" seemed very much like African "possession" of the devout by spirits "whom they favored," a phenomenon which was "a vital part of African traditional religion," and which was "an experience greatly sought after."[3] The conversion experience, so valued by white Evangelicals as the primary authenticating act of their rituals, therefore, became the most important contact point between traditional African culture and the Evangelical movement. For reasons suggested below, it is doubtful that tormenting self-doubts, a sense of sinfulness, or self-castigation afflicted blacks as they did many

whites, but the two peoples began to respond to Evangelical
preaching in the same joyous sense of release and celebration—the
preachers called it "liberty," significantly enough. That the whites
believed the experience to be God's gift, and that the blacks
perceived it as possession does not detract from its binding and
recruiting functions, for both blacks and whites could agree that
the other people, no matter how foreign in appearance and
language, was responding to the preaching of God's word in the
same fashion, thus revealing that they shared the same God and
perhaps even the same Mediator. That the images and moods
within the minds of the converts should differ according to culture
is obvious, but the fact remains that with the Evangelical movement, a new means of contact between the two races had been
established.

Blacks elaborated the meaning of their conversion experience in
ways which eventually differentiated black from white churches.
But in the transports of the first quarter-century of Evangelical
expansion, "African" and "European" practices and expressions
interacted in such a way as to make difficult any attempt to
distinguish the culture of origin. The incantational preaching
which New Light Baptists brought from New England was very
much like the interaction between leader and worshipers in African religion. The same similarity existed with regard to Methodist
preaching, which in the southern colonies, as in Great Britain,
often became a litany between preachers who promised salvation ad
worshipers whose cries, moans, and tears indicated the efficacy of
the exhortation and the presence of the Holy Spirit. When blacks
saw whites' engaging in familiar religious activities that triggered
behavioral responses which were almost the same for both whites
and blacks, they began to participate in a volatile interaction with
whites. This almost uncontrollable phenomenon seems to have had
a sobering effect upon both peoples because both apparently
believed that the impact of the "conversion experience" on the
other was proof of God's power. Other similarities between African
patterns and European practice also helped to bind converts from
the two cultures. Baptism, for example, whether by immersion,
sprinkling, or pouring was similar to some African initiation rites.
And enthusiastic congregational singing, to which Methodists were

almost fanatically devoted, elicited positive responses among Africans, whose singing became a special contribution to Evangelical meetings just as it had been in African rites.

The important thing to keep in mind about the contact which the Evangelical movement made possible for the two races is that there was a movement on the part of each people toward the other. Whites did not simply convey a set of ideas and practices which were humbly and gratefully received by blacks; nor did blacks coldly expropriate white forms in which to pour African substance. Something quite different and new was happening, the significance of which cannot be understood apart from the framework of slavery and blacks' experience with whites prior to the Evangelical movement. Then, white priests and missionaries had attempted to dictate religious moods and ideas by catechizing, a process which expects nothing of the student but a correct answer. In the teachers' eyes, African practices and beliefs were simple barbarism and superstition—an arrogant, demeaning view difficult to disguise and reinforced by the fact that the church in no way questioned slaveholding. In the arena of contact between "white Christians" and "black heathen," the former could easily become an adversary to whom blacks were to surrender everything whites had not already taken—soul, relations with ancestors, family, perhaps even tribe. It is not surprising, therefore, that so few blacks converted.

Evangelicals, however, were different from other white people. Their religious exercises were similar enough to those which blacks valued to make the transition to Christian rites much easier. Even more important, these whites, quite unlike the careful and fastidious teachers of the church, eagerly invited blacks to participate in religious meetings much more actively than they had ever been able to before. Thus conveying an interest which may have surpassed their actual feelings, Evangelicals encouraged blacks to be receptive to "conversion" as "experience," rather than as cognitive transformation. True, the experience had to be related to the congregation in orthodox language, but even if correct theological formulae eluded the black convert, he was not demeaned and rejected by the group. He was encouraged to try again and again until able to explain what was happening inside himself in terms which whites could understand. And when he did finally witness to the power of

the Holy Spirit in a promiscuous congregation of whites and blacks,
he and through him other blacks had the unique experience of
whites' listening while blacks spoke, and in instances by no means
rare, of those whites responding "with freedom" and in awe that
God's word could come from persons, regardless of social "condition." The contempt with which churchmen dismissed such
preaching reveals the importance of the innovation for blacks.
"The most illiterate among them," wrote a rector about the New
Light Baptists in 1766, "are their teachers; even Negroes speak in
their Meetings."[4]

Blacks became especially important to Evangelical preachers—as
opposed to lay persons—who often measured the success of their
preaching and exhortation by the expressive behavior, ecstatic
shouts, and tears of the congregation. And if whites were sometimes "dumb" or "unfeeling," blacks could almost always be
depended upon to provide the kind of audience which preachers
treasured. "To see the poor Negroes so affected," wrote Francis
Asbury in 1771, "is pleasing; to see their sable countenances in our
solemn assemblies ... affected me much." Nineteen years later
one of Asbury's assistants could mention the same kind of responsiveness. "Met the D[ea]r black people in the morning," wrote
William Mckendree "in a flaim of love, a sweet heart melting time
indeed. A large congregation, preached with more than common
degree of liberty. The D[ea]r Lord attended the word with power."
And forty years later one Baptist clergyman could write a friend:
"The poor negroes lifted up their voices and wept so that 3 times I
had to sit down ... O ... my business is plain, a humble preacher
among the poor & destitute—for this only have I voice, mind, or
heart."[5] In the early revivals this kind of attitude projected by the
white preachers—whether or not it was sentimental, patronizing,
and self-dramatizing—clearly revealed an interaction between
whites and blacks which members of both races thought important.

More important still for blacks was the new status possible for
black leaders and the assault upon slavery which accompanied
Evangelical innovation. How soon blacks began to preach is
unknown. Samuel Davies's Presbyterians certainly left no record of
black preachers, but as the Anglican priest mentioned above
observed, they were active among Baptists by 1766. Indeed, by the

Revolution a black Baptist preacher such as George Liele could preach in the area around Savannah, creating a constituency which in 1788 would constitute the first independent black Baptist church in the United States. It should be understood that whites did not give blacks a new elite. Blacks created their own leadership, but they did so in a situation which required whites' sponsorship, lest they arouse the suspicion and displeasure of the civil authorities. This relationship between patron and client did not guarantee freedom of worship and assembly, to be sure. James Meacham learned the lesson in a vivid and dramatic manner. A white man and an itinerant Methodist preacher, Meacham was particularly devoted to his black congregations. One night at meeting, as he recalled in his journal, "the dear black people was filled with the power & spirit of God" whereupon they let out a "great shout" which "vexed the Devil," who appeared in the form of a mob to disperse the meeting and beat the blacks. Meacham was aghast! "A poor black bro[ther] lucked [sic] me in the face," he wrote, "with bursting grief tears of blood rolling down his bruised face, and cryed, 'this is what I have got for praising of my dear Jesus.' O how can I rest," wondered the preacher, "when I see my bro[ther] unhumanely treated?"[6] The blacks would have remembered that night for the cruelty of the local magistrate, which was probably no surprise to them, but they and others like them had learned that whites were divided, and that some, like Meacham, ostensibly hated slavery because of their religious piety.

   This discovery made the Christian gospel all the more important to blacks, who began to convert in great numbers during the time when white southern Evangelicals were most outspoken against slavery. No matter how disguised or debased, Christianity contains a message which liberates those who are bound, frees those who are oppressed, and promises to revolutionize social ranking in God's kingdom: the "last shall be first, and the first last" (Matt. 20:16). Resentment aginst the false values of the world and the unjust ordering of society was expressed over and over again in early Evangelical statements and meditations. William McKendree's response to the attendance of a few gentlemen at preaching is a case in point. He thought that they were secretly taunting him and inferred all manner of slight from the things they did or did not do during worship, confessing triumphantly in his diary that the

humble would be exalted and those who exalted themselves would
be "debased."[7] Men like James Meacham made even more specific
the opposition between pure Christianity and social ranking.
"While the proud whites," he wrote, "can live in luxury and
abomination, making a mock of God and his word, the African
upholds him by his Swet and labour of his willing hands.... O
blood, blood, how awful it Cryes up before God against my poor
unjust professing Bro[ther.]"[8] Such homely responses, when
added to antislavery harangues and the many battles with slaveholding fought by Evangelicals for over a generation, could reveal
to blacks that Christianity was a religion of freedom. And in their
practical, unabstract cast of mind blacks could begin to discover two
very important things—that the freedom promised by the gospel
was real and that Christianity was not solely the white man's
possession.

This last discovery was essential for the further development of
black Christianity, for as Francis Asbury found as late as 1795, it
was exceedingly difficult to convert black people "held by professors of religion."[9] The difficulty was transcended, however, as
blacks discovered the discrepancy—alien to their cultural heritage—between the white man's actions and his religion. Slaves
seemed bent on formulating a new Christianity, freed from the
compromises dictated by social mobility and the consequent necessity to make distinctions between sacred and secular affairs. And as
they became even more familiar with the gospel of freedom, they
discovered it also as a gospel of hope, a discovery which added a
significant new dimension to their lives. Traditional African religion was not structured to provide a sense of cosmic hope or
ultimate vindication. History moved backwards for Africans, in the
sense that the future was projected at most only a few years ahead of
the present. In African religion, much more important than a
future event was the continuing contact with the spirit world
through the living memory of those who had recently died, on into
the realm of those only vaguely remembered, and beyond that into
impenetrable mystery. Africans had no way of conceiving of history
as a linear progression toward a valued, sublime goal in which true
believers would be vindicated for all the persecution that they had
suffered in God's name.

As for a life after death, traditional African religions could offer no change in status, no rewards, no freedom from the constraints which bound one in this life, no comfort for the sorrow which afflicted him as a slave. Christianity altered this cosmology in offering blacks freedom. The most tangible example of that freedom was of course actual emancipation, which would occur when whites were willing to abide by Christian principles. Should that never come to pass, however, Evangelical Christianity still offered hope in the final vindication at the end of history which would come with terrible vengeance upon the unjust, and also in the reward of Heaven to all who were faithful disciples and had called upon the name of the Lord. The first impact of this belief system was not to vindicate slavery, and certainly not to leave blacks satisfied with their lot, for at every point it promised a hope quite beyond the ability of traditional systems to produce.[10]

It should be clear from the discussion thus far that two common misconceptions about the conversion of slaves have to be rejected. The first is that blacks joined Methodists and Baptists because these groups were "more emotional" than others. This explanation hardly deserves serious consideration because it is so hopelessly vague and subjective; some people find a Catholic high mass and others find a Quaker meeting to be highly emotional experiences, and yet neither attracted Africans in great numbers in the United States. But we know from the experience of Africans in the New World outside English America that they were attracted to Catholicism when priests and missionaries made an effort to convert them. The extent of their success depended upon blacks' seeing in Roman Catholic ritual and belief those practices, images, and symbols familiar enough to attract interest and meaningful enough to be appropriated. Neither in Catholic nor in Protestant America was the amount or intensity of emotion the issue, but rather the way in which emotion—an elemental force in all religion—became a part of religious exercises. The similarity of Evangelicalism to highly valued aspects of African tradition—especially the awesome "possession" perceived in the conversion experience—combined with the collective interaction between black and white at worship to help convert Africans to Christianity.

The other misconception, like the first, is not so much incorrect as misleading; it argues that Methodists and Baptists attracted blacks because they were close to blacks in social status. This could have been true only if one assumed the vantage point of the aristocracy; but the slaves' perception was quite different. They often came to meeting with their masters, who were careful to maintain social distinctions between freedom and bondage, white and black. If slaves appropriated the language which masters had once used against worldly elites, this reveals not parity of social status, but blacks' attraction to the same value system which enhanced the self-esteem of whites. It would be recalled, too, that proximity in social rank, far from evoking brotherly love and empathy, often induces increased antagonism in the battle for social position. Both of these common misconceptions, however, contain elements of truth insofar as they convey the fact that blacks converted to Evangelicalism because they found it a satisfying, hopeful, and liberating idea system which made sense to them in their social condition. They took Christianity from the whites because they had discovered that it was not the sole possession of whites; indeed, just because they had discovered that it passed cosmic judgment upon whites and promised something far better for black people than the world which the slaveholders had made.

Conversion to Evangelical Christianity was as long a process for southern blacks as it was for whites and occurred at an irregular tempo which has never been carefully analyzed. There were surges of recruitment and troughs of declension throughout the ante-bellum period, a fact which suggests that speculation about African continuity and Christian innovation in the conversion experience is limited by ignorance of many psychological, social, and demographic factors. It is a matter of record, however, that blacks had by the end of the Revolutionary era laid claim to their right to hear and preach the Gospel. The same ideological and economic conditions that made it possible for southern whites to preach against slavery also made it possible for black preachers to build independent black churches here and there, and for whites and blacks together to establish black congregations associated with local or regional organizations of white churches. In Silver Bluff, South Carolina (1773–75); Savannah, Georgia (1788); Williamsburg, Virginia, and Augusta, Georgia (1793), for example, independent Baptist churches were constituted, and almost every southern circuit of the Methodist Episcopal church had black membership by 1800. Doubtless the same could be said of Baptist churches, all of which were willing and some of which were eager to accept blacks as members. Even rumors of insurrectionary conspiracies in eastern North Carolina in 1789 and 1802 could not for long make whites deny blacks their own preachers, teachers, and assemblies.

The impressive growth of black Christianity did not mean that such growth was easy. James Meacham's account of the brutal attack by a white mob upon his black congregation on a hot August night in 1788 is a case in point. And the torment of Andrew Bryan is an even better example of the remarkable commitment and violent reality which existed behind generalizations about "growth" and "development." Bryan was a slave from the area near Savannah who had been converted under the preaching of George Liele, a freedman who accompanied the British to Jamaica when they evacuated the city in 1782. Bryan assumed Liele's role and by 1785 had a nucleus of eighteen believers and important contacts with slaves on farms and plantations along the Savannah River. There, away from white surveillance, Bryan and his nameless allies formed "societies"—a term borrowed from the Methodists—guided by watchmen who often presided over secret night meetings. To white believers and ministers such as Abraham Marshall, who helped Bryan constitute the African Baptist Church in Savannah in 1788, these society meetings and the church itself were outposts of Christianity among the "heathen," a term which was applied to white and black alike. Their dogmatic insistence on the separation of church and state reinforced white Baptists' view of the black church as purely religious, but to black communicants and suspicious masters they were that and much more.

For blacks who made no distinction between sacred and secular, the plantation societies and the church could indeed be thought of as political because they were the means by which blacks created a public life for themselves. The hope of every authoritarian regime is to force its subjects to relate to each other only through channels of communication approved, monitored, and guided by the rulers. Any organizations which exist independently of the ruling elites, select their own leadership, and are able to attract loyalty from dependent groups, even in the guise of religious worship, provide an important basis for social solidarity and personal security. To the extent this sense of unity against outsiders and the self-esteem it generates are able to limit the power of ruling elites, the organization serves rudimentary political purposes which, if realized, may serve as the basis for more sophisticated and direct political action. It is not surprising, therefore, that an outraged police patrol should seize and whip blacks who were on their way to meeting without appropriate passes. Finally, Bryan and his brother, Sampson, were captured by authorities, whipped until blood flowed from their lacerated backs, and thrown into prison with about fifty of their fellow church members. The Bryan brothers' master and several other whites obtained the prisoners' release and eventually helped them to raise money to build a meetinghouse. By 1800 Bryan could write: "We enjoy rights of conscience to a valuable extent"; but he had bought them, as would many black preachers after him, by pain as piercing as that suffered by his Christ.[11] Indeed, the memory of white authorities' erratic brutality created a martyrology for the black tradition quite unlike anything white churches could recall.

Bryan's persistence as well as his pain suggest how the black church grew. He enlisted the patronage of influential white people to create a buffer between his church and further persecution. White Baptist preachers vouched for him, the Georgia Association accepted his church as a member, and Bryan himself circulated a petition for endorsement by the "leading men of the city and country." The document pointed out the church's connection with "Friends of Religion" in two states, the socially beneficial impact of Christianity upon black people, the indispensability of Bryan's leadership, and the importance of the church's continued independence.

To understand the petition and the position of black churches in the South for over one hundred fifty years, it is important to remember that it was addressed to authorities who, as Bryan knew from the scars on his back, were very suspicious of people like him. Thus he had to establish himself as associated with powerful white people—hence the reference to "Friends of Religion"—and the endorsement by members of the local gentry. He also had to emphasize that the continued existence of a disciplined black church would, as had already been demonstrated, create a people whose "meek and inoffensive carriage" and "peaceable and quiet behaviour" guaranteed social stability. The church's black leadership was, Bryan insisted, to be relied upon to prevent, or at least to warn of, any potential "disorder." Anticipating the authorities' suggestion that Savannah would be better off if blacks attended white churches, Bryan dismissed it as "impracticable" because the worship of black people was often so "disagreeable" to whites. The petition ended with an appeal to allow the blacks to worship "according to the dictates of their consciences and in their own way."

All black congregations in the antebellum South had to solve the problems which Bryan faced. Even "independent" churches were never so free of white surveillance as their special status implied. Depending on time and place, these churches were sometimes required to have white sponsors or "trustees" to legitimate their existence; sometimes white "missionaries" visited them at stated intervals to meet legal requirements for whites to be in "control" of black churches; a few had white pastors who preached every Sunday, but who left the actual management and pastoral work to black officials and preachers, as did the famous African Baptist Church in Richmond.[12]

Despite white sponsors and allies, however, separate black churches could always be disbanded if white authorities became alarmed at their independence, as they did in New Orleans in 1857 and 1860 when the city council first closed separate black churches and then forbade any independent meetings of black Christians. Despite the whites' suspicion and caution which spawned such actions, black Christians who were associated with or were members of white churches were never quite so much under whites' control as their formal institutional status may suggest. Prayer groups, special preaching services, separate revivals, and secret meetings could make black members of white or mixed churches as independent as the ingenuity and determination of blacks and the trust or carelessness of whites would allow. Actually the dialectic between white direction and discipline at one extreme and black autonomy and expressiveness at the other was a constant theme in the dynamic process which shaped southern Evangelicalism.

At the beginning of the Evangelical movement, the dialectic was not so evident as it was to become. Then, blacks were in important positions as a rough division of labor developed, possibly differing with locality but generally leaving whites in supervisory roles and blacks in positions of actual leadership. White "supervision" was not the kind of direction one would expect in a modern bureaucracy, but a loose arrangement in which white Methodist circuit riders and Baptist preachers occasionally addressed black assemblies while their black "assistants" actually maintained the continuity of the societies, meetings, or congregations. Within the white church these preachers had various official titles—local preacher, local exhorter, class leader, elder, deacon—but within the developing black church they were the acknowledged leaders. White congregations and ministers could sometimes be amazingly *laissez-faire* in their relations with black Christians. For example, in 1815 the Edenton, North Carolina, Methodist Station allowed their black members to exercise discipline on their own responsibility in disregard of official prescription. Further south, a group of white Methodist ministers in 1808 sent black missionaries from Charleston to outlying plantations with authority to "admit and exclude members," even though the action was considered illegal by South Carolina law and irregular according to Methodist rules. The blacks were "good men," recalled William Capers in the Methodist jargon that meant "efficient" and "charismatic:" "The work was one of the most sacred obligations to be done."[13]

As suggested by Capers' enthusiasm about his experiment, independent black preachers were important and impressive enough to become part of the oral tradition of white clergymen, who could never quite rid themselves of an elemental fascination with these extraordinary men. Henry Evans, for example, a free black shoemaker and local preacher, became one of the heroes in the lore of both races for establishing Methodism in Fayetteville, North Carolina, despite the opposition of violent and hysterical whites. Or consider the story of Black Punch, who consecrated himself to Christianity because of Francies Asbury's earnest conversation, and who eventually developed a following of two hundred people quite independent of the bishop's jurisdiction, a congregation which endured fifty years before Methodist officials heard of it. And if that accomplishment were not remarkable enough,

Punch also converted his overseer.[14] Such conversions as this became an important part of southern Evangelicalism because whites as well as blacks recalled the power and authority of black preachers. For the sensitive and troubled whites these men seemed somehow to pacify troubled consciences and justify past relationships; for blacks they were the focal point and expression of the folk who would endure despite persecution.

This open interaction between white and black clergy was but one of the several characteristics which fashioned a "historical period" from the time between the earliest Evangelical conversion of blacks to about 1820. The importance of black preachers to their white counterparts can scarcely be overestimated, as blacks' legendary exploits became vicarious sacrifice which transformed the first fifty years of Evangelical expansion into an "apostolic age." Journals and diaries of first-generation preachers reveal a persistent and sometimes forced identification with the Apostolic age of the New Testament, when Paul was jailed, starved, mobbed, and shipwrecked for the faith. A constant persecutorial theme runs through the memoirs. Virginia Baptists' preaching from their jail cells provided fare for one hundred years' hagiographic celebration; ruffians' stoning revival meetings and mobs' chasing outspoken preachers became heroic incidents in recounting the "sufferings," "experiences," and "labours" of the first Evangelicals. But none of these white men could match the pain and brutality which black preachers suffered under the lash or the seemingly impossible burdens of ignorance, superstition, fear, and hatred which confronted them. Sambo Deas was but one of the many whose lives shamed the white clergy, for he had once sold his only pair of shoes to buy a Bible, and later, while exercising the powers granted him by a license to preach, was seized by a patrol and "severely whipped." "He said before the church afterward," recalled a white man, "that the Lord so strengthened him he scarcely felt the lashes as they laid open his flesh. That he could bear ten times as much for Christ."[15] Awed by this undeniable bravery and determination and probably shamed by their own inability to demonstrate the same staying power and courage in fighting slavery, influential white clergy and lay people enlisted with the supporters of Savan-

nah's Andrew Bryan to defend the black church throughout the
South as best they could with money, legal counsel, and personal
influence.

This support should not be thought of as a bounty which made
the black church possible, but as the positive response of a few
whites to black leaders who were pushing against the confining
walls of slavery. The weaker the walls, the easier for black preachers
to establish independent churches. In Philadelphia, Baltimore, and
New York during the 1790s and on into the following quarter
century, black congregations became ever freer of white domination
until they became the African Methodist Episcopal and the African
Methodist Episcopal Zion churches.

The same kind of independence became evident in Charleston by
1815, when white Methodists charged that the African societies had
not properly exercised discipline, although it is not clear what the
whites were concerned about other than a steady trend of black
independence. As a result, white Methodist officials deprived the
Africans of their own governing quarterly meeting conference and
later expropriated property which the black Methodists claimed was
legally theirs. In response to these acts, black leaders sent two men
to Philadelphia to be ordained by Richard Allen, bishop of the
African Methodist Episcopal church, and led a secession of over
4300 blacks—ninety percent of the black membership—into association with the northern church (1817). Patriarch of the Africans was
Father Morris Brown, who would one day be fond of preaching
about how the same "mysterious Providence" which had led the
children of Israel into Egypt had also provided them a Moses. In
anticipation of our own Moses, he would say to his people: "Run
with patience the race which I now set before you."[16] But more
patience was required in the South than in nonslaveholding states.
The sense of certain deliverance could not make black churches as
independent as they would have liked, for a number of changes were
taking place which would stall the blacks' trend toward autonomy
within southern Evangelicalism.

Interaction between Christians of the two races had reached a
critical point of assertiveness on the part of blacks and a frightened
realization on the part of whites that this boldness threatened their
control. This awareness on the part of whites developed over a long

period of time. Blacks and whites had differed in church meetings long before confrontations became political enough to change general behavior patterns among whites. To be sure, Esther Boulware's slave, Winnie, could not get away with saying that Christians could not own slaves, or that "Thousands of white people [were] Wallowing in Hell for their treatment to Negroes," for she was excluded from the church—her wish that twice as many whites might writhe in eternal torment probably sealed her fate.[17] But by 1815 in Charleston such individual confrontations as Winnie's had become collective, and southern white Christians were wary of the growing independent church movement among blacks in Maryland as well as in the nonslaveholding states. When in 1822 Charleston authorities discovered a plot among blacks to seize the city and execute the white people, they were alarmed at the great number of conspirators who were members of the African Methodist Episcopal church, which had seceded from the white Methodists.

Worse still, Denmark Vesey, the free black from whose fertile mind and proud will the plot had unfolded, was a religious lay leader in the church. And its native African minister, Morris Brown, who had no active role in the conspiracy, was obviously revered by those who had. Vesey and thirty-four confederates were hanged, Brown was ordered out of town, the African church was dissolved, and its members were sent back to churches controlled by whites. The wisdom of this solution was demonstrated in 1831 when white southerners learned what could happen when conspiracies went undetected and black religious leaders gained power apart from "proper supervision." Nat Turner's religious visions led him to terrorize not only southeastern Virginia and eastern North Carolina, but the entire South. In response, old laws were resurrected and new laws passed to put black religious assemblies under constant surveillance of white people, limit freedom of movement and other privileges of black clergymen, and impede still further the education of black leaders by denying to slaves in most southern states the opportunity of learning to read and write. State and local authorities answered the defensive plaints of white churchmen that Turner was not a regular preacher with demands to keep all religious leadership "regular" and all religious expression contained within boundaries approved by whites.

Changes within the white religious community also altered the
relationship between the two races. Black assertiveness paralleled
that of whites themselves, who were self-consciously rising above
and repudiating the ''poverty'' and powerlessness of their own past
and expressing their own sense of importance and respectability by
building new institutions. As one of these institutions, the Mission
to Slaves was developed to combat African heathenism, foil
abolitionism, and continue the earliest commitments made to
blacks during the early antislavery impulse. That the missionary
ideal was honorable and benevolent or that it elicited the devotion
of admirable men like William Capers and Charles Jones does not
diminish the fact that it was also in conception and implication an
extension of invidious distinctions between true believer and
infidel, the knowledgeable and the ignorant, the wise and the
foolish, the superior and the inferior. These inherent, inadvertent
distinctions, when fused with middle-class aspiration, easily reinforced the tendency to consign the black people to the periphery of
whites' concerns—the back of the church, the galleries, the missions. The implications of the Mission were clearly contradictory—it
was both a benevolent reaching out and a defensive holding off.

Racial egalitarianism in southern churches was always limited to a
few whites and a majority of black Christians, but at least in the
early period of Evangelical expansion, blacks were thought of as an
integral part of the church—as *fellow* Christians. With the rise of
missionary ideology came also a change in the mood of many
whites, an edge to conversation about black Christians, a selective
recounting of black clergymen not as suffering apostles of the
common faith, but as exemplary models of humility and deference.
At other times whites would project a view completely alien to this
one, discounting black piety as pretense, as if acknowledgment of
its authenticity would call into question the whites' religious
commitment. Once a compelling example of the fact that God was
''no respecter of persons,'' blacks' Christian devotion had become
offensive to many whites for that very reason.

The transformation can be seen in a minor but symbolic episode
of Evangelical history; and, as with so many symbolic events in
southern history, this one, too, happened in Charleston. It began
on a hot summer (1833) sabbath in a Methodist church when some
arrogant young white men threw two mulattoes—father and

son—out of the sanctuary for sitting on the main floor. "This gave great offence," sneered one of the insolent toughs, "to some of the whites who were more careful for the accommodation of the colored persons than for respectable gentlemen."[18] But the youths had felt compelled to take such action because of the proud intransigence of their pastor, William Capers, who was one of the whites to whom they referred. The fact of the matter was that free blacks had been sitting with whites on the main floor of the meetinghouse since time immemorial—at least it must have seemed so to those under the age of thirty—while slaves sat in the gallery. For some reason, perhaps a stinging remark from a nonbeliever about Methodists' "love" for blacks, a few young men had told Capers to stop the "offensive practice" of seating "coloured persons . . . among the whites." His refusal led to the outrage against the two black men. Instead of calling the whites to account, the quarterly meeting conference asked the board of trustees to make alterations in the seating arrangements and entrances to the sanctuary in order to prevent blacks from "intermixing with whites." Once again Capers found a way to fend off the young dissidents' demands, and a few days afterward spoke to a meeting of the white members about showing "charity and kindness towards the people of color"; he emphasized the claims on Christian brotherhood made by blacks who gave "evidence of sincere piety" and were "otherwise respectable in their station."[19] When once they would have been an effective appeal to pious whites, Capers's words were now received as insults. Finally the trustees caved in to pressure from the majority of whites and reluctantly granted permission to separate the free black members from the whites, an action that eventually drove many black people from the church.[20]

Revealed in the controversy was a transformation of whites' attitudes—repudiation of a past which valued black people as fellow church members, and the affirmation of a future of racist arrogance. Although there had always been a distinct color line in the church, there had also been a sensitivity to the dignity of black people and a habit of judging them on the basis of their piety and respectability, rather than on their color—at least this was the view of older members and their minister. But among younger members

there was an undercurrent of resentment and hostility against
blacks and their champions which led to sarcastic comments about
Capers's inability to take any action without first having "taken
counsel . . . *of mulattoes.*" Sure that their refusal to associate with
black people would commend them to the people who counted,
the swaggering dissidents taunted Capers. By refusing their demands, they said, he would reveal to all Charleston that he favored
mulattoes over white people, and he would pay dearly! "What
would become of *your* black classes," they demanded. "Aye, what
would become of *your* black missions?"[21] In the younger peoples'
view, the participation of blacks in whites' religion was not the
doing of young whites, but that of the old, despotic preachers;
in the former's view, the classes and missions did not belong to "us
Methodists," but to someone else's generation and foolishness.
Ironically, one of the ringleaders of the group who attacked Capers
was the son of John Honour, first Methodist missionary to slaves on
the South Carolina coastal plantations.

The Charleston affair was a minor event in southern history,
passing almost unnoticed by most historians except as an unimpor-
tant, intramural squabble so characteristic of religious folk. But it
was far more than that; it was one of those moments which reveal so
much about a people. No one really emerges as heroic: Capers was
willing to keep slaves in the gallery even as he fought for the free
blacks' rights on the floor; the free blacks resented being forced to
choose between standing during the service or sitting with slaves;
and the latter disliked the free blacks so much that they would not,
as one man complained, "permit us to rest in peace."[22] But the
young white men, aspiring to purge themselves of contamination
by black people, exhibited the dull, brutal white arrogance and
rejection of the past which could no longer appreciate or respect the
heroism of Andrew Bryan, the valiant determination of Henry
Evans, the unparalleled devotion of Sambo Deas, or the piety and
dignity of two black men who knelt in prayer at Trinity Methodist
Church in Charleston.

The "white reaction" of the 1820s and 1830s—given impetus by
black assertiveness, maintained by fear of abolitionists, and shaped
by class aspirations and anxieties—helped to provide a rough

periodization for black religious life from Revival to Emanicipation. After the "apostolic age" (1760-1820) came the generation (1820-1845) from Vesey's conspiracy to the white Evangelicals' schismatic demonstration of their southern loyalties. In the first period, churchmen, through their activities in the Mission, had tried to develop a practicable, safe, and effective way to convey their form of Christianity to blacks. In a process which varied with locality and season, they negotiated with each other, civil authorities, and black people in an attempt to fashion a framework which would guarantee blacks the kind of religion whites thought they should have. After the ecclesiastical divisions of the 1840s until Emancipation (1845-1870), there was a period of further maturation, as black Christianity became for white Evangelicals a vindication of slavery.

Attractive as such periodization may be, however, it reflects only the mental construction of whites. Blacks experienced the century before Emancipation much differently, as they found in Christian commitment and communal identity shelter from the slave system, an institutional framework to confound the logic of their social condition, an ideology of self-esteem and an earnest of deliverance and ultimate victory. For the last one hundred years of legal slavery, all events which whites saw as sequential were experienced by blacks as persistently contemporaneous, as if history were an objective drama of subjective perception and meaning. The process of conversion to Christianity, the wrath of Vesey and Turner, the dialectic of white Mission and black piety were always present from the first fusion of African "possession" and European "experience" to the vindication of Christian blacks' faith that they would one day be delivered in an apocalyptic event—one in which eternity and time crossed radically and violently. The Bible had promised the final act in the Valley of Armageddon, but some would see it in the march from Atlanta to the sea.

Black religion in the Old South was a churning suspension of ideas and behavior patterns fed by African and Christian traditions. The process which throughout the period worked to transform the suspension into a more stable compound unfolded essentially through four channels: folk religion, autonomous black congregations, black constituencies associated with white churches, and black memberships of mixed, white-controlled churches. The

relation of each channel of blacks' religious expression to the two
main traditions they contained cannot fairly be placed on a
spectrum. True, African influence persisted most in folk religion,
and was probably expressed in direct proportion to the amount of
contact that folk religion had with whites' religious life. But the
idea that African forms express Christianity less well or faithfully
than European forms is absurd, as well as impossible to demonstrate. The richness of early black religion may in part inhere in its
openness to two separate strains from the past which became fused
into a profound restatement of the Christian dialectic between the
burdens which enslave humanity and the hope of freedom.

To many whites and to a few literate southern blacks, the folk
religion of blacks was "superstition." This belittling tag is often
applied by peoples with an advanced science and technology to
others who explain good fortune, misfortune, illness, death, and
mysterious phenomena as the work of spirits. But the difference
between this explanation and that which attributes such things to
the Providence of God is a matter of how directly the supernatural
is seen as affecting everyday events and experiences. The slaves lived
in a world much closer to the supernatural than that of whites who,
for all their talk about the presence of the Holy Spirit in conversion,
were children of a technology and theology which had taken much
of the mystery out of life and had, for all intents and purposes,
placed human destiny in the hands of men who manipulated the
environment by mechanical means. Personal events might be
attributed to a general Providence or even to a special plan which
God had for individuals, but there was among whites very little
thought of actual give-and-take between humans and spirits, and
certainly by the nineteenth century little thought of actually
appropriating God's power for personal use.

In black folk religion, however, there was a realm of spirits less
transcendent than that of the Christian God and close enough to
humanity to allow considerable traffic between the two worlds.
Personal events as ordinary as a sprained ankle and as disappointing
as an unfaithful lover were often explained as the work of
unfriendly spirits, who might have been set upon the victim by a
witch in the service of some unknown enemy. With the boundaries
between this world and that of the dead seen as being so easily

crossed, people had to find some way to remain open to visitations by dead relatives, but free from the malevolent power of hostile spirits. Slaves often turned to root doctors or conjurers, who provided various potions, charms, and prayers, for protection. These specially gifted people supposedly understood both the supernatural and natural worlds so well that they could employ the powers of the latter to confound the power of the former, and they were successful enough in the eyes of many blacks to have maintained a constituency even after Emancipation.[23]

Another aspect of black folk religion, and one which impressed some whites as a peculiar sensitivity to God, was the persistent report by black believers of visions and dreams in which the spirit world impinged upon the historical. These visitations were of friendly spirits, often dead relatives who indicated by their presence an enduring care and love which were no less strong in death than in life, thus making the vision personally reassuring and supportive. Such experiences undoubtedly helped to reinforce a sense of continuity with the past, a matter of no small importance for a people who needed all the spiritual, intellectual, and social resources they could muster to fend off the crippling impact of slavery.

According to African traditions, memory of and contact with ancestors are extremely important in maintaining personal and communal identity, giving visions of the recently departed dead social as well as personal significance. Moreover, as a way for God to communicate to man, visions like "possession" could become a bridge from African past to Christian future. Indeed, blacks' cultural predisposition to receive truth in vivid, sometimes traumatic visions often seemed to observers to have given them a more intense experience of Christ's salvation than that of whites. The intensity of the experience and its perception as having come from completely outside the person had the kind of authenticity which made sensitive white clergymen respond in simple awe; it was almost as if black culture provided ways to express the meaning of divine grace better than the doctrines of election or justification by faith. Indeed, former slaves recalled a feeling of utter dependence and helplessness during some visions. "I fell out on the floor flat on my back," recounted one woman. "I could neither speak nor

move, for my tongue stuck to the roof of my mouth; my jaws were
locked and my limbs were stiff." And then she felt herself being
elevated to heaven; the whole experience was explained in a single
phrase: "God struck me dead!"[24]

Religious life inherited from Africa was not necessarily sloughed
off at conversion, even though the word connotes radical renunciation of past loyalties and views. To be sure, there is much evidence
to show that some black people consciously rejected "superstition" for faith for Christ. In black Christianity there has always
been a dialectic between orthodox and "pagan" elements, as well
as between disciplined morality and antinomian celebration.[25]
Significantly, however, the dialectic took place *within* the black
churches, which appear to have been less likely than their white
counterparts to hold fast to the dichotomy between world and church
or to excommunicate members. The reason should be obvious,
since Christian blacks who wished to maintain the Evangelical
disjunction would have been compromised by a social condition
which made racial and class disjunction more important. During
slavery, the orthodox-discipline continuum of the dialectic sometimes seemed dangerously close to the views of whites, who were
thought to have surrendered any claim to Christian purity by
owning slaves. When a group in one autonomous black church
threatened to leave the congregation because of the minister's
"scandalous" behavior, he taunted them for running to the whites.
If you want to "sit by the door when the white folks have
communion, an' wait there 'til they get through 'fore you get
some. *Come now,* an' get your letter!" When six people actually
did so, the ridicule from the congregation was loud and clear.[26]

What appeared as a familiar dialectic between restraint and
expressiveness, or "superstition" and faith, could never be identified completely as a conflict between Africa and America. Black
Christians met in brush arbors to worship, like their African
ancestors, who had set aside sacred groves for the purpose; like
Africans they sometimes met at night to pray around an inverted
pot or tub, and often expressed their freedom in the Holy Spirit
through the chant or dance. Almost always they responded to black
preaching in a pattern which recalled Africa much more than
England or Scotland. This fusion took place within individuals as a

microcosm of the church, sometimes producing someone as exotic and yet as American as a Christian root doctor who had the confidence of whites as well as blacks.

Such a person was Elihu. Every Sunday of his long adult life, he had paraded to church and worshiped in a manner as "punctilious as a Pharisee." He relied upon his religion as a power to protect him against evil spirits and to heal the sick. Over his door he nailed an inverted horseshoe to ward off witches. "What witches?" he was asked, and he explained the case of a neighboring white man whose horses had been ridden into the ground by witches. Cutting a piece of paper into the shape of a man whom he believed was responsible for the act, he tacked it to the door with a nail through the "heart." Sure enough, Elihu reported, the wicked suspect died and the horses were saved. "Mars Suttle," affirmed the black man "know how to fetch'em that time." Elihu himself had special knowledge that enabled him to heal beasts and humans alike. Once urgently demanding a pass from his master in order to go to someone's aid, he was challenged about his supposed healing powers. Agitated and eager to leave on his errand of mercy, Elihu replied, "Sent for by the white folks, Sir, all roun' the country." He got his pass.[27]

The folk wisdom of blacks helped to create a world that was uniquely theirs, one valued just because it was their own. If a few whites like Mars Suttle, or those who in their pain called upon Elihu, or others who carried charms "just in case" were touched by knowledge and beliefs not rooted in Europe, they at least had in a small way acknowledged their common nature as human beings assailed by those mysterious demons which possess all men and those things which, as the ancient Anglo-Saxon prayer said, "go bump in the night." But whites were still seen as being foreign to black knowledge, interlopers into the world of people fascinated by their African roots even if they could not always remember them. Words, phrases, stories, beliefs, and rites were passed on from one generation to the next, and if a native African should appear in the quarters, he or she would be looked upon as exotic, perhaps even as possessing a strange and awful power made familiar to children and grandchildren through tales of Africans' being raised up in the air like Elijah and flying off to Africa.[28] More potent still was the art and mystery of the African sorcerer Gullah Jack, who conspired

with the stern and vengeful Vesey to kill the whites, having first
presented his confederates with charms to spare them from the
oppressor's bullets. But even this sorcerer knew his power could not
affect the whites in a more effective way. For the most part, black
folk religion could only perpetuate the mystery of Africa, the
wisdom that made the black world different from that of the
whites; it could not assail slavery, since it explained away many of
the problems of life as the work of evil spirits or a prankish devil.[29]

What was needed, therefore, was a religion which could provide
a sense of ultimate justice, establish a claim upon the oppressor for
recognition of the slaves' dignity as human beings, enhance their
self-esteem, order their daily lives in an ultimately meaningful way,
and create a special identification with the Supreme Being and His
Mediator. This special relationship would have to sustain the
people until their deliverance, creating all the while a sense of
confrontation within the slaves themselves until it should be
projected as an objective reality into the very cosmos. The need was
defined by interaction between the slaves' social situation and the
religion which was more clearly available to them. Had the slaves
been subject to Muslims or Roman Catholics, their needs probably
would have been defined and met by Islam or Catholic Christianity. As it was, however, slaves in the southern United States
developed their religion in interaction with Evangelical Protestantism.

No religion could have met all black peoples' needs equally; men
cannot share exactly the same faith with an equal amount of psychic
intensity when more than two or three are gathered together, which
is why doctrines develop and dogma is promulgated. In black
Christianity, social status, race, and illiteracy performed many of the
functions of dogma by channeling faith, so we are left with an
experience incapable of exemplification in doctrines, and only
approximated by talking about hope, faith, courage, power,
celebration, expectation, and freedom as ultimate vindication. This
is not to say that blacks did not understand the Christian message,
but that they received it as the primitive Christians had—as a
message transmitted orally about God's act in history which
proclaimed "liberty to the captives." "The folks in them times
didn't have nobody to worship," recalled one old man in Alabama;
"an' then one come who said, 'Father, hand me a body, and I'll

die for them.' That's Christ, an' He was baptized, an' God give
Jesus this whole world" (John 1:1, 14).[30] It was the same Christ
nailed to a cross even though He had done no wrong—perhaps
precisely because He had done no wrong—with whom blacks could
identify, knowing who it was had put Him there and pierced His
side and killed Him, hoping that He would come again in glory.

As it is clearly impossible to reconstruct black religious life by
analyzing doctrine, the only alternative is to tease out themes and
images which helped to make it the expression of black community
within southern society. The only word of admonition must be a
reminder that the religion never lost the dynamic of the early
"apostolic age"—it was always changing, adapting, appropriating,
moving between poles—mirroring as it did so religious themes of
the crucified Christ and the Lord of the Apocalypse, Daniel and
Joshua, Moses and Jesus, present experience and hope.

The best expression of this dynamism was found in black
worship. Every white observer or participant who commented on it
agreed with black people that black worship was radically different
from that of most whites, even when those whites were in the same
church at the same time. Autonomous black congregations and
those associated with and meeting separately from white churches
were best able to express themselves as they wished. By the 1830s,
emotional breakdown of white people under Evangelical preaching
became much less common than it had been, limited for the most
part to special revival seasons or camp meetings. Moreover—and
this may be the crux of the matter—impressions of whites'
conversion experiences differ markedly from those left by blacks'
religious exercises. Blacks shared with whites, especially sentimental white Methodists, the initial emotional explosion of conversion as well as a persistent emotionalism afterwards, but blacks'
"possession" and visions appear to have been qualitatively different from whites' experiences. For whites, the emotional fire-
works resulted from relief at being saved from God's wrath, the
release of tension brought to a breaking point by contrast between
God's expectation of perfection and man's inability to achieve it. In
whites' view, only if persons were convicted of sin, broken as was
Christ upon the cross, could they be made ready to receive
assurance of salvation; and for the rest of their lives, whatever

emotional response was triggered by preaching probably came in the form of tears of gratitude for having been saved from the sin that tainted them still. Encouraged to celebrate their salvation, whites were more often than not inhibited from doing so by their persistent sense of sin and the heavy trapping of guilt which it perpetuated, as if they could not really believe that they had been saved.

Black Christians, on the other hand, did not have that sense of original sin which so confused and burdened white Evangelicals. Like latter-day Methodism and liberal Christianity, the taint was not imbedded into their very souls; but unlike members of those two forms of "white Christianity," blacks did not lapse into optimistic sentimentalism. Their social condition made that change impossible. Using a formula they learned from white Christians, they prayed to be released from sins, but unlike the masters, they were locked into a form of bondage which could be objectified, cast outside the self in a manner unavailable to whites. The emotional toll of slavery was much more effective than the doctrine of original sin in creating self-contempt.

As a black sociologist, Paul Radin, wrote many years ago: "To a man seeking union with God it is immaterial how his soul has become befouled, and one can always rely upon an unanchored humility and a feeling of inferiority to discover that the suppliant has himself been responsible for the befoulment."[31] And yet, despite the logic of the slave system, black Christians did not dwell on the taint of their bondage; they celebrated their release from it. While whites might rightfully be said to have "broken down" under preaching, blacks were lifted up, enabled to celebrate themselves as persons because of their direct and awful contact with divinity which healed their battered self-esteem with the promise of deliverance, the earnest of which was the vision itself.

These religious exercises separated blacks from whites by creating a psychic world from which whites were excluded because they were simply irrelevant. Blacks often danced and clapped and shouted in joyous expression of their humanity in a "black" world, a phase of worship which sometimes frightened whites, who undoubtedly sensed that if the psychic power was translated into political terms, it could become all too dangerous. The preaching of blacks to

blacks, too, was part of their communal solidarity, with incantational cadences eliciting responses which united worshipers in
affirmation of freedom both present and future. The religious
festivity which characterized blacks' worship was so alien and yet so
resonant with the secret hopes of many whites that in some mixed
congregations it became a vicarious celebration for them. These
whites could sometimes grasp the supreme irony of the masters'
looking to the slaves to teach them joy and the true "consolation of
religion," as they would have put it, but thought of it as part of the
mysterious paradox of blacks' tortured existence.

Black preachers, too, like the worship they led, helped to define
the differences between black and white and to rally blacks in
celebration of their psychic unity. Whites often preached to blacks,
although many fugitive slaves remembered such instances as lectures about behavior, rather than as sermons about salvation. But
even whites who could genuinely move blacks—such as the brilliant
Richard Fuller of Beaufort, South Carolina, and Baltimore, Maryland—could never establish the identity between congregation and
preacher which was so important in black religion. Throughout the
antebellum years, white churchmen had to deal with the galling
knowledge that try as they might to "reach" the slaves, they could
never do so. Black congregations could be aroused only by black
preachers, no matter how illiterate or suspect whites thought those
preachers to be. In the 1850s, authorities complained about black
preachers in the mixed tones of disgust and envy which had once
been spat out by Anglican priests about Shubal Stearns and Francis
Asbury, and for the same reason. Blacks had created their own
leadership. Their leaders possessed varied talents, intellects, and
motivations, but they exercised a power, craft, or mystery which
elevated them, despite any shortcomings they might have had, as
the expression of the folk. "It made us proud," recalled one
believer of John Jasper, "to look at him."[32]

Indeed, Jasper is as important a representative of black preachers
as the illustrious saints of the "apostolic age." A "quick witted and
alert" worker in a Richmond tobacco factory, Jasper was converted
one day while stemming the sot-weed's leaves. He was the son of
Philip Jasper, a preacher, and the last of twenty-four children born
to his mother, who was a nurse and driver over women on a

plantation in Fluvanna county. Both parents were leaders in the
slave quarters, and Jasper himself was quite resourceful, as evi-
denced by his finding someone to teach him to read. His subsequent conversion prepared the way for his answering the "call,"
and he eventually became popular for his remarkable talent of
preaching funeral sermons. Throughout the South, blacks were
granted special privileges to memorialize the dead, and these
occasions became exceedingly important public events that drew
huge crowds—one reportedly drew five thousand people in Louisiana—and required the finest and most moving preachers. Jasper
was one of the best of the best. It is not surprising that after
Emancipation the enterprising and fascinating man should have
transformed a group of nine people into a congregation of two
thousand. Over the years, he became something of a legend for
preaching a sermon which embarrassed young black ministers and
attracted large crowds of curious people who came to hear the
preacher prove "The Sun do Move." This thoroughly unscientific
thesis, when combined with Jasper's crucifixion of the English
language, should have served to make him appear ridiculous, yet it
was delivered with such personal magnetism and natural eloquence
that after hearing the sermon scoffers would have to admit, almost
without realizing it, that Jasper was "right."[33]

The white Baptist preacher who recounted the story about Jasper
did so to prove the former slave's eloquence, for he was occasionally
a brilliant speaker. But the point of Jasper's sermon was much more
important than his ability to preach it; simply put, it was to
present "The Lord as the defender of His ancient people." This
theme, far more than scientific questions, characterized Jasper's
preaching, for the issue of the sun's movement must be understood
in the context of one of the most universal themes in black religion:
the deliverance of the Jews from Egyptian slavery. After having led
the Children of Israel into the land of Canaan through the ashes of
Jericho and Ai, Joshua won the Gibeonites as allies. For their
cooperation with the invader, the Gibeonites were attacked by the
five Amoritish kings, an action which sent the vengeful Joshua into
battle with a fury that plunged his enemies into a bloodbath. To
guarantee that he would kill them all, the victorious general
appealed to the Lord to keep the sun up until he had accomplished

his grisly task. "And the sun stood still, and the moon stayed, until the people had avenged themselves upon their enemies" (Joshua 10:13). Obvious to Jasper was the identification between Joshua's troops and his own people, between Moses' people and blacks. He had learned to preach as a slave, and if his art meant anything at all to blacks it meant enabling his black congregation to transcend their social situation and enter the realm in which their rage could be expressed in such a way that it saved them from execution, but created an impenetrable psychological shield against their enemies, transforming blacks all the while from victims into "conquerors"— indeed, as Jasper emphasized, as "more than conquerors."[34]

The themes of "conquest" flowed through his preaching: Shadrach, Meshach, Abednego in the fiery furnace as more than conquerors; Daniel among the lions as more than a conqueror; Joshua slaying the Amorites, as more than a conqueror. Perhaps Jasper chose the scientific question of the sun's movement because it was so absurd, and because black preachers had a finely tuned sense of the absurd when confronted by whites, who had a knack for becoming sidetracked from matters of faith to matters of fact. Jasper had preached all his life about the evil of slavery in full view of a white audience, for he had learned what all black preachers had to learn—how to preach the truth to people who needed it without triggering the vengeance of people who feared it. He did not know, but he would have understood, the fugitive slave from North Carolina who addressed a postwar black congregation by reminding them about how "we used to have to employ our dark symbols and obscure figures to cover our real meaning." Jasper would have joined the congregation as they shouted "Amen. Hallelujah! That's so!"[35]

Jasper was master of the art of disguising meaning. Recalling his own conversion, he would anticipate meeting his former master in Heaven: "He'll say, 'John, call me master no mo'; we're brothers now," and the congregation would be "stirred" as if swept by a "celestial gale."[36] Only a fool or a white man would have seriously believed that Jasper or his congregation meant to postpone expressing their humanity until they were dead. Talking about the future to a people oppressed by the present is a classic way of evoking anger against the social system without inviting punishment from authority. And in this manner he consistently reminded his people of their essential equality with whites:

> Ev'body got to rise to meet King Jesus
>   in th' morning
>   Th' high and th' low
>   Th' rich and th' po'
>   Th' bond and th' free
>   As well as me.

But beyond the doggerel and the "obscure meanings" Jasper always came back to two themes: Joshua's avenging army before the stationery sun, and that text—one of his favorites—which he had discovered when he first began to preach funeral sermons as a slave, the Revelation of St. John, in the second verse of the sixth chapter. There, while his congregation's attention was fixed on that fragile boundary between life and death, when they were most susceptible to summing up the meaning of their own mortality, when they most desired to reach beyond the barrier of death to touch the face of God, Jasper had learned the truth about himself and his people: "And I saw, and behold a white horse: and he that sat on him had a bow; and a crown was given unto him: and he went forth conquering, and to conquer." He preached all his life that his people should become "more than conquerors," for he knew how history would end and how that future affected the present.[37]

These strains in Jasper's preaching were but part of the whole thematic structure of southern antebellum black Christianity and deserve to be understood in that context. Undoubtedly the most important theme of all was the equality and dignity of human beings no matter what their race or social condition. "God is no respecter of persons" (Acts 10:34) was one of the most popular biblical passages in black Christianity, cropping up as it did in sermons, conversations, reminiscences, and confrontations with white people. When they first heard the statement from white preachers at the beginning of the Evangelical movement, blacks adopted the orthodoxy of the politically weak and oppressed, for the Christian canon was closed, while the primitive church was still proclaiming "liberty to the captives"—the outcasts of the ancient world. Thus, for black Christians, the theme of equality was not a principle to be believed, but the general assumption upon which preaching was made possible and the conversion experience understood. Indeed, within the African tradition even more than the European pietist tradition from which Evangelicalism had come, the emotional trauma of possession/conversion was authentication of the person's contact with the divine and therefore undeniable confirmation of his importance as a human being.

The strengthening of one's self-esteem, battered and damaged by the psychic and physical brutalities of slavery, became one of the most important psychological supports which Christianity could offer the slaves. That the self should be celebrated in corporate worship helped to reinforce time and time again the sense of one's value, which was so regularly assaulted; and this was precisely what many white people complained about. The blacks' religion, instead of teaching humility, as missionaries had promised it would, only invited blacks to think more highly of themselves than they should have. To more sensitive whites, the blacks' celebration was even more unsettling, for they sensed, as did their slaves, that the assumption that "God is no respecter of persons" was judgment upon the system which admittedly rested upon invidious social distinction and was therefore judgment upon them as whites and as slaveowners. White discomfort was no doubt increased by discovering that even though most slaves could not read the Bible, they knew some very significant passages: "Thou shalt love thy neighbor as thyself," "Whoso stoppeth his ears at the cry of the poor, he also shall cry, and shall not be heard," "Call no man master, neither be ye called master."[38]

Every statement about equality and human dignity necessarily included the theme of deliverance; preachers could not "proclaim liberty to the captives" without someone's taking them seriously. Jasper's sermon on Joshua's league with God against the Amorites was an extension of the best-known and most vividly remembered story in the black "canon"—Moses's leading the Children of Israel out of bondage. In song, story, and vision Moses was a constant figure in blacks' thought about their corporate relation to God. It was not memory of the past which captured their imagination, but promise of the future with its awful judgment. This sense was buttressed by other favorite biblical passages: "Do justice to the afflicted and needy, rid them out of the hand of the wicked," "Let the oppressed go free."[39] At prayer, too, the sense of injustice was intense. "A slave," explained William Thompson, who had been one, "cannot pray right: while on his knees, he hears his master, 'Here, John!'—and he must leave God and go to his master."[40] No wonder sensitive whites felt uncomfortable in the presence of black faith, even when they heard the slaves' songs, which many whites professed to love. The spiritual "Go down, Moses" comes to us neither in the past tense nor the historical present, but in the future tense, which is to say as a moral imperative. Few obeyed; but Moses remained nonetheless one of the constant reminders that, as a maid told her mistress, "*God never made us to be slaves for white people.*"[41]

If God had not made blacks slaves, neither had He been very specific about when he would redeem them. The servant girl was certain her deliverance was at hand because the year was 1865, and she knew that the Yankees were coming. For many years her people had awaited the day; but the length of time between promise and fulfillment was not so important as the moral certainty that deliverance should and therefore would occur. The earnest of ultimate vindication was the same experience which reinforced self-esteem and which was either witnessed or participated in at most worship services. Heaven, the Last Judgment, and the experience of Grace were contemporaneous and immediate in their psychological impact upon believers. They would be delivered upon their death; their people would be delivered at the final judgment; they had already been delivered by the Holy Spirit through participation in the death and resurrection of Christ Jesus at baptism.

The formula was not a way of avoiding or compensating for present bondage, but of meeting it head-on. The most important impact of Evangelical Protestant Christianity upon both blacks and whites was the transformation of the way in which they thought of themselves, their rejection of social canons in favor of ethical and moral understanding based on Christian experience. The promise of a future life which—unlike its counterpart in African tradition—rejected historical inequalities and injustices and provided separate destinies for the faithful and unbelievers helped blacks to fend off some of the most destructive psychological consequences of slavery. The reasons are both obvious and subtle. The Christian message has always been that the ultimate judgment of history has already been clearly pronounced in the life-death-resurrection of Christ Jesus, so that whatever happened to people who affirmed Jesus as the Christ should not be thought to be the ''last'' word on their value as human beings. That value was decided at their conversion and would be confirmed in the next world.

But as one must expect with matters eternal, there has been some confusion among those burdened by time and space as to ''where'' the next world is: just beyond our grasp in Heaven (or Hell) or at the end of time after the general resurrection. No matter, actually, for the message conveyed by the vivid images of Heaven and Hell or the Last Judgment is the same. And African culture may have intensified the power of the Christian message by foreshortening time in the minds of black converts, instead of allowing it to extend into an indefinite future. That is to say, the future in African culture is practically imminent, just as it was to the ancient Christians, just as it is to most premodern peoples. Moreover, unlike modern Western views, the spirit world in African culture was seen as being very close to the temporal, so Heaven and Hell, if incorporated into one's view of his personal destiny, seemed, as did the Last Judgment, very close indeed. Add to this the knowledge that sacred and secular find no distinction in the African background and interpret this fact with a respect for the concrete way of thinking which characterized the slaves—and deliverance becomes immediate! Thus, the religion which whites hoped would reconcile the slaves to their condition was actually fashioned by blacks as a way to transcend it.

But what of Moses? After all, it would be much better to have crossed over the Red Sea with Pharaoh's pursuing charioteers gasping for air than to await a deliverance that was just beyond one's grasp. Slaves obviously would have preferred to follow Moses out of slavery if they could have done so, but there was the troublesome matter of who he was or would be. Bishop Morris Brown, who had been exiled from Charleston after the execution of Denmark Vesey, had firsthand knowledge of what would happen if one assumed Moses' mantle at the wrong time and place, and so he urged his people to believe that what God had done once, He would do again; but until He did, Brown counseled patience and forbearance. Had black preachers done otherwise, great numbers of black people would have met the same fate as the heroic Vesey. But even Vesey, and Nat Turner after him, found that the social situation could not initiate or sustain a broad-based, expanding movement aimed specifically at getting free of whites.

Despite this fact, Christian blacks possessed the symbolic material for a millennial movement. Such movements have occurred throughout the Christian era and across the modern world in places where cultures are in conflict and where people in chaos discover a leader who through them will establish the ideal society. The word *millennial* is associated with such movements because their mixture of religious and political elements, of supernatural and historical events, promises a radical alternative to present society, much like the thousand years of perfect order connected with Christ's Second Coming. The millennium may be seen as the result of a gradual perfection of extant social structure and ideology or as a revolutionary encounter which establishes a completely new order. The distinction between the two is usually defined in their temporal relation to the return of Christ. Movements or groups are postmillennial and reformist if Christ is expected after the ideal society is established through the extension of present ameliorative social trends; but they are premillennial or revolutionist if the good society can be established only by destroying the present one. Premillennialist commitments may not be political if for some reason—usually social—the true believers await Christ's direct intervention in history, rather than claim for themselves the role of ushering the millennium in by violence. If this quietist solution is dictated by circumstances, it must not be assumed that believers become pliable, passive, or happy with their position. Rage must be channeled in other ways, some of which—as in all oppressive situations—could become self-destructive.

Black Christians became of necessity premillennial quietists. The primary reason was the power and ubiquitous surveillance of civil and religious authorities. After two traumatic experiences with black religious leaders who had not been under effective supervision of whites, southern authorities became much more careful not to allow religious assemblies and leaders to get out of hand again. From 1831 to the Civil War whites did their best to keep in direct contact with all religious activities of blacks, who in their turn were very much aware of the whites' power and their ability to use it. Other matters, too, may have prevented premillennial violence. Since millennial movements have occurred in black Africa, it would be silly to assume that the persistence of African culture helped to preclude them in the New World by subverting the discipline-inducing qualities of the Christian doctrine of original sin. The celebratory quality of black religion did not make people so happy-go-lucky that they dissipated their anger in expressive group behavior, but it might have made the problem of discipline more complicated by providing immediate gratification through the personally reassuring experience of the Holy Spirit. The idea is suggestive, but it also ignores the fact that millennial movements have occurred in Africa, where similar religious patterns have been found. Even the idea that Evangelicalism provided a Christianity which focused more on the individual's personal salvation than that of the collective does not grapple with evidence that suggests blacks' sense of salvation was more collectivist than that of whites. Moreover, Evangelical sects have been the basis for millennial groups in Africa.

Attempts to explain the problem of black quietism will have to remain either blatantly ideological or admittedly tenuous until we know more about the inner structure of antebellum black Christianity than we do now. There are factors, however, which will have to be taken into account even if their interrelatedness within the matrix of causality is unknown. Millennial movements can develop only if oppressive authority is far enough away for leaders to organize and for organizations to meet undisturbed by the police, and southern whites' authority was anything but distant. In addition to the restrictive character of black-white interaction, the possibility of violent collective confrontation was probably diminished by the intellectual structure of early black Christianity. Blacks inherited from Evangelicalism a belief system which valued the disciplined person within a disciplined community instead of a grand vision of the good society. And in negotiations between white and black Christians about the nature of their respective faiths, this emphasis was reinforced because it was so effective in eliciting from whites the frequently reluctant admission of the

blacks' moral dignity. But self-discipline was important also because it elevated blacks above their oppressors by demonstrating
their participation in a community not of this world—one in which
the rules of slave society did not apply, one so radically different
that belonging to it meant the sublimation of an anger that dare
not have been either repressed or expressed. This commitment did
not imply surrender to the slave system or collusion with the whites
to strengthen it, but it did acknowledge that deliverance would be
completed only by Him who had promised it in the conversion
experience. God would have to do it; and there were many who
would live to believe that He had.

In addition to the themes of equality and deliverance, the theme
of Gospel discipline was present in black Christianity. It might be
supposed that a person whose worship was often celebratory and
whose social life was dictated by the worst kind of human "order"
would have rejected out of hand a religion that set about ordering
the world. But moral order was precisely what slavery could not
provide and was precisely the means through which white Evangelicals had first institutionalized their love for one another in Christ;
it was what blacks needed to gain public recognition of their
humanity. Acknowledgment of one's moral status in society is acknowledgment of his claim to be honored as an independent, adult
person with ability to distinguish between right and wrong, to
choose options, order priorities, and to answer for the conduct resulting from these decisions. By submitting themselves to discipline, the
first black respondents to Evangelicalism were putting themselves in
a position to demand that whites deal with them according to standards which transcended masters as well as slaves and were equally
binding on both.

The sociologist may bridle at this idea, for he must be sure that
the "transcendent" ethic was an extension of the whites' social
situation—which is true but irrelevant. By agreeing to be bound by
rules they themselves had made, whites demonstrated the "transcendent" quality of the rules insofar as interaction between the two
people was concerned. In cases where whites were put on probation
or excluded, the moral responsibility of the person was not only
admitted, but insisted upon. The same was true for slaves. That
blacks were and would continue to be suspicious of whites'

demanding standards which masters themselves did not obey is true and signifies the importance of Christian disicipline because it turned the nice psychological trick of using the white man's ethic against him, at once assuming and transcending his moral position. By becoming "more Christian" than whites, blacks were confirmed in the knowledge of their own moral superiority and further strengthened in their claim to ultimate vindication. This was no mean accomplishment in the moral anarchy of slavery. But possibly even more important, Christian discipline made possible transactions hitherto impossible between people of different races, professing different ethics and religion. Without its influence, masters would not have admitted the authenticity of moral claims against them, and the result would have been to keep most transactions at the level of force and exploitation. With the development of their own Christianity, however, blacks could in many circumstances elicit from Christian masters acknowledgment of their common humanity and moral accountability. Over seventy-five years of church records contain the matter-of-fact evidence of that most important of human interactions—moral conflict and debate—which whites did not always win, and which, in a psychological sense, blacks could never lose.

Self-discipline, rather than that imposed from without, was the goal of black Christian leaders, just as it was the goal of white Evangelical theorists. If this end seemed to many blacks to be yielding too much to the master class, it was to those who preached and practiced it the strengthening of their dignity, honor, and resolve, for the emphasis was upon the creation of a responsible self within that social framework which most corrupted the ideal. The means of creating the responsible person was the same for black Eavangelicals as it was for white—the Christian family. Blacks won even from irreligious masters the privilege—some could even admit the right—of sanctifying marriage through a Christian wedding, infant baptism (if Methodist or Presbyterian), and rules which were designed to keep the slave family together and to protect its members from harm.

White preachers did not always respond well to differences between them and blacks about morality, especially in the early stages of the Evangelical movement. The earnest William McKen-

dree was often angered by the moral impact of slavery, but equally
hostile to the people who suffered it. In his journal for June 26,
1790, he wrote about "how abominable cruelty did appear and
how Irrational did Slavery appear." Over a week later the general
complaint became more specific when "two black women presented their child to be baptized and each lay their child to one
man who stood up between and professed religion." McKendree
was outraged, the blacks were puzzled, especially when the
preacher told them "To repent or they would all go to Hell
together & sent them away Shocked."[42] Even greater difficulties were
presented by whites who violated black women or broke up
families, and most congregations had to create procedures for
allowing remarriage of a slave whose spouse had been sold contrary
to ecclesiastical regulation. Conditions of remarriage varied with
locality and reveal both draconic expectations of self-discipline for
slaves and sympathetic understanding and respect.

In personal morality, too, self-discipline was the goal, although
there could be some fairly outspoken confrontations between black
and white over what constituted disciplinable offenses. The points
at issue were often theft and running away, and when black
members refused to prosecute slaves for charges brought by whites,
white committees sometimes recommended probation or expulsion,
though they did so without the moral legitimacy which blacks could
claim. Again, practices differed with locality, not denomination,
but the ideal was to have discipline in the hands of black
committees, with appellate jurisdiction residing in white churchmen. As with whites, black preachers and their allies valued
honesty, responsibility, sobriety, perseverance. Also emphasized
was the kind of pride in self, which was for those blacks who
exhibited it a truly remarkable achievement because it was completely at odds with the moral implications of slavery.

The religious and economic prestige of a few free blacks may have
helped to reinforce the attractiveness of this impossible ideal of self
pride, but it was also expressed by slaves. Josiah Henson, for
example, a convert at 18, a Methodist preacher, and an unofficial
overseer, embodied the ideal. Enterprising and self-reliant, he
extracted from his master a promise to allow Henson to buy his
freedom. He traveled widely on his master's business, even into the

free soil of Ohio, but he did not run away. His self-respect and personal pride would not allow him to act in any but the most responsible manner. As so often happened when whites made agreements with slaves, his master reneged on the promise to free Henson and kept the $350 that Henson had given as down payment on his freedom. Because of this treachery, Henson believed his commitment to the devious white man abrogated; he fled and later returned to take his wife and children to Canada.[43] The discipline which Henson exemplified revealed the kind of pride in self which black Christianity could support, a pride which was not emulation of whites—Henson's master was not exactly the model of Christian honor—but the determination to live a morally responsible and disciplined life for the personal victory it was.

Association with whites whom blacks actually respected could also result in reinforcement of commitment to the ideal of Christian respectability. Cato Jones, who served his master as an assistant overseer, was one of the fortunate few. Thorough, careful, responsible, and pious, Jones possessed great dignity and proud devotion to a job well done. He explained it all this way: "I wish to live right, and Serve God faithfully & be prepared, let death come Sooner or Later, and I know I can't be unfaithful to my Earthly master, and faithful to God, but I feel it in me If I am faithful to my heavenly master the best I can, then Every Thing Else goes right."[44] He also wanted to pass on his sense of disciplined respectability, for, as he explained to his master, "I want my child to behave better and be Smarter or as Smart as anybody's children."[45] In the American nightmare, there it was—the American Dream.

By isolating the themes of equality, deliverance, and discipline we can begin to appreciate the remarkable quality of black Christianity. None of these themes could waft from the ideal realm into social experience through the perfection of institutions and beliefs; each was an impossible imperative. And each should have seemed all the more impossible when expressed in the preaching of Jasper and his fellows, in their urging black people to become "more than conquerors." The words would seem to be so utterly absurd, so shamefully taunting. Their meaning, however, was clear and inspiring, for they were addressed to a chosen community of love, forbearance and hope. Although black Christians did not believe themselves chosen by God to usher in a new age, there is a great deal of evidence to suggest that they did believe that God had selected them for some mysterious purpose. And it is possible to go further than this and hypothesize that this purpose was, in the view of many pious blacks, to demonstrate in one people the full maturation of Christianity. God's power had been made manifest before in a despised Jew executed as a common criminal, in the "last"' who would be "first," in those who labored and were heavy-laden, in the meek, in the captives, in people who knew that the oppressor would be judged and the prisoners set free just because of the Gospel which the oppressor himself had given his slaves.

In that message forgiveness and forbearance were clearly the attitudes which enabled the weak and powerless to make the oppressor and his instruments psychologically irrelevant. Blacks did not deny they had been wronged, but their Christianity kept them from being destroyed by that fact. Hatred of the master class would only have reinforced the moral disintegration so endemic to the system which governed slaves, for it would have transferred their moral focus from themselves to their oppressor and made every defeat at his hands an ultimate defeat. Black Christians tried as best they could to transcend the brutalizing effects of their servitude by acting on a higher moral plane than did their captors. Consistent with their commitment to equality, they expressed Christian love for all people, including white people. Moreover, they could offer forgiveness, but not in an obsequious or superficial way; if they were to maintain their dignity, the offer would have to be made self-consciously, proudly, and with restraint, conveying by their manner the terms upon which whites would be enabled to receive such a terrifying and revolutionary gift. In the civil rights movement of the next century, whites would still be startled by the offer of forgiveness and the affirmation of love from people they had wronged; but these were not mere tactics of a social protest movement—they were the essential expression of the black Christian faith.

If love and forbearance are the only guiding principles of subject peoples, the oppression of those people can very easily transform these ideal attitudes into instruments of enslavement. By emphasizing such principles to the exclusion of other ideals, white missionary theorists promised to make blacks into docile, tractable, and efficient slaves, an intention which has often been employed as proof of the result. The view of black Christianity has been further distorted because of limits imposed by conventional analysis: accommodation, compensation, and survival have been the acceptable categories of evaluation. The pejorative connotations of such a view are striking, and Uncle Tom, the symbolic figure of this religion, has earned the scorn and taunts of generations of blacks. More "real" than many historical figures, Shelby's Tom was created by Harriet Beecher Stowe to be the image of the suffering servant, who through love and forbearance in the face of personal destruction would be the means of redemption for his people, including the two slaves who beat him to death on the orders of Simon Legree. Pious, dignified, and wise, Tom becomes the archetypical loving black, eliciting either awed respect or apoplectic rage from the whites whom he encounters. Sold as the result of economic and moral failure on the part of good white folks, Tom is finally bought by the displaced Yankee, Legree, who orders him to beat a fellow slave. Realizing that the order is a test of loyalty and faith and assault upon him as much as upon his possible victim, Tom refuses: "My soul an't yours, Mas'r." The resulting contest of wills could end only in Tom's death: "After ye've killed the body, there an't no more ye can do." Each confrontation results in brutality for Tom and defeat for Legree, who is unable to break the slave's will, unable even to make Tom retaliate in kind. Fellow slaves offer to help kill Legree and flee to the swamps, but Tom refuses their aid, telling the bewildered and frustrated Cassy that Jesus had taught us to love our enemies. Such piety eventually provokes Legree to the final act of violence from which Tom dies, forgiving, as he does so, Legree and the two slaves who beat him. Tom is not the only hero of the story, to be sure, but he becomes the most remarkable one, the image of the perfect slave, one whom the wrathful Denmark Vesey would no doubt have said deserved to be a slave.

The contrast between the historical rebel and the fictional victim is striking. Vesey did his best to elicit and direct the anger of his people against whites, hoping that by seizing the city of Charleston he could raise the countryside and gain support from the North or St. Domingue. Vesey's religion enabled him to conceive, plan,

organize, and justify his rebellion; and it strengthened him on the
gallows just as it did Tom under the lash. Vesey's planning was
impressive, for he was able to channel his anger into productive,
goal-oriented behavior. But Tom seems to have no anger, a fact
which deprives him of authenticity. The creation of a white person,
he expresses only in fleeting moments a theme which if developed
would have redeemed him from sentimentality—apocalyptic
judgment.

In fact, it is the Apocalypse which is missing from most
evaluations of black Christianity. The issues of accommodation,
compensation, and survival, like the figure of Uncle Tom, ignore
the fact that the chosen community of love and forbearance is also
that of hope, but not a flaccid expectation that everything will turn
out right in the end. The hope is Apocalyptic; that is, it is based on
the vision of a future, violent struggle in which Evil is destroyed.
The judgment is clear, the psychological and moral distance
between the masters and slaves emphasized. Throughout the slaves'
Christianity the themes of the Apocalypse were evident. They were
in John Jasper's preaching at funerals—"he went forth conquering,
and to conquer"—and in the sermon on Joshua's execution of
God's enemies. They were in the visions of those who glimpsed the
future and the prayers of those who believed that the past deserved
more than a Deliverer. Moses was the symbol of deliverance and as
such was very important; but escape was not enough. Slaves hoped
also for justice which could not be given by the crucified Christ who
gripped Mrs. Stowe's imagination—it could come only from the
Lord of the Apocalypse. In the slaves' spirituals, the images tumble
out: "I take my text in Matthew, and by the Revelation," "Meet,
O Lord on th' milk-white horse," "Out of his mouth come a
two-edged sword," "Earth shall reel and totter; Hell shall be
uncapped, Th' dragon be loosed," "On th' Day of Judgment—
moon turn to blood," "King Jesus rides on a milk-white horse/No
man can hinder him."[46]

It is in conjunction with these images that sense can be made of
one of the most dramatic events in antebellum history: Nat
Turner's famous revolt in Southampton county, Virginia, during
the latter part of August in 1831. With fewer than seventy men,
Turner terrorized southeastern Virginia for seventy-two hours,
killing infants, women, and men until his followers were killed or

captured. After weeks of hiding, he himself was finally caught in
October. Before his trial and execution, Turner dictated to Thomas
R. Gray a "confession" which reveals his profound religious
sensibility.[47] The man thought of himself in two complementary
ways: as a prophet in the Old Testament tradition and as the
instrument of God's apocalyptic wrath. When asked his motives,
he replied that all his life he had believed—as his parents had told
him—that he had been "intended for some great purpose" as a
prophet, for he had extraordinary psychic and intellectual powers.
As Turner grew older, his insatiable curiosity, vivid imagination,
and superior intellect made him something of a leader among
blacks, but one who kept aloof from his fellows, consciously
disciplining himself physically—"the austerity of my life and
manners"—and psychologically: "I . . . wrapped myself in mystery, devoting my time to fasting and prayer."

Turner's arrival at manhood and his calling as a prophet were
closely associated in his memory. At religious meetings he was
constantly "struck with that particular passage which says: "Seek ye
the kingdom of Heaven and all things shall be added unto you.'"
The passage obsessed him, and he doubtless contemplated the
entire chapter in the Gospel of St. Luke in which it is found. What
things would be added or provided, he would have wondered, and
the answer would have come: food, drink, clothing, and the
Kingdom of God itself (Luke 12:31–32). Indeed, it would come
upon him unaware—"Be ye therefore ready also: for the Son of
Man cometh at an hour when ye think not." With the promise of
the kingdom came ominous warning of the end. And then the
words which had troubled him for so long became part of his
private sense of destiny, as if the Spirit spoke them not as a promise
to all humanity, but as a specific command to him. "What do you
mean by Spirit?" Gray asked. "The Spirit that spoke to the
prophets in former day," answered the man in irons, adding that
he had been astonished, too.

For two years, he recalled, he had thought about this terrifying
event, and, curious and intelligent as he was, must have searched
the scriptures for word of other prophets who like him had been
confronted by God Himself. He could not have escaped that one
passage which every minister knows as the expression of his own
calling, the passage which was especially popular among Methodist

circuit riders and Baptist preachers: "The Spirit of the Lord is upon
me; because the Lord hath anointed me to preach good tidings to
the meek; he hath sent me to bind up the broken hearted, to
proclaim liberty to the captives, and the opening of the prison to
them that are bound; To proclaim the acceptable year of the Lord,
and the day of vengeance of our God" (Isaiah 61:1-2).

Searching and reading, praying and thinking, he was finally
confirmed in his belief that he was "ordained for some great
purpose in the hands of the Almighty" when the Spirit came to him
a second time. Thereafter, and despite the fact that white Baptist
officials would have nothing to do with him, he began to develop a
following among his fellow blacks which, he insisted, was quite
unlike that of the conjurers. In emphasizing this peculiarity of his
authority, Turner was not repudiating his African heritage so much
as raising the level of intercourse with the spirit world above that of
simple manipulation and trickery; he was talking about the very
cosmos itself, the Ultimate God and His plan for His enslaved
children. To them, Turner promised that "something was about to
happen that would terminate in fulfilling the great promise that
had been made to me." Before the secret could be revealed,
mundane affairs intervened; Turner's master appointed an overseer
whom the prophet could not abide and he ran away. After thirty
days in the wilderness he returned because, as he explained, he had
not been chosen by God simply to run away; a greater future lay in
store for him. His fellow slaves were understandably skeptical and
taunted him.

Ashamed that he had been more concerned for the "things of
this world" than for the Kingdom of Heaven, and stung by the
criticism and suspicion of his former disciples, Turner was sensitized
to further apocalyptic visions. "Seek ye the kingdom" he had
heard over and over again; words and images intertwined as he saw
himself ever more surely as one of the line of Old Testament
prophets. He stood with Amos and Isaiah, and then all at
once—shriven of his shame and hurt—he stood before the awesome
vision of the final great battle foretold in the Revelation of St. John
when the hosts of the Christ should be locked in ultimate combat
with those of Satan; but Turner saw something which John did not
see—the *color* of the opposing armies: "*White* spirits and *black*
spirits engaged in battle." Throughout his confession, Turner used

the words and images of the anonymous enslaved Christian on the isle of Patmos (Rev. 6:12, 19:11–21) and of St. Peter in his sermon at Pentecost (Acts 2:20). "The sun was darkened," Turner recalled, "and blood flowed in streams." And then came the voice: "Such is your luck, such you are called to see, and let it come rough or smooth, you must surely bare it." "Such is your luck!"—the words came not only from God, but from Africa, whose western nations believed that every man had a unique destiny ordained for him from before his birth. This destiny was made known to him, as it had been to Turner, upon his initiation into manhood; and from that time forward he was subject to this personal benevolence or destiny, or as it is best translated into English, "Luck."[48] And if Turner had no "good destiny shrine" as had his ancestors in Africa, by the time of this vision (1825), the whole universe seemed to the sensitive man to have enshrined his "luck": "the elements, the revolution of the planets, the operation of tides, and the changes of seasons."

Turner's "luck" became ever more clearly defined as he became more introspective and the visions became more ominous. He saw Christ crucified against the vast expanse of night sky. In the morning he discovered blood like dew on the corn, and later saw shapes "portrayed in blood." The blood of Christ once shed on earth, he mused, the Christ whom Turner believed was even now returning to announce the final judgment. In anticipation Turner baptized himself, becoming by that act crucified and raised with Christ Jesus. The orthodox interpretation—just as the sound of the Spirit's voice—became utterly real for him. Scriptural allusions to judgment and blood, darkness and vengeance, were congealing into specific and imperative actions. In May 1828 God told him that Satan had been set loose (Rev. 12:9–12) and that the last days were "fast approaching when the first should be last and the last should be first" (Mark 10:31; Matt. 20:16). This prophecy was associated in scripture with the day of final judgment and was placed in the context of Christ's foretelling His own death and resurrection. But now the Spirit told Turner that Christ, far from looking ahead to His part in the plan of salvation, "had laid down [His] yoke" and that the prophet himself should take "it on and fight against the Serpent." From vision to act, the Serpent (Satan) was revealed in reality as the white man, and when in February

1831 there was an eclipse of the sun, Turner knew that his time had come. He "communicated the great work laid out for [him] to do" to four confidants, and in August they and their fellows became the instrument of God's wrath.

It is easy to ask irrelevant questions of Nat Turner. Gray himself asked one: "Do you not find yourself mistaken now?" And Turner responded with another question which revealed his disdain for Gray's frame of reference: "Was not Christ crucified?" The centrality of Christ in the black man's thinking about judgment links his New Testament eschatology with his calling as a prophet in the Judaic tradition, for Turner was especially attached to those passages of scripture which link Divine judgment, Christ's mission, and the new ordering of society—"the last shall be first." Apocalyptic passages associated so easily with the Book of Revelation were also obvious in Jesus' statement about the meaning of His life and ministry as recorded in the Gospels. One of the events which Turner associated with his final act of vengeance was his self-baptism, an act through which he became crucified in Christ and raised with Him, thus repudiating the pragmatic morality of unbelievers. Therefore, when he came to that act which was his final destiny, he could not weigh consequences. Perhaps he was, as some historians have suggested, hoping to reach the swamps of eastern Virginia or North Carolina, which had harbored fugitives for over fifty years. But he himself could not be bothered with such irrelevancies. He had seen and heard the reality of Divine judgment. And should it have been asked if it had been God's will that infants, children, and women should have been slaughtered, the prophet could well have recounted the vengeance of God upon his enemies as related in the Book of Ezekiel: "Go ye . . . and smite; let not your eye spare, neither have ye pity: slay utterly old and young, both maids, and little children, and women." (Ezek. 9:5-6).

In Nat Turner the Apocalyptic vision is revealed as if the anger of every Christian who had ever been a slave had been unleashed. To dismiss him as nothing but an exception—which he certainly was—is to miss the point, for Turner's acting out his personal vision of the Apocalypse reveals the mental framework which made possible the chosen community of love, forbearance, and hope. The anger and judgment of the Apocalypse were necessary to prevent the theme of a disciplined Christian life from becoming accommodation, to prevent the themes of equality and deliverance from becoming compensation, to prevent the personal achievements within black American religion from becoming mere survival, to prevent love and forebearance from becoming dehumanizing pap. But Apocalyptic anger if undisciplined by faith in Christ's ultimate vindication of His people and love for one's fellows would become self-destructive in one of two ways. Either the anger would consume those frustrated by their inability to act, or it would drive the isolated person into acts of violence which were compromised by their apparent senselessness and perverted by their inevitable failure. The tension between Uncle Tom and Nat Turner was tremendous. The demands made upon the human spirit by such an ethos were great, and many were destroyed by being pulled too far in one direction or the other. But for many people the demands were themselves liberating, as their discipleship to Christ made them into the people of Jasper's constant refrain: "more than conquerors." Somehow their anger and hope had been redeemed, and they awaited Gabriel's trumpet—their final vindication—but until then, a marvelous transformation had already taken place:

> The trumpet sounds within-a my soul
> I ain't got long to stay here.

6

"To Proclaim Liberty to the Captives"

Proclamation of liberty is not the theme that conventional historical analysis would tease out of the religious experience of the Old South. The notion seems patently absurd, and stubborn insistence upon it seems perverse because of the brutal fact of black slavery and the distortions of the slaveholding ethic. The discrepancy between naive exhortation to free the slaves and the shameful inability to respond to that exhortation positively predominate most views of ante-bellum southern religion. Consequently, sympathetic interpretations of the South, if they have taken any account of religion at all, have elaborated the themes of sin, guilt, irony, and suffering because these themes represent the tension between profession and act which has theoretically characterized sensitive southerners. For those presumably insensitive to such tensions, southern religion has been a dismal, rigid fundamentalism unconcerned with social injustice and firmly locked into what one scholar has called "cultural captivity." Nowhere in this cluster of ideas and themes does the concept of liberty have relevance, except perhaps by its absence, to confirm everything already assumed about the sense of failure endemic to southern religion.

Contrast between ideal and actual behavior is admittedly one way to understand the past, but in the case of southern Evangelicalism it is useful only if we do not assume the vapid, self-dramatizing posture of moral outrage. There are more relevant attitudes, such as an empathetic openness to the vitality of southern religion. The promise of liberty had an undeniable magnetism when Evangelicalism first invaded the South, and its force cannot be appreciated if we ignore early Evangelicals' belief that their cause liberated thousands from their low estate to establish them eventually as refined and enlightened people. Once redefined, white Evangelicalism channeled its energies into restricting the liberty of its original Gospel. For blacks, however, the restriction never came. By ignoring this fact, a persistent infatuation with the inevitable moral failure of the powerful continues to distort our understanding of the South. It is as if the inability of whites to be true to the liberating promises of Evangelical Christianity was more significant for understanding southern religion than the admirable accomplishments of black Christianity—which is to execute Nat Turner and lash Uncle Tom all over again. Without including blacks and their religion in the southern experience, discussion of that rich tradition, no matter how suggestive or brilliant, will continue to be one-sided.

Liberty was admittedly not the only thing on the minds of southern converts during the eighteenth-century revivals, but it was the concept that caught their attention; and it was never completely lost in southern Evangelicalism. Its expression and implications were, however, shaped by the social status and aspirations of those who believed it. Once attracted by the Evangelical promise, women, blacks, and relatively powerless white men had to discover how liberty could be achieved within limits set by other people. If each of these three constituencies had had a specific leadership to speak to and for them, and to devote its energies to creating a special sense of bondedness apart from the rest of the Evangelical community, the rhetoric of liberty would have had social support to make it effective. Black people had their own leadership; lower-class white men did not. Although there continued to be persons who resented the tendency of ministers to court prominent men, there were few enough maverick preachers to provide leadership to shape resentment into action. After the first antislavery impulse, the liberty which white clergymen preached would never have for white men the kind of revolutionary implications it had had in the eighteenth century, nor would it have the bonding and enriching power of that preached by black ministers.

Liberty for women was also compromised by the want of a visible,

universally acknowledged leadership to develop self-consciousness
that could in turn support their liberation as a group. Not until
after the war did regional women's religious organizations begin to
provide the sense of solidarity and common interest so obvious in
black churches. But before secession in local churches throughout
the South women were developing their own networks of leadership.
Ministers were often condescending and patronizing to "the Ladies,
God Bless 'em,'' but many also helped to educate them in
academies and colleges and to make it possible for women to claim
a special role in family and church. From the perspective of the
present, this is not much of an achievement, but to people whose
public life was limited to the church, this ideal could prepare the
way for public activities in the last generation of the nineteenth
century. The complaints of overbearing and self-important ministers reveal that in the decade before the war, pious women were
not always so submissive as men would have liked—many took their
Evangelical usefulness much too much to heart.

Within the local church these pious Evangelical women could
become influential through the force of their own characters or
through their "calling" as preachers' wives. It could be argued that
once the Evangelical movement had stabilized enough to curtail the
itineracy of preachers and missionaries, becoming a preacher's wife
became a vocational goal quite apart from the woman's relationship
with her husband. The minister's wife was in effect the leader of
the women of the church—if she chose to be—and as such
personified the interaction between the preacher and a majority of
his parishioners. Many young ladies who were not called and who
thought they were marrying a man instead of an institution
complained bitterly of their lot, but others made their status as
minister's wife into a position of leadership which not even their
husbands could assail. Even when their advice to others seemed to
indicate submissiveness, these women through their many activities—teaching, visiting, writing, organizing missionary societies—
provided role models of independence and responsibility for
younger women. The amount of interaction between women and
men in the churches is still a matter for speculation, but even if
rude and insensitive preachers did attempt to keep women in their
place, and even if others more well-meaning and essentially good-

hearted did not always display an appreciation for women's burdens and the captivity imposed by "women's sphere," women themselves were capable of using the church as a supportive institution. There they could "find themselves," and perhaps be consoled, too, if their great numbers in the sanctuary were thought to be representative of the demography of heaven.

Anyone who wished to be liberated from worldly standards which demeaned him or her would obviously be susceptible to a movement which honored the individual member. Gospel standards which required self-discipline may not appear to buttress liberty at all, but for many people they were liberating indeed. Within the small group of believers, the bondedness of love and intimate conversation about what a later day would call "personal problems" helped to keep the church together. The establishment of objective standards of conduct was also very important because it erected boundaries between Evangelicals and the rest of society. The rules, ideas, and behavior patterns which objectify differences between groups may be understood as boundaries to keep outsiders out and insiders in. If a group is established on the basis of common loyalties, ideas, and behavior rather than kinship patterns, cultural distinctions, proximity, or the like, there will be a discussion about boundaries as long as there are challenges to the ability of ideology to keep the group together. Constant recruitment such as Evangelicals engaged in would pose such a challenge. Thus discussion about boundaries—an exclusivist orientation—likely occurred with the Evangelical movement as long as the inclusivist missionary impulse continued. The discussion was facilitated by each individual member's commitment to beware any breach in the boundaries on his own part or that of his neighbor, and to recommit himself over and over again to the life of disciplined piety. Self-discipline in establishing one's own personal boundaries and deference to the moral judgment of the community were rewarded with approval and support of other Evangelicals and reinforced by participation in the process of recruitment.

It is relatively easy to see the boundaries between Evangelicals and worldlings on an individual level, but the task becomes more difficult when trying to define the difference between Evangelicals as a cohesive people and the world which they professed to scorn.

As with many social movements in our history, the Evangelical movement began as a repudiation of traditional authority and standards, an act which evoked a greater clamor for liberty than many Evangelicals had bargained for. The first great debate over the social boundaries of Evangelicalism ended with the rejection of antislavery activity, thereby guaranteeing that the religious mode would not undermine class distinctions. Subsequently, Evangelical leaders and spokesmen were constantly on the move to become more responsible, refined, and influential, attempting at the same time to maintain their contacts with the past by celebrating, often with oozing sentimentality, the common but ''respectable'' folk from which they had sprung. This sense of transition and aspiration reflects the role of Evangelicalism in mobilizing a large constituency held together by membership in churches, commitment to self-discipline and piety, and loyalty to such institutions as denominational colleges and slave missions. But these matters indicate the gravitational center of the Evangelical constituency—not the outer limits, which were in constant need of redefinition throughout the antebellum period.

This need resulted in conflict among the faithful as well as with the world, for Evangelical leaders could never dictate belief and action as they would have liked to do. Among the religious themselves, isolated, uneducated, and relatively powerless whites would often complain about the aloofness of denominational authorities and resist as best they could the professionalization of the clergy. Many preferred to have leaders who could identify with them and evoke the cathartic and healing ritual of self-discovery and forgiveness, rather than clergymen who would preach careful sermons of correct understanding and refined sentiments. When Evangelicals were not disagreeing over who their real leaders were, they might be found enlisting aid for assaults on drinking liquors, breaking the sabbath, and yielding to the lasciviousness regnant in dancing, circuses, plays, and novels. Such things had always presented problems, but as Evangelicals became more influential they wanted more than ever to make their values legally binding upon the whole society. The battle with the world was never over, they knew, and if they could not enter politics to affect relations between masters and slaves, they could at least try to do so by regulating private behavior. After the Civil War, moral surveillance, which had once been the churches' responsibility, would be transferred to the legal code. But victory still eluded antebellum Evangelicals. They would have to wait until laws ordering behavior—such as those regulating whiskey-drinking—could be seen as the functional equivalent of the old slave codes.

Much conflict about Evangelical boundaries was expressed in theological discourse and denominational rivalry, although it was not necessarily an angry confrontation. Relations among ministers of different denominations were usually cordial. Sometimes Evangelical unity was formidable, especially if an Episcopal bishop should make an exaggerated claim for Apostolic succession; and then he was in danger of losing some of his own ministers to other denominations. There were nevertheless many examples of denominational friction. Baptists and Presbyterians might complain of Methodist hysteria and illiteracy; Methodists would sometimes smoulder with intense resentment at Presbyterian arrogance and shake their heads at Baptist "bigotry," defined as the insistence that baptism meant immersion of adult believers. Sometimes there were public theological debates for intellectual exercise, but everyone already knew the arguments anyway, so that these occasions were often merely opportunity for a young minister to reveal his intelligence, or—as it turned out all too often—to reveal the exact opposite.

Religious controversy frequently was indicative of social division seeking ideological confirmation, or of intellectual disagreement settling into class conflict, and the result would be serious and prolonged debate within denominational boundaries. The Disciples of Christ probably grew out of social as well as theological dissatisfaction; and the seeds of postwar schism and controversy may have been planted by the very refinement of which Evangelical publicists were so proud. The social divisions revealed in the anti-Mission and Landmark controversies would never entirely disappear; and the Holiness and Pentecostal movements in the late nineteenth century continued the tendency of southerners to express class conflict through religious ideology. Debates in the 1850s reveal the same divisions, for they centered on the desirability and possibility of recapturing the solidarity of the past, the simplicity of the founders, the essential humility of the first Evangelicals. Some of these conflicts even got entangled in the sectional controversy, indicating in the resulting confusion that the assurance, expansiveness, and power of the first revivals were beyond the grasp of a more complex age. Much debate would eventually return to discussion of the first issue to compromise distinctions between Evangelicals and the world—slavery. And once again Evangelical theorists would restate the terms on which the boundaries had been negotiated: liberation of slaves from moral degradation, masters from the brutalizing effects of their own power, and clergy from northern criticism and the taint of their own sin.

To display the conflation of liberty and slavery in the minds of southern white Evangelicals is to expose the absurdity with which people of both races lived. Liberty? When those who were faithful to the religious heritage of humility, simplicity, and piety were demeaned and insulted by coreligionists who pretended respectability with colleges, periodicals, slave missions, wealth, and pianos in the sanctuary? When those who were seen as the guardians of morality were treated little better than chattel, herded into female colleges at best, into secondary roles in their churches at least, and into deferential dependency to unbelieving husbands at worst? When those who awaited the Lord of the Apocalypse were forced to swallow their anger, but still fight for their pride? Liberty? Yes! Precisely because of Biblical warrant for it; because of the persistent promise of it in the face of failure to achieve it. For in the conversion experience, the possession of the Spirit, or the assurance of salvation, men and women of both races found the psychological and ideological resources to endure, to structure their pride not on their own power, but on the power which would one day be provided. The promise was as fruitless as mere psychological compensation and as potent as God's earnest that those who were not yet fully liberated would one day be freed and vindicated.

This tension between hoped-for liberation and present bondage was what made the revivals so important for black and white alike. It may seem insufferably idiosyncratic for a discussion of southern religion to postpone serious consideration of revivalism until the final argument. The fault seems to be intensified by the common assumption that revivals were the means through which Evangelical expansion took place. This assumption has yet to be demonstrated empirically, although most Evangelical ministers in the Old South swore that it was true. The evidence of church growth does not, however, verify their belief. Churches proliferated throughout the South without mass meetings and mass conversions, establishing through less dramatic means the structures upon which the subsequent, more stylized revivals could be based. Evangelicals throughout the antebellum South were notoriously imprecise when they reported revivals. Checking membership figures against such reports, one finds that frequently a revival was nothing more than a reaffirmation by outwardly pious people of their faith. At other times, of course, a revival was definitely a recruiting impulse, though it may have been uncontrollable. A Methodist, for example, could honestly report an explosive outburst of religious activity on his circuit, only to admit sometime later that most converts had joined the Presbyterian and Baptist churches. On other occasions ministers would report heartrending failure in trying to raise a revival, only to have some young whippersnapper scarcely old enough to shave ignite wild expressions of collective religious hysteria to the greater glory of God and his own reputation. The revival impulse was obviously erratic.

There is no doubt, however, that revivalist preaching, whether like Davies's, Stearns's, or Jasper's was important throughout the nineteenth-century South. It was a style which could be adapted to time, place, and audience—a style associated not so much with exceptional events as with those events which occurred with predictable regularity. The style helped to direct within potential as well as mature believers the internal drama of the soul's liberation through psychological breakdown, ecstatic vision, or intense inner conviction. And it is this message, delivered in the familiar argot of revivalism, that was so important to the continuing vitality of southern Evangelicalism. Gradually the revivalistic mode became limited to special seasons or campaigns which believers and their children could look forward to. The social function of revivals is often overlooked by focusing upon them as quaint, exotic, irrational forms of collective behavior that reveal southerners' lack of sophistication. By the 1820s, however, camp meetings, protracted meetings, and revivals had become for the devout significant bonding and purgative occasions. They were the reenactment of older believers' conversions and the appropriate process through which younger people rejected the carelessness of youth and assumed the somber and delicate responsibilities of adulthood. In brief, through the style of preaching—which was often referred to by its practitioners as "liberty"—and the heightened expectation which accompanies special sacred events, revivals institutionalized liberty. They became the means through which Evangelicals could recapture the emotional vitality of the movement's early career, when spontaneity and ecstasy had not yet given way to the routine and order of successful institutions.

Revivals not only helped Evangelicals to recapture the subjective sense of liberty, but also to maintain the boundaries between themselves and the world. To have publicly experienced the New Birth was and continued to be the most important thing which distinguished believers from worldlings throughout the antebellum period. With the growth of churches, however, boundaries sometimes became blurred by the fact that they ran through families, often separating women from their husbands and brothers, and children from their fathers. Such divisions meant that sometimes within the same family the debate over responsibility, morality, and policy resulted in assigning the Evangelical ethos to weakness, naivete, and emotion—characteristics identified with women, children, and blacks. But with the rise of sectional conflict and the ambitious and energetic institution-building during and after the 1830s, Evangelical leaders began to establish their importance as educators of the South and as indispensable publicists of the slaveholders' ideology. Through their Mission to Slaves and the elaboration of a slaveholding ethic, Evangelicals were attempting to fuse the strength of the slaveholding elites—Evangelicals were always trying to convert "influential and powerful men"—with the religious sensibilities of their women. Slaveholding could be justified, preachers argued, only among Christians. It was in the pulpit rather than the tract or book that the ideology of southern paternalism was born.

Of course, a majority of slaveholding men did not convert to Christianity. But the conservative impact of such preaching was obvious. This, combined with the fact that most education was under Evangelicals' control, and reinforced by the obvious need to keep blacks under constant surveillance through religious institutions, seems to have encouraged nonbelieving men to support Evangelical missions and local churches as a sign of their responsibilities as citizens and masters. The movement to socialize black children in values acceptable to the slaveholding regime was of such obvious advantage that it seemed only logical to sponsor the churches' activities in many areas. In this gradual manner were the boundaries between believers and worldlings blurred. During the years when the southern ideology was taking shape, therefore, Evangelicalism became in the view of many Christian theorists one of the distinguishing marks of what it meant to be a southerner.

The conflict between worldlings and believers, however, remained. Having become the guardians of public morality and private decorum insofar as responsible conduct between the races was concerned, white Evangelicals nevertheless failed to prevent sexual exploitation of black women or assault of black men. To be sure, they could sometimes prevent such violence, and they might gradually prevail upon a few lawmakers to reform slavery during the war; but they were not successful in this policy, nor were they able to facilitate the transition from slavery to freedom on the part of either race. This powerlessness was rooted in the southern social system. First of all, many southern men—the people who held power—were not church members; ecclesiastical rules were not binding upon them. Moreover, any movement for reform growing out of the churches would be identified with women and blacks, who by law were under the authority of men; it would therefore have to be commended to the powerful, as was the Mission, on the basis of their own self-interest—and to that extent compromised. Based on a survey of surviving church records, there is reason to believe that if all slaveholding men had been church members, blacks would have been far better off than they actually were because they could have brought charges against masters and debated the relative responsibilities of the two races in ecclesiastical courts. That this practice would have been uniform throughout the region is doubtful because of the many different ways in which diverse localities presided over race relations. To have held

the master accountable in any local church in a significant manner
would have required the force of civil law, a solution quite
impossible in the nineteenth-century South. Separation of church
and state was axiomatic there, and the idea that slaveholders would
limit their own power through a church has a forbidding naive
innocence to it.

In the minds of many historians, however, one question demands an answer. Why did the churches not pass their own slave
codes to monitor whites' relations with blacks? The question
assumes that formal rules would have been more effective than an
unwritten tradition in protecting black people; it also assumes that
there was no Christian code of behavior regulating relations
between the races. As it was, many Evangelical churches did
attempt to discipline members who treated slaves badly or unfairly,
but the standards applied in such disciplinary action were always
those of the masters. Southern Evangelical leaders had learned
during the last days of the Revolutionary antislavery impulse that
religious groups would not be allowed to intervene in the master-
slave relationship and therefore concluded that an indirect approach
to the problem of slavery was dictated. Through moral influence and
the conversion of both masters and servants, the churches could avoid
opposition which formal rules, even if not obviously aimed at
weakening slavery, would have elicited. Circumspection was made
even more logical as more and more Evangelicals—and Evangelical
leaders—became slaveholders. In the process of responding to this
transformation and to the assaults of northern reformers, a few
southern white Evangelicals tried to define the ethic upon which a
Christian slave code could have been based. By the time more than
a few people saw the necessity of such a code, slavery had ceased to
be an issue.

The tragedy of southern Evangelicalism was not that its institutions were unable to make white men behave as they should
have, but that they could not allow black people full liberty in their
Christian profession. The logic of Evangelicalism was to elevate and
discipline the self within a strong community, under the aegis of a
leadership which was seen as the projection of its followers. If black
Evangelicals had been as free as whites to follow the logic of their
Christian faith, they would have been able to demand for them-

selves what was rightfully theirs. As it was, in almost every Evangelical church where there was a significant black membership there were always opportunities for blacks to fend off, with varying degrees of success, complete domination by whites. By being too absorbed with wishing whites had acted differently in our common past, historians have too often ignored the achievements of blacks. And yet it is the development of black Christianity in direct, local, every-Sunday interaction with white Evangelicalism which sets off the religious experience of southerners.

Even Evangelicals who owned no slaves usually worshiped with slaves, since most white churches had black members. In addition, many churches with a racially mixed constituency had a predominately black membership. Wherever white Evangelicals met, therefore, black Christians were there, too. This ubiquity of blacks tended to remind the nonslaveholder of his debt to slaveholders for keeping black people under control, but it also meant that interaction between the two peoples through religious assemblies and ritual actions provided a means of communication and a set of common symbols—even if experienced in different ways—which affected whites and blacks alike. The significance of this interaction is difficult to trace because of our own frustrations and entrapment in the maze of history; conclusions are likely to be shaped as much by ideology as by empirical evidence. But our thinking about this matter must proceed out of the knowledge that whites and blacks needed each other, through their victories as well as their failures, to become what they were by secession.

The most significant impact of religious interaction has often been overlooked for its being so simple. Through common participation in holy things, black and white alike—master, nonslaveholder, slave, and freedman—discovered people of the other race whom he or she could respect and admire on the basis of ideals which they held up to each other. The nonslaveholding whites who were converted under the preaching of black ministers, the white man whom Nat Turner baptized, the white congregations who relied upon black members to express the joy of conversion received images as significant and displayed emotions as basic as those received and displayed by blacks. Even more obvious, but less creditable, is the fact that by making religious institutions the

means by which blacks were to be given values that would
guarantee the stability of southern society, whites reinforced the
claims of Evangelical theorists that their churches were the foundation of social order. Indeed, more than anywhere else in the United
States—with the exception of Mormon Utah—religion became
identified with an essential, public reaffirmation of social solidarity. Going to church became not merely a religious act, but a
civic responsibility. No wonder that pious southern whites could so
easily and honestly condemn Yankee heretics as anarchists and
madmen. When thinking of impending social chaos and outside
threat, the presence of black people always made it easy for white
Evangelicals to thank God for southern piety.

But those black Christians in all those white churches had an
even greater impact upon their white brethren. To the sensitive
woman whose moral domain seemed so hopelessly compromised by
the licentious exploitation and cruel brutality of the slave system,
the piety of black people was important for supporting her own
courage and ability to endure. And of course the power and dignity
of black religion helped to stir in sensitive whites—men and women
alike—that sense of guilt which afflicted them from the time when
their grandfathers first admitted that emancipation required too
great a sacrifice; after all, it was really Christ's sacrifice and not that
of ordinary mortals which perpetrated the church. But the question
of guilt can become, as it has all too often, a beguiling diversion
from the significant achievement of Evangelicalism in the Old
South: the liberation of the captives, the blacks. Through their own
experience, black Christians in the Old South expressed the
Christian theology of suffering, hope, and victory in a way that
transcended their own social situation. True, in black slavery, as in
the ante-Nicene church, experience was flawed by cultural and
social realities that limited its most profound articulation. But
nothing is quite so irrelevant in understanding the experience of
southerners as a historian who wants Gregorian chants instead of
spirituals, or the abolitionist missionary who complained that the
slaves thought that Christ was a Second Moses. The missionary's
earnest and orthodox desire was to explain to the poor benighted
heretics the true meaning of the atonement.[1] But who in all
honesty would tell them that they did not already know it?

Even as whites scurried South to repair the damage that southern Christianity had already done, black preachers were beginning to build their new Church with tools they had already crafted. The full model of southern Evangelicalism was the creation of blacks themselves; it was they who made southern religion different. Somehow sensing this as a grave responsibility in the moment of the white South's defeat, black Christians offered the right hand of fellowship to those who had been their patrons and fellow Christians. But it was refused. Most whites could not understand that by retreating to their white churches, they had, like the priests of the Establishment before them, given over the measure of Christian experience to those whose authority came from the fact that, as one lonely southern white clergyman reminded his offended fellows, "God hath chosen the weak things of the world to confound the things which are mighty—that no flesh should glory in His presence."[2] It had been true of Shubal Stearns and Francis Asbury, Andrew Bryan and John Jasper. It would be true again, for one in their tradition would write: "If today's church does not recapture the sacrificial spirit of the early church, it will lose its authenticity, forfeit the loyalty of millions, and be dismissed as an irrelevant social club with no meaning. . . . If the inexpressible cruelties of slavery could not stop us," he would write, "the opposition we now face will surely fail. We will win our freedom because the sacred heritage of our nation and the eternal will of God are embodied in our echoing demands."[3] That those demands were based on the proclamation of liberty, he had no doubt, for his own personal experience had taught him that, and so had his father—the elder Martin Luther King.

Notes

1   *"Disallowed Indeed of Men,*
                                    but Chosen of God,
                                    and Precious"

1.   George Maclaren Brydon, *Virginia's Mother Church and the Political Conditions under Which It Grew* (Richmond: Virginia Historical Society, 1948), 1:370ff, 426–42.
2.   Ibid., pp. 90–93, 97–105, 174–76, 326, 352, 397ff.; Paul Conkin, "The Church Establishment in North Carolina, 1765–1776," *North Carolina Historical Review* 32 (January 1955): 1–30; Frederick Dalcho, *An Historical Account of the Protestant Episcopal Church in South Carolina from the First Settlement to the War of the Revolution* (Charleston: Thayer, 1820), pp. 75–167; Henry Thompson Malone, *The Episcopal Church in Georgia, 1733–1957* (Atlanta: Protestant Episcopal Church in the Diocese of Atlanta, 1960), pp. 3–32; William Seiler, "The Church of England as the Established Church in Seventeenth-Century Virginia," *Journal of Southern History* 15 (November 1949): 478–508; Seiler, "The Anglican Parish in Virginia," in *Seventeenth-Century America: Essays in Colonial History*, ed. James Morton Smith (Chapel Hill: University of North Carolina Press, 1959), pp. 119–42.
3.   Charles Woodmason, *The Carolina Backcountry on the Eve of the Revolution*, edited and with an Introduction by Richard J. Hooker (Chapel Hill: University of North Carolina Press, 1953), p. 12.
4.   George William Pilcher, *Samuel Davies, Apostle of Dissent in Colonial Virginia* (Knoxville: University of Tennessee Press, 1971), pp. 29–32.
5.   Samuel Davies, *Sermons on Important Subjects* (Boston: Lincoln and Edmands, 1811), 1:92.
6.   Samuel Davies, *Sermons on Important Subjects* (New York: T. Allen, 1794), 3:396, 398.

7.   Ibid., pp. 381, 383, 384.

8.   Davies, *Sermons* (1811 edition), 1:154.

9.   See ibid., pp. 105–63.

10.   Davies, *Sermons* (1794 edition), 3:363–87.

11.   Robert B. Semple, *A History of the Rise and Progress of the Baptists in Virginia* (1810; rev. ed. by G. W. Beale, Richmond: Pitt and Co., 1894), p. 16. The most accessible sources for information about Separate Baptists is Semple's classic study and Robert A. Baker's *The Southern Baptist Convention and Its People, 1607–1972* (Nashville: Broadman Press, 1974); William Latane Lumpkin, *Baptist Foundations in the South: Tracing through the Separates the Influence of the Great Awakening, 1754–1787* (Nashville: Broadman Press, 1961), pp. 3–83; David T. Morgan, Jr., "The Great Awakening in North Carolina, 1740–1775: The Baptist Phase," *North Carolina Historical Review* 45 (Summer 1968): 264–83; Ronald Wilson Long, "Religious Revivalism in the Carolinas and Georgia, 1740–1805" (Ph.D. diss., University of Georgia, 1968). For the New England background, see Clarence C. Goen's excellent scholarly work, *Revivalism and Separatism in New England, 1740–1800* (New Haven: Yale University Press, 1962).

12.   Jarratt, *The Life of Devereaux Jarratt*, p. 89.

13.   Ibid., pp. 126ff.

14.   See Joseph Biggs and Jesse Read, *A Concise History of the Kehukee Baptist Association from Its Original Rise to the Present Time* (Tarboro, N.C.: G. Howard, 1834), pp. 34–45.

15.   Elmer T. Clark, ed., *The Journal and Letters of Francis Asbury* (Nashville: Abingdon Press, 1958) 1:168 (November 14, 1775).

16.   Virginia Annual Conference of the Methodist Episcopal Church, Manuscript Journal, February 2, 1809, Randolph-Macon College Library. This is not a quotation from the record, but a paraphrase of the proceedings.

17.   Clark, *Asbury's Journal*, 1:346 (April 23, 1780).

2   *"To Set in Order the
                               Things that are Wanting"*

1.   Mattrimony Baptist Church Record, August 16, 1794: "The church met to do the work of the lord and to set in order the things that are wanton." Southern Historical Collection, the University of North Carolina at Chapel Hill.

2.   William Davidson Blanks, "Corrective Church Discipline in the Presbyterian Churches of the Nineteenth-Century South," *Journal of Presbyterian History* 44 (June 1966): 91.

3.   For discussions of church discipline, see William Davidson Blanks, "Ideal and Practice: A Study of the Conception of the Christian Life

Prevailing in the Presbyterian Churches of the South during the Nineteenth Century" (Th.D. diss., Union Theological Seminary, Richmond, 1960); Cortland Victor Smith, "Church Organization as an Agency of Social Control: Church Discipline in North Carolina, 1800–1860" (Ph.D. diss., the University of North Carolina at Chapel Hill, 1966). Original local church records in the following archives may also be examined: Duke University Library; Department of Archives and History, Raleigh, North Carolina; South Caroliniana Library, the University of South Carolina; Southern Historical Collection, the University of North Carolina.

4.   *Minutes of the Annual Conferences of the Methodist Episcopal Church for the Years 1773–1828* (New York: T. Mason & G. Lane, 1840), 1:95–101, 122–34, 142–52.

5.   Charleston Baptist Association, *A Summary of Church-Discipline Shewing the Qualifications and Duties of the Officers and Members of a Gospel-Church* (Charleston: Markland, M'Iver & Co., [1794]), pp. 25–28.

6.   Jesse Mercer, *A History of the Georgia Baptist Association* (Washington, Georgia: n.p., 1838), p. 213.

7.   Ibid., p. 213; 2 Corinthians 13:14.

8.   *Minutes of the Roanoke District Association, Virginia* (Hillsborough, N.C.: R. Ferguson, 1789), p. 12.

9.   See, for example, Biggs and Read, *A Concise History of the Kehukee*, pp. 75–76; Mercer, *A History of the Georgia Baptists*, pp. 39, 56–57, 101; Semple, *A History of . . . Baptists in Virginia*, pp. 64ff.

10.   Quoted in H. J. Eckenrode, *Separation of Church and State in Virginia: A Study in the Development of the Revolution* (1910; reprint ed., New York: Da Capo Press, 1971), p. 108.

11.   Thomas Reese, "Essay on the Influence of Religion in Civil Society," *American Museum* 9 (June 1790): 325. The essay was first published in 1783; see Fred S. Hood, "Revolution and Religious Liberty: The Conservation of the Theocratic Concept in Virginia," *Church History* 40 (June 1971): 170–81.

12.   Stephen B. Balch to Ashbel Green, May 15, 1805, Simon Gratz Autograph Collection, Pennsylvania Historical Society, Philadelphia. Balch was writing from Washington, D. C.

13.   John Leland, *The Writings of John Leland*, ed. L. F. Greene (1845; reprint ed., New York: Arno Press, 1969), p. 172.

14.   Diary of William McKendree, September 18, 1790, Vanderbilt University Library.

15.   Ibid., September 13, 1790.

16.   Charles Colcock Jones, "The Death of Aaron," manuscript of sermon preached July 31, 1842, C. C. Jones Papers, Historical Foundation of the Presbyterian and Reformed Churches, Montreat, N.C.

17.   Richard Baxter, *The Saints Everlasting Rest; or, A Treatise of the Blessed State of the Saints in Their Enjoyment of God in Glory*, ed. John Wesley (New York: Carlton & Phillips, 1854), p. 53, 110, 112, 135.

18.   Donald G. Mathews, *Slavery and Methodism: A Chapter in Amer-*

ican Morality, 1780-1845 (Princeton: Princeton University Press, 1965), pp. 7-8.

19.   Andrew E. Murray, *Presbyterians and the Negro—A History* (Philadelphia: Presbyterian Historical Society, 1966), p. 17.

20.   *Minutes of the Baptist General Committee at their Yearly Meeting, Held in the City of Richmond, May 8, 1790* (Richmond: T. Nicolson, 1790), p. 7.

21.   Daniel Grant to John Owen, Jr. (son-in-law), September 3, 1790, David Campbell Papers, Duke University.

22.   William K. Boyd, ed., "A Journal and Travels of James Meacham —Part I, May 19-August 31, 1789," *Historical Papers* (Trinity College Historical Society) 9 (1912): 94.

23.   Winthrop D. Jordan, *White over Black: American Attitudes toward the Negro, 1550-1812* (Chapel Hill: University of North Carolina Press, 1968), pp. 137-78.

24.   Philanthropos [David Rice], *Slavery Inconsistent with Justice and Good Policy* (Lexington, Kentucky: J. Bradford, 1792). Francis Asbury was so pleased with Rice's pamphlet that he put the author's name on it and had John Dickins publish it as an official publication of the Methodist Episcopal Church the same year it appeared in Kentucky. David Barrow, a Baptist minister from southeastern Virginia had worked against slavery for 20 years when he published an antislavery broadside and left for Kentucky in 1798; see David Barrow, *Circular Letter, Southampton County, Virginia, February 14, 1798* (Norfolk: Willet & Connor, 1798). Freeborn Garretson put his ideas down on paper much later, but the trend of his thought may be found in Freeborn Garrettson, *A Dialogue between Do-Justice and Professing-Christian* (Wilmington: n.p., n.d.). There is a photostatic copy in the Duke University Rare Book Collection. Association, presbytery, and conference records, as well as those from local churches are sprinkled with the discussion of slavery as defined in the above works.

25.   James O'Kelly, *Essay on Negro Slavery* (Philadelphia: Prichard & Hall, 1789), p. 34. Pamphlet in Rare Book Collection, Duke University.

26.   Devereaux Jarratt to Edward Dromgoole, March 22, 1788, Dromgoole Papers, Southern Historical Collection, University of North Carolina at Chapel Hill.

27.   O'Kelly, *Essay on Negro Slavery*, p. 31.

28.   Minutes of the Roanoke Association, June, 1790, Virginia Baptist Historical Society, University of Richmond. See also Mathews, *Slavery and Methodism*, pp. 20, 293-94; Biggs and Read, *A Concise History of the Kehukee*, pp. 59-60.

29.   Mathews, *Slavery and Methodism*, pp. 28-29.

30.   Baxter, *Saints Everlasting Rest*, p. 195.

3   *"An Enlightened
                                    and Refined People"*

1.   Charles Force Deems, *The Annals of Southern Methodism*
(Nashville: Methodist Episcopal Church South, 1857), p. 116.
2.   William Maxwell, *A Memoir of the Rev. John H. Rice, D. D.*
(Philadelphia: J. Whetham, 1835), p. 174.
3.   Jeremiah Bell Jeter, *Recollections of a Long Life* (Richmond:
Religious Herald Company, 1891), p. 57.
4.   *Minutes of the United Baptist Association, formerly called the
Kehukee Association, October 1791* (Edenton: n.p., 1791), p. 6.
5.   John Weaver, "The Formation of Voluntary Associations in
Hillsborough, North Carolina, 1816-1825" (Seminar paper, University of
North Carolina, Department of History, January 1975).
6.   Sylvanus Milne Duvall, *The Methodist Episcopal Church and
Education up to 1869* (New York: Bureau of Publications, Teachers
College, Columbia, 1928), pp. 39-40.
7.   George J. Stevenson, *Increase in Excellence: A History of Emory
and Henry College* (New York: Appleton-Century-Crofts, 1963), p. 67.
8.   William Hooper to James C. Furman, August 8, 1837, James C.
Furman papers, Furman University.
9.   Z. G. Henderson, Circular from Marion, Alabama, June 1857,
Manly Family Papers, Furman University.
10.   Basil Manly, Jr., to Basil Manly, Sr., May 5, 1851, Manly Family
Papers, Furman University.
11.   William Wightman, "Address of the Reverend William M.
Wightman...," in *Documentary History of Education in the South before
1860*, ed. Edgar Knight (Chapel Hill: University of North Carolina Press,
1953), 4:372.
12.   "Review of Theodore Dwight Woolsey's *Discourses and Addresses*," *Quarterly Review* (Methodist Episcopal Church, South) 1 (April
1847): 239.
13.   Bertram Wyatt-Brown, "The Ideal Typology and Antebellum
Southern History: A Testing of a New Approach," *Societas* 5 (Winter
1975): 7.
14.   *Minutes of the Virginia Portsmouth Baptist Association ... May
24, 1800* (n.p., 1800), p. 10.
15.   Clark, *Asbury's Journal*, 1:538 (April 26, 1787).
16.   Davies, *Sermons* (1811 edition), 2:38-56.
17.   *Minutes of the Virginia Portsmouth Baptist Association ... May
24, 1800*, pp. 6-11.
18.   *North Carolina Christian Advocate*, March 10, 1859; December 5
and 25, 1860; April 2, 1863.
19.   David Hay, *Home; or, The Way to Make Home Happy* (Nashville: Methodist Episcopal Church, South, 1871), pp. 143, 164-78; see also

Charles Force Deems, *The Home-Altar: An Appeal on Behalf of Family Worship with Prayers and Hymns for Family Use* (New York: M. W. Dodd, 1851). Deems was a North Carolina Methodist minister.

20.   *Minutes of the Virginia Portsmouth Baptist Association . . . May 24, 1800*, p. 7.

21.   Biggs and Read, *A Concise History of the Kehukee*, pp. 48-49.

22.   Clark., ed., *Asbury's Journal*, 1:310 (August 16, 1779).

23.   Diary of Jeremiah Norman, May 29, 1796, Stephen B. Weeks Papers, Southern Historical Collection, University of North Carolina at Chapel Hill, 3:199.

24.   Ibid., 2:149 (January 11, 1796).

25.   Racoon Swamp Baptist Church Book, August 14, 1831, Virginia Baptist Historical Society, University of Richmond.

26.   South Quay Baptist Church Record Book, March 4, 1809, Virginia Baptist Historical Society, University of Richmond, p. 98.

27.   Frances Trollope, *Domestic Manners of the Americans*, ed. Donald Smalley (New York: Alfred A. Knopf, Vintage Books, 1960), pp. 173-75; also pp. 107n, 107-15.

28.   See, for example, *The Doctrines and Disciplines of the Methodist Episcopal Church, South* (Richmond: John Early, 1846), p. 51.

29.   Charles C. Jones, "Charge," manuscript of sermon, C. C. Jones Papers, Historical Foundation of the Presbyterian and Reformed Churches.

30.   Mrs. Eliza M. Cuttino to Iveson L. Brookes, May 20, 1820, Iveson L. Brookes Papers, South Caroliniana Library, University of South Carolina.

31.   Mill Swamp Baptist Church Minute Book, 1780-1811, May 17, 1793; June 13, 1794; October 10, 1794. Virginia Baptist Historical Society, University of Richmond.

32.   Register of the Baptist Church in Suffolk [Virginia], "At a conference held the 30th day of April 1829," Virginia Baptist Historical Society, University of Richmond.

33.   Basil Manly [Sr.], Church Journal, June 22, 1829; December 1833, Basil Manly Correspondence, Furman University.

34.   Carroll Smith-Rosenberg, "The Female World of Love and Ritual: Relations between Women in Nineteenth-Century America," *Signs* 1 (Autumn 1975): 9, 1-29 passim.

35.   Virginia Cary, *Letters on Female Character Addressed to a Young Lady on the Death of Her Mother* (Richmond: Ariel Works, 1830), p. 14.

36.   Rufus William Bailey, *The Family Preacher; or, Domestic Duties* (New York: John S. Taylor, 1837), p. 53. Bailey was a minister in South Carolina.

37.   Augusta J. Evans to J. L. M. Curry, July 13, 1863, J. L. M. Curry Papers, Library of Congress.

38.   Basil Manly, Jr., to his parents, July 20, 1848, Manly Family Papers, Furman, University.

39.   James Osgood Andrew, *Family Government: A Treatise on Conjugal, Parental, and Filial Duties* (Philadelphia: Sorin & Ball, 1847), p. 79.

40.   Mary McGehee to John W. F. Burruss, May 29, 1836, John C. Burrus Papers, Louisiana State University.

41.   Luther M. Smith, *Thorough Female Education, An Address...* (Atlanta: C. R. Hanlecter & Co., 1856), p. 5.

42.   Mary McGehee to John W. F. Burruss, May 29, 1836, John C. Burruss Papers, Louisiana State University.

43.   Angelina Grimke, *Appeal to the Christian Women of the South* (New York: American Antislavery Society, 1836).

44.   Harriet Davis Furman to Maria Furman, November 11, 1840, Furman Family Papers, Furman University.

45.   Charles Wesley Andrews, *Memoir of Mrs. Anne R. Page* (Philadelphia: Herman Hooker, 1844), p. 20.

46.   Ibid., p. 69.

47.   Ibid., p. 26.

48.   Ibid., pp. 29, 49.

49.   Smith, *Thorough Female Education*, p. 6.

50.   Basil Manly, Jr., "Jottings Down," July 21, 1844, Manly Family Papers, Furman University.

51.   W. S. Webb to Charles Wesley Andrews, March 15, 1844, Charles Wesley Andrews Papers, Duke University.

52.   Diary of Joseph Buck Stratton, June 16, 1850; February 2, 1851, Louisiana State University.

53.   See, for example, Jeremiah Bell Jeter, "Address to Young Men," in Miscellaneous Notebooks, 1828-47, Virginia Baptist Historical Society, University of Richmond; Robert Lewis Dabney, "Carnal Intimacies Forbidden" in Sermons 102-300, Robert Lewis Dabney Collection, Spence Library, Union Theological Seminary, Richmond, Virginia.

54.   See chap. 1, n. 14; Diary of William McKendree, September 18, 1790, Vanderbilt University Library.

55.   Journal of Peter Doub, January 24, 1830, p. 29 (Sermon on Romans 8:13), Doub Papers, Duke University.

56.   See note 33.

57.   Wyatt-Brown, "The Ideal Typology and Antebellum Southern History...," pp. 1-29. For an Evangelical man's disapproval of the southern popular ideal, see Charles C. Jones to Mary Jones, September 8, 1829, C. C. Jones Papers, Tulane University.

58.   Anne Firor Scott, *The Southern Lady: From Pedestal to Politics, 1830-1930* (Chicago: University of Chicago Press, 1970), pp. 135-63.

59.   William Swan Plumer to Samuel Miller, May 15, 1841, Samuel Miller Papers, Princeton University.

60.   Robert Ryland to James C. Furman, September 25, 1847, James C. Furman Papers, Furman University. Ryland was an educator who was, in this letter, discussing the common complaints of people who opposed college-educated ministers.

61.   *The American Telescope, by a Clodhopper of North Carolina* (Philadelphia: n.p., 1825), p. 4.

62.   Keith R. Burich, "The Primitive Baptist Schism in North

Carolina: A Study of the Professionalism of the Baptist Ministry'' (unpublished M.A. thesis, the University of North Carolina at Chapel Hill, 1973), p. 81.

63.   *The American Telescope...*, p. 6.

64.   John Donald Wade, *Augustus Baldwin Longstreet: A Study of the Development of Culture in the Old South* (Athens: University of Georgia Press, 1969), pp. 249-53.

65.   Charles Wesley Andrew to William Nelson, July 15, 1837; to Miss Ellen Henry, January 2, 1850; to Mrs. ——— McEndree, January 2, 1850, Charles Wesley Andrews Papers, Duke University. Edward Clowes Chorley, *Men and Movements in the American Episcopal Church* (New York: Charles Scribner's Sons, 1946), pp. 107, 108.

66.   Matthew Page Andrews to Anna, January 20, 1861, January 27, 1861, Charles Wesley Andrews Papers, Duke University.

67.   See James R. Graves, *Both Sides: Full Investigation of the Charges Preferred against Elder J. R. Graves by R. B. C. Howell and Others, September 8 and October 12, 1858* (Nashville: Southwestern Publishing House [Graves, Marks, & Co], 1859). See also Robert B. C. Howell to Morton B. Howell, May 5, 1858, Morton B. Howell Papers, Tennessee State Library and Archives. For one of the most boring, wordy, contrived, and elaborate religious tracts of the 1850s see Graves's *Theodosia Ernest; or, The Heroine of the Faith* (Nashville: Graves, Marks & Rutland, 1856), which should not be confused with *Theophilus Walton; or, The Majesty of Truth. A Reply to Theodosia Ernest* (Nashville: Southern Methodist Publishing House, 1859).

4   *"We Who Own Slaves*
                          Honor God's Law

1.   James C. Furman to W. E. Bailey, December 18, 1848, Furman Family Papers, Furman University.

2.   Donald G. Mathews, "The Methodist Mission to the Slaves, 1829-1884," *Journal of American History* 51 (March 1965): 615-31. William M. Wightman, *Life of William Capers, D.D., One of the Bishops of the Methodist Episcopal Church, South...* (Nashville: J. B. M'Ferrin, 1858).

3.   Charles Colcock Jones to Mary Jones, September 8, 1829, C. C. Jones Papers, Tulane University. See also Donald G. Mathews, "Charles Colcock Jones and the Southern Evangelical Crusade to Form a Biracial Community," *Journal of Southern History* 41 (August 1975): 299-320.

4.   [Charles Colcock Jones], *Report of the Committee to Whom Was Referred the Subject of the Religious Instruction of the Colored Population, of the Synod of South-Carolina and Georgia* (Charleston: n.p., 1834), p. 26.

5.   *Eighth Annual Report of the Association for the Religious*

Instruction of the Negroes in Liberty County, Georgia (Savannah: Thomas Purse, 1843), p. 37.

6.   Charles Colcock Jones, *The Religious Instruction of the Negroes in the United States* (Savannah: Thomas Purse, 1842), p. 186.

7.   Charles Colcock Jones, *Suggestions on the Religious Instruction of the Negro in the Southern States* (Philadelphia: Presbyterian Board of Publication, 1847), p. 31.

8.   Charles Colcock Jones to Mary Jones, June 26, 1837, C. C. Jones Papers Tulane University.

9.   Jones, *Suggestions on Religious Instruction*, p. 35.

10.   South Quay Church Book, 1775-1827, August 1780; May 5 and July 1, 1786; April 2 and 31 [sic], 1791, Virginia Baptist Historical Society, University of Richmond.

11.   Salem Baptist Church (South Carolina) Book, South Caroliniana Library, the University of South Carolina, Columbia.

12.   John Witherspoon to Samuel Miller, January 7, 1836, Samuel Miller Papers, Princeton University.

13.   John W. F. Burrus to Sarah, December 5, 1837, John C. Burruss Papers, Louisiana State University.

14.   Basil Manly [Sr.], "On the Emancipation of Slaves, April 1821," Basil Manly Correspondence, Furman University.

15.   Stephen Symonds Foster, *The Brotherhood of Thieves; or, A True Picture of the American Church and Clergy* (Boston: Antislavery Office, 1844), p. 40.

16.   James Henley Thornwell, "Slavery and the Religious Instruction of the Coloured Population," *Southern Presbyterian Review* 4 (July 1850): 109.

17.   Augustus Baldwin Longstreet, *Letters on the Epistle of Paul to Philemon; or, The Connection of Apostolical Christianity with Slavery* (Charleston: B. Jenkins, 1845), pp. 37-45.

18.   James Floy to John McClintock, November 19, 1839, John McClintock Papers, Emory University.

19.   Mathews, *Slavery and Methodism*, p. 142.

20.   For the Baptist schism, see William Greer Todd, "The Slavery Issue and the Organization of a Southern Baptist Convention" (Ph.D. diss., University of North Carolina at Chapel Hill, 1964).

21.   George M. Marsden, *The Evangelical Mind and the New School Presbyterian Experience: A Case Study of Thought and Theology in Nineteenth-Century America* (New Haven: Yale University Press, 1970). Hubert Vance Taylor, "Slavery and the Deliberations of the Presbyterian General Assembly, 1833-38" (Ph.D. diss., Northwestern University, 1964).

22.   Calvin Colton, *Abolition a Sedition* (Philadelphia: G. W. Donohue, 1839).

23.   Larry Edward Tise, "Proslavery Ideology: A Social and Intellectual History of the Defence of Slavery in America, 1790-1840" (Ph.D. diss., University of North Carolina, 1974).

24.   Ibid., pp. 283–87, 302, 312, 489–90, 538–66.

25.   J. B. Adger, "The Christian Doctrine of Human Rights and Slavery," *Southern Presbyterian Review* 2 (March 1849): 573.

26.   Methodists as well as Presbyterians were saying such things. See, for example, "The Scriptural Argument for Slavery," *Quarterly Review* [Methodist Episcopal Church, South] 11 (January 1857): 30–44; "Dr. Smith's Philosophy and Practice of Slavery," *Quarterly Review*, 11 (April 1857): 242–58; William Sasnett, *Progress: Considered with Particular Reference to the Methodist Episcopal Church South* (Nashville: Southern Methodist Publishing House, 1855).

27.   Frederick A. Ross, *Slavery Ordained of God* (Philadelphia: J. B. Lippincott & Company, 1859), pp. 55–58, 124–25. Ross was a minister of the Presbyterian church in Huntsville, Alabama.

28.   William Andrew Smith, *Lectures on the Philosophy and Practice of Slavery as Exhibited in the Institution of Domestic Slavery in the United States*, ed. Thomas O. Summer (Nashville: Stevenson & Evans, 1856), p. 72.

29.   Josiah Priest, *Bible Defence of Slavery: and Origin, Fortunes and History of the Negro Race* (Glasgow, Kentucky: W. S. Brown, M.D., 1852), pp. 228–29.

30.   James Henley Thornwell, *Report on the Subject of Slavery, Presented to the Synod of South Carolina ... November 6, 1851* (Columbia: A. S. Johnston, 1852), p. 5.

31.   Richard Fuller and Francis Wayland, *Domestic Slavery Considered as a Scriptural Institution...* (New York: L. Colby, 1845), p. 163.

32.   George M. Fredrickson, *The Black Image in the White Mind: The Debate on the Afro-American Character and Destiny, 1817–1914* (New York: Harper and Row, 1972), pp. 84–90. See also ibid., pp. 43–70 for other matters relating to this discussion.

33.   Fuller and Wayland, *Domestic Slavery*, p. 202.

34.   Bell Irwin Wiley, "The Movement to Humanize the Institution of Slavery during the Confederacy," *Emory University Quarterly* 5 (December 1949): 207–20.

35.   Thornton Stringfellow, *Scriptural and Statistical Views in Favor of Slavery* (Richmond: J. W. Randolph, 1856), pp. 100–117.

36.   Basil Manly, Jr., to Basil Manly, Sr., May 27, 1847, Manly Family Papers, Furman University.

37.   Basil Manly, Sr., to Basil Manly, Jr., May 18, 1849, Manly Papers, University of Alabama.

38.   Basil Manly, Jr., "Notes for a Lecture on Slavery," Richmond, 1850, Basil Manly, Jr., Papers, Furman University.

39.   James C. Furman to the Bushy Creek Baptist Church, October 18, 1863, Furman Family Papers, Furman University.

40.   See Dorothy Ann Gay, "The Tangled Skein of Romanticism and Violence in the Old South: The Southern Response to Abolitionism and Feminism, 1830–1861" (Ph.D. diss., University of North Carolina at Chapel Hill, 1975).

5   *"The Trumpet Sounds
                                                      within-a My Soul"*

1.   Stanley Elkins, *Slavery: A Problem in American Institutional and Intellectual Life* (Chicago: University of Chicago Press, 1959), pp. 195, 195n.

2.   Peter H. Wood, *Black Majority: Negroes in Colonial South Carolina from 1670 through the Stono Rebellion* (New York: Knopf, 1974), pp. 138–40, 188–89; Joseph B. Earnest, Jr., *The Religious Development of the Negro in Virginia* (Charlottesville: The Michie Company, 1914), pp. 12–39; Charles Colcock Jones, *Religious Instruction of the Negroes*, pp. 16–34; *Drums and Shadows: Survival Studies among the Georgia Coastal Negroes*, with an Introduction by Elliott P. Skinner and a Foreword by Guy Johnson (Garden City, N.Y.: Doubleday & Company, Anchor Books, 1972).

3.   Leonard E. Barrett, *Soul-Force: African Heritage in Afro-American Religion* (Garden City, N.Y.: Doubleday & Company, Anchor Books, 1974), p. 25.

4.   Quoted in Lawrence Lee, *The Lower Cape Fear in Colonial Days* (Chapel Hill: University of North Carolina Press, 1965), p. 226.

5.   Clarke, *Asbury's Journal*, 1:9 (November 11, 1771); Diary of William McKendree, November 6, 1790, Vanderbilt University Library; Richard Fuller to Basil Manly, Sr., October 1834, Manly Family Collection, University of Alabama.

6.   Boyd, ed., "A Journal and Travels of James Meacham...," p. 94.

7.   Diary of William McKendree, October 31, 1790, Vanderbilt University Library.

8.   Boyd, "A Journal and Travels of James Meacham," p. 88.

9.   Clark, *Asbury's Journals*, 2:46 (April 3, 1795).

10.   John S. Mbiti, *New Testament Eschatology in an African Background* (London: Oxford University Press, 1971), pp. 24–31, 63–74, 80, 86.

11.   James M. Simms, *The First Colored Baptist Church in North America* (Philadelphia: J. B. Lippincott Company, 1888), pp. 18–26; John W. Davis, "George Liele and Andrew Bryan, Pioneer Negro Baptist Preachers," *Journal of Negro History* 3 (April 1918): 119–27; "Letters Showing the Rise and Progress of the Early Negro Churches of Georgia and the West Indies," *Journal of Negro History* 1 (January 1916): 69–92.

12.   Simms, *The First Colored Baptist Church*, p. 29.

13.   William M. Wightman, *Life of William Capers* ... (Nashville: J. B. M'Ferrin, 1858), p. 139; Edenton Methodist Episcopal Church Minutes, Fourth Quarterly Meeting, January 7, 8, 1815, Microfilm in the Southern Historical Collection, the University of North Carolina at Chapel Hill.

14.   Albert Deems Betts, *History of South Carolina Methodism* (Columbia: Advocate Press, 1952), pp. 223–42.

15.   Basil Manly [Sr.], Church Journal, May 6, 1826, January 18, 1829, December 29, 1829, Basil Manly Correspondence, Furman University.

16.   Daniel A. Payne, *History of the African Methodist Episcopal Church*, ed. C. S. Smith (Nashville: AME Sunday School Union, Nashville, 1891), pp. 263–65. F. A. Mood, *Methodism in Charleston: A Narrative* (Nashville: Methodist Episcopal Church South, 1856), pp. 130–31.

17.   William Warren Sweet, *The Baptists, 1783–1830: A Collection of Source Materials* (New York: H. Holt and Company, 1931), pp. 328–30.

18.   *An Exposition of the Causes Which Led to the Secession from the Methodist Episcopal Church in Charleston, South Carolina* (Charleston: E. J. Brunt, 1834), pp. 3–4.

19.   *Exposition of the Causes and Character of the Difficulties in the Church in Charleston in the Year 1833* (n.p., 1833), p. 5.

20.   William Thomas Catto et al. to the South Carolina Conference, February 11, 1836, Manuscript in Wofford College Library.

21.   *Exposition of the Causes and Character*, p. 10.

22.   William Thomas Catto et al. to the South Carolina Conference, February 11, 1836.

23.   "The Religious Life of the Negro Slave," *Harper's New Monthly Magazine* 27 (November 1863): 816–20.

24.   Clifton H. Johnson, ed., *God Struck Me Dead: Religious Conversion Experiences and Autobiographies of Ex-Slaves* (Boston: Pilgrim Press, 1969), p. 59.

25.   See, for example, Orishatukeh Faduma, "The Defects of the Negro Church," *The American Negro Academy Occasional Papers*, no. 10 (1904) (New York: Arno Press, 1969); William E. B. Du Bois, ed., *The Negro Church: Report of a Social Study Made under the Direction of Atlanta University* (Atianta: Atlanta University Press, 1903).

26.   "The Religious Life of the Negro Slave," p. 485.

27.   Ibid., p. 487.

28.   *Drums and Shadows*, pp. 6, 15, 22, 25, 26, 31, 38, 40, 54.

29.   Eugene D. Genovese, *Roll, Jordan, Roll: The World the Slaves Made* (New York: Random House, Pantheon Books, 1974), pp. 217–32.

30.   WPA Federal Writers Project, Typescript of Narratives of American Slaves: Alabama, p. 152, Library of Congress.

31.   Paul Radin, "Status, Fantasy, and Christian Dogma," in *God Struck Me Dead*, p. vii.

32.   William E. Hatcher, *John Jasper: The Unmatched Negro Philosopher and Preacher* (New York: Fleming H. Revell Co., 1908), p. 80.

33.   Ibid., p. 160.

34.   Ibid., p. 119.

35.   L. S. Burkhead, "History of the Difficulties of the Pastorate of the Front Street Methodist Church, Wilmington, N.C. for the year 1865," *Historical Papers* (Trinity College Historical Society), ser. 8 (1908–9), p. 43.

36.   Hatcher, *John Jasper*, p. 29.

37.   Ibid., pp. 36ff.

38.   William G. Hawkins, *Lunsford Lane; or Another Helper from North Carolina* (New York: Negro Universities Press, 1969), pp. 67-68.

39.   Ibid.

40.   Benjamin Drew, *The Refugee: North-Side View of Slavery* (1856; reprint ed., Reading, Mass.: Addison Wesley Publishing Company, 1967), p. 95.

41.   M. L. S. to Iveson Brookes, March 2, 1865, Iveson Brookes Papers, Samford University.

42.   Diary of William McKendree, June 26, July 8, 1790, Vanderbilt University Library.

43.   Robin Winks, "Josiah Henson and Uncle Tom," in *An Autobiography of the Reverend Josiah Henson* (Reading, Mass.: Addison Wesley Publishing Company, 1969), pp. v-xi.

44.   Cato Jones to Charles Colcock Jones, March 3, 1851, C. C. Jones Papers, Tulane University.

45.   Cato Jones to Charles Colcock Jones, September 3, 1852, C. C. Jones Papers, Tulane University.

46.   William Francis Allen et al., comps., *Slave Songs of the United States* (1867; New York: Peter Smith, 1929), p. 43; Howard Odum and Guy Johnson, *The Negro and His Songs: A Study of Typical Negro Songs in the South* (Hatboro, Pa., 1964), pp. 44, 53; John Lovell, Jr., *Black Song: The Forge and the Flame* (New York: Macmillan Company, 1972), p. 253.

47.   For a compilation of source material, including Nat Turner's confession, see Henry Irving Tragle, *The Southampton Slave Revolt of 1831: A Compilation of Source Material including the Full Text of the "Confessions" of Nat Turner* (New York: Vintage Books of Random House, 1972).

48.   Meyer Fortes, *Oedipus and Job in West African Religion* (Cambridge: Cambridge University Press, 1959), pp. 34-55.

6   *"To Proclaim Liberty to the Captives"*

1.   *American Missionary*, July 1864, p. 179.

2.   Richard Hugh Bagby, "Article on the Colored People after the War," in Virginia Baptist Historical Society, University of Richmond.

3.   Martin Luther King, Jr., *Why We Can't Wait* (New York: Signet Book of New American Library, 1963), pp. 93, 94.

Note on Sources

The study of southern religious history must begin with surveys of denominations and the bibliographies upon which they were based. Most impressive of this genre is the magisterial series by Ernest Trice Thompson, *Presbyterians in the South* (Richmond, Va.: John Knox Press, 1963, 1973), 3 vols. The Methodists have not fared so well because their most complete history was written by so many different people; see Emory Stevens Bucke, ed., *The History of American Methodism* (Nashville: Abingdon Press, 1964), 3 vols. For the latest survey of Southern Baptists see Robert A. Baker, *The Southern Baptist Convention and Its People* (Nashville: Broadman Press, 1974), but the work of John Lee Eighmy, *Churches in Cultural Captivity: A History of the Social Attitudes of Southern Baptists* (Knoxville: University of Tennessee Press, 1972), published posthumously, should also be consulted. For the Disciples, see David Edwin Harrell, *Quest for a Christian America: The Disciples of Christ and American Society to 1866* (Nashville: Disciples of Christ Historical Society, 1966). For other bibliography that is both more general and more specialized, see Nelson R. Burr, *A Critical Bibliography of Religion in America* (Princeton: Princeton University Press, 1961), 2 vols; Larry E. Tise, ''Proslavery Ideology: A Social and Intellectual History of the Defence of Slavery in America, 1790-1840'' (Ph.D. diss., University of North Carolina at Chapel Hill, 1974), and Milton C. Sernett, *Black Religion and American Evangelicalism: White Protestants, Plantation Missions, and the Flowering of Negro Christianity, 1787-1865* (Metuchen, N.J.: Scarecrow Press, 1975), pp. 239-88.

There are also denominational histories for every state, and even studies of individual associations, presbyteries, and conferences. Some, like Jesse Mercer's *History of the Georgia Baptist Association, Compiled at the Request of that Body* (Washington, Ga.: n.p., 1838), are really documentary histories. These will lead the curious in turn to the many biographies, memoirs, autobiographies, and obituaries in which the subjects have all but been canonized. Some, like John Donald Wade's *Augustus Baldwin Longstreet: A Study of the Development of Culture in the Old South* (Athens: University of Georgia Press, 1969 edition of an earlier publication), are well written and penetrating; others, like George G. Smith's *Life and Times of George Foster Pierce, D.D., LID.* (Sparta, Ga.: 1888), contain enough original source material quite apart from the narrative of the subject's life to compensate for their filiopietistic posture. Religious periodical literature contains a wealth of information, and the guide to some of it is Henry Stroupe, *The Religious Press in the South Atlantic States, 1802–1865* (Durham, N.C.: University Press, 1956). Almost every synod, conference, and state convention at one time or other attempted to publish its own periodical, but the best of the lot were the *Biblical Recorder* (Baptist, Raleigh, N.C.), *The Religious Herald* (Baptist, Richmond), *Richmond Christian Advocate* (Methodist, Richmond), *Southern Christian Advocate* (Methodist, Charleston), *Southern Churchman* (Alexandria and Richmond, Protestant Espiscopalian), *Southern Presbyterian* (Columbia), *Southwestern Christian Advocate* (Methodist, Nashville). There are also, among many others, two truly distinguished quarterlies. *The Quarterly Review* of the Methodist Episcopal Church, South (Louisville, Ky.) and the *Southern Presbyterian Review*, which was sponsored by a group of ministers associated with the Columbia (S.C.) Theological Seminary.

Once all the above material has been surveyed, one must begin to make sense of the data and impressions which will be accumulated from research. One of the best places to begin is the *William and Mary Quarterly* and two exceptional articles by Rhys Isaac: "Religion and Authority: Problems of the Anglican Establishment in Virginia in the Era of the Great Awakening and the Parson's Cause," *William and Mary Quarterly*, 3d ser., 30 (January 1973):

3-36, and "Evangelical Revolt: The Nature of the Baptists' Challenge to the Traditional Order in Virginia, 1765 to 1775," *William and Mary Quarterly*, 3d ser., 31 (July, 1974): 345-68. Three other studies that may prove helpful are Peter L. Berger, *The Sacred Canopy: Elements of a Sociological Theory of Religion* (Garden City: Anchor Books, Doubleday and Company, 1969); Neil Smelser, *Theory of Collective Behavior* (New York: Free Press, 1962); John Wilson, *Introduction to Social Movements* (New York: Basic Books, 1973).

None of the above studies will introduce students to the way in which Evangelicalism became part of the southern ethos unless they go to the archives where printed and manuscript sources are kept. The best collections of printed materials of religious organizations are housed at the Baptist Historical Commission in Nashville; Church Historical Society in Austin Texas at the Theological Seminary of the Southwest (Protestant Episcopal Church); Duke University; Furman University; Historical Foundation of the Presbyterian and Reformed churches at Montreat, N.C.; Union Theological Seminary at Richmond, Va.; the University of Richmond; and Wake Forest University. The Baptist Historical Commission and the Union Theological seminary have mircrofilmed many manuscripts of the Southern Baptist and Presbyterian denominations which makes research less demanding for scholars who prefer to work in semi-darkness in their home libraries. Until all manuscripts are on microfilm, however, it is good to know where the best collections are. In the acknowledgments of the Preface there is a list of the repositories which were visited to do research for this book. Among the most impressive collections were the Amistad Research Center, Dillard University; Charles Wesley Andrews Papers (Duke University); Iveson L. Brookes Papers (Duke University, Samford University, University of North Carolina); Robert Lewis Dabney Papers (Union Theological Seminary, Richmond, and the University of Virginia); Edward Dromgoole Papers (University of North Carolina); James C. Furman Papers, Richard Furman Papers, and the Furman Family Papers (Furman University); Simon Gratz Autograph Collection (Pennsylvania Historical Society, Philadelphia); Jeremiah Bell Jeter Papers (Virginia Baptist Historical Society, University of Richmond); Charles Colcock Jones Papers (Historical

Foundation of the Presbyterian and Reformed Churches, Montreat, N.C. and Tulane University); Basil Manly and Manly Family Papers (Furman University); Samuel Miller Papers (Princeton University); James Hervey Otey Papers (Tennessee State Library and Archives); Robert Ryland Papers (Virginia Baptist Historical Society); James H. Thornwell Papers (South Caroliniana Library, Columbia); Virginia Conference Papers (Randolph-Macon College, Ashland, Va.); William Winans Papers (Millsaps College).

These are but a few of the collections in which research was done for this book. Aside from the collections oriented to a denomination (Furman, Wake Forest, Randolph-Macon, Richmond University) the best repositories of information about southern religion are at Duke University and the University of North Carolina at Chapel Hill, where diaries, letters, journals, unpublished manuscripts, and even survey data such as that accumulated by North Carolina Methodists in anticipation of the American Centennial (Duke) are available. But one cannot appreciate the nature of southern religious history by reading only those manuscripts which are specifically "religious"; all of the important letter collections which reveal the inner life of people must be consulted as well.

Indispensable for the writing of this book were the local church records scattered in repositories throughout the South. Although only a few of these were cited in the footnotes, they all were the foundation upon which the argument of the book was based. Many students think they have "looked" at church records, only to find nothing in them; but a calm and careful evaluation of these minutes reveals the interaction of people over a long period of time. Each church, society, and congregational record must be analyzed as evidence of a process of social interaction and projection of self into a public personality. Over a period of time—at least one hundred years—one can almost see the psyche of a given church change with the passing of generations. An appreciation of church records is enhanced by following names on membership lists through the land, tax, and estate records. This search is not so easy as the analysis of literary sources, but it is no less important and rewarding.

Index

Abolitionists, 153–55; and pamphlet
  campaign, 155–56; as Jacobins, 165;
  as subversives, 166
Academies, Evangelical, 87
Accommodation, as questionable
  analytical tool, 230–31
Act of Toleration, 17–18
Adultery, as disciplinable offense, 44
African Baptist Church of Savannah,
  198–99
African Baptist Church of Richmond,
  201
African conversion, 188. *See also*
  Conversion experience
African culture: whites' view of, 141;
  as danger to whites, 141; persistence
  of, 188; and white Christianity,
  191–92; and religion, 208–13; and
  Nat Turner, 234
African Methodist Episcopal Church,
  203
African Methodist Episcopal Church
  Zion, 203
Africans, in early revivals, 66–67
Age of Reason, 49
American Baptist Home Missionary
  Society, 162
American Colonization Society, 79
Ancestors in African religion, 210
Andrew, Bishop James Osgood, 160–61
Andrews, Charles Wesley, 117, 131
Anger, black, 218–19, 223, 231*ff*
Antiabolitionists, 155–56, 159–60

Antislavery activity, 66–80, 72–74, 195;
  persistence of in mountain areas,
  75–76; failure of, 75–80; attractiveness of to blacks, 194
Antislavery past, as problem for
  southern Evangelicals, 150, 153–54,
  156
Apocalypse, 231*ff*, 243
Arminianism, 31, 60
Asbury, Francis, 29, 33, 48, 98, 103,
  193, 250
Augusta College, 89
Axson, I. S. K., 143

Baptism, 24; and blacks' social
  condition, 188; similarity of to
  African rites, 191
Baptist organization, 53
Baptists, 7, 22–28, 32–33, 49, 51, 52,
  133–34, 161–63, 198*ff*; innovations
  of, 25–26; attitude of, toward church
  and state, 56–58; against slavery, 69;
  ministry of, 85–86; and conflict over
  missionary societies, 125–29
Barrow, David, 254 n 24
Baxter, Richard, 63*ff*, 77
Benevolence, as women's duty, 116–17
Bible: and slavery, 157; and Declaration
  of Independence, 157; Southerners'
  belief in, 158; and racial inferiority,
  170; and defense of southern
  Evangelicals, 175–76

Black Christianity: and impact on
    whites' piety, 114, 117; "buffoon-
    ery" of, 187; morphology of, 208-36;
    as experience instead of doctrine,
    213-14
Black churches, 197-98; white "super-
    vision" of, 201-2. See also Indepen-
    dent black churches
Black preachers. See Ministers, black
Black Punch (black preacher), 201-2
Blacks as chosen people, 228-30
Board of Managers of the Baptist
    General Convention, 162
Boundaries between Evangelicals and
    the world, 240-41
Brothels, contrasted favorably with the
    Methodist Episcopal Church, 154
Brown, Morris, 203, 204, 222-23
Bryan, Andrew, 198-200, 207, 250
Bushyhead, Jesse, 162

Caldwell, David, 87
Camp Meeting, 51-52
Campbell, Alexander, 132-33
Capers, William, 138-39, 140, 201,
    205-7
Chapel Hill, N.C., 92
Charleston, S.C., and racial unrest,
    205-7
Children, Evangelical view of, 98-99
Church discipline, 42-46; versus family
    discipline, 100-101; and relations
    between blacks and whites, 146-48;
    and blacks, 197-98; important for
    relations with whites, 225-26
Church of England, 2-10; and Society
    for the Propagation of the Gospel in
    Foreign Parts, 5, 6, 188
Circumstances said to vindicate southern
    Christian slaveholders, 158, 159
Class: conflict and disestablishment,
    56-57; identification, 37-38;
    differences among Evangelicals on,
    64; Evangelical view of, 89-97, 118,
    119, 166, 182
Class conflict, 194-95; and Evangelical-
    ism, 79; as religious conflict, 124-29,
    135; and racism, 172-73, 183
Colleges, Evangelical, 88-97
Colonization, 79, 117-18, 153, 154
Columbia Theological Seminary, 88

Community, 2, 4, 10, 13, 15, 16, 18, 19,
    20, 24, 26-28, 35, 38, 39, 41, 43, 44,
    54, 64, 65, 240
Compensation, as questionable
    analytical tool, 230ff
Competition between churches, 55-56
Conjurers, 210-13
Conversion experience, 11, 12, 13, 14,
    19, 24, 32, 33, 34, 46, 59-61; of
    blacks, 67-68, 70; and emancipation,
    70; and family religion, 78-79; and
    nurture, 99-100; of women, 104-5,
    109, 115; white attitude toward
    blacks', 145; impact on self-esteem,
    150-51; of blacks, 189; and African
    "possession," 190-91, 192, 210-11
Cultural inferiority of blacks, 171-72
Cumberland Presbyterian Church, 51

Davidson College, 90
Davies, Samuel, 17-23, 66, 99
Deas, Sambo, 202, 207
Deliverance, as theme in black
    Christianity, 220ff, 225
Denominational structure, 52-58
Devotional diaries of women, 113, 114
Disciples of Christ, 132-33
Discipline, Christian, 24, 25, 42-46;
    among blacks, 22ff; as an Evangelical
    value, 241-42
Disestablishment, 55-58
Dissent, religious, 5, 7; restrictions on,
    8, 16; growth of, 16
Dissidents, Evangelical, 125-35
Domestic slavery, 100, 173, 174
Domesticity, as feminine ideal, 112-13
Doulos, 157

Edenton, N.C., black control of
    discipline in, 201
Education and Evangelicals, 87-97;
    goals of, 89-97; of women, 119-20;
    attacked, 125; of blacks, 141ff
Emory and Henry College, 90
Emory College, 90
Emotionalism in conversion experience,
    59-60; and blacks, 196, 197
Equality: in Evangelicalism, 25, 35, 37,
    67, 70; limited in conversion
    experience, 151; rejected by
    Evangelicals, 168; theme of in
    black Christianity, 219

Evangelical education, 94-96

Evangelical movement, 10-11, 12, 13, 14, 15, 18, 30, 34; and expansion, 46-50; family as cadre for, 99; innovation for blacks, 189

Evangelical style, 124

Evangelical woman, as ideal, 111-24

Evangelicalism: defined, xvi-xviii, 11, 12, 14, 15; preaching and conversion in, 18; ideas of, 21, 34-38, 58-80; changes in, 82-83, 94-97; persistence of, 124-25

Evangelicals, 34-38, 40-41; identified, 14, 15, 16-17, 21-22, 27; authorities' distrust of, 16-17

Evans, Henry, 201, 207

Expansion of Evangelicalism, 26-27, 46-50; and failure of antislavery impulse, 77

Family: Evangelical view of, 44, 45, 97, 97-101; and family religion, 98-101; life of, subject to discipline, 104

Federalism and proslavery thought, 164-68

Folk religion, 208-13

Foot-washing among Baptists, 42

Fornication, as disciplinable offense, 44

Fredrickson, George, 172, 173, 179

French Revolution, seen as enemy of Christianity, 49, 165, 166, 177

Funeral sermons of blacks, 217

Furman College, 90

Furman, James, 136, 183

Garrettson, Freeborn, 68, 70

Garrison, William Lloyd, 138, 154

General Conference of the Methodist Episcopal Church (1844), 160-63

Georgetown College, 90

"God is no respecter of persons," 219

Gooch, Governor William, 16

Graves, James G., 133, 134

Great Revival, 49-52

Grimke', Angelina, 116, 184

Guilt, 19, 20-21, 249; and failure of antislavery activity, 79-80, 150, 152; Adam's imputed, 163-64; and slaveholding ethic, 173; resolved, 182

Ham, 171

Hampden-Sydney, 88

Heaven, not mere compensation, 221-22

Henry, Reverend Patrick, 16

Henson, Josiah, 227-28

Hillsborough, North Carolina, 88

History, extended for blacks in Christian belief, 195-96, 221-22

Holiness, 62

Home, analogy of to heaven, 101

Homosocial solidarity of women, 110

Honour, John, Jr., 207

Hooper, William, 91-92

Hope, in black Christianity, 195-96, 222-23

Howard College, 90, 93

Independent black churches: white support of, 199-200; white suspicion of, 203ff; movement of, 203-5

Individualism in Evangelicalism, 13, 19, 39-40, 43-44, 60-61, 64-65, 77-78; and antislavery, 98

Inequality in southern Evangelicalism, 168-69

Insurrections. See Slave insurrection; Turner, Nat; Vesey, Denmark

Itineracy, 30, 48, 103

Ives, Silliman, 131

Jarratt, Devereaux, 28-30

Jasper, John, 216ff, 250

Jeter, Jeremiah Bell, 84

Jones, Charles Colcock, 139, 141, 143, 180

Joshua, 27

Judgment. See Last Judgment

Justice, 213, 220, 221. See also Last Judgment

Justification, 59

Kentucky Revival, 49-52

King, Martin Luther, Sr., 250

Landmark controversy, 133-34

Last Judgment, 195, 196, 197, 219-20, 221-22

Leaders, black, 145-46, 193-94. See also Ministers, black

Leland, John, 60

Liberator, 138

Liberty: as response to Evangelical
    preaching, 190–91, 193; Evangelical
    movement and, 238; women and,
    238–40; revivalists preach about, 245
Liberty Hall, 87
"Liberty to the captives," 219–20,
    236–50
Liele, George, 194, 198

Manhood, Evangelical ideal of, 120–24
Manly, Basil Jr., 93, 94, 121, 182, 183
Manumission, 151
Marshall, Abraham, 198
Masters: and conversion of slaves,
    139–41; responsibility of, 178, 179;
    urged to treat slaves with respect, 180
Master-slave relationship, 140–42
McKendree, William, 62, 63, 122, 193,
    194–95, 226–27
McNemar, Richard, 51
Meacham, James, 194–95
Meade, William, 117, 130, 139
Mercer College, 90
Methodist ideology, 30–34
Methodist organization, 52
Methodist Protestant Church, 129
Methodists, 28–37, 49, 51, 52; and
    slavery, 66–67, 68, 73–74, 75; and
    complaints about demise of class
    meeting, 100; and schism of 1844,
    160–61, 163; and blacks in Charles-
    ton, S.C., 205–7
Migration, and church's role in
    providing order, 25
Milennium, and blacks, 223–25
Ministers: and Church of England, 5, 6,
    7, 8, 14; authentic, 16–17; Evan-
    gelical movement and, 18; and New
    Light Baptists, 27–28; Methodist
    characterized, 29, 30; talents among
    Evangelicals, 58–59; character of,
    83–87; training of, 85–86; Presby-
    terian, 85; Methodist, 85; Baptist,
    85–86; under suspicion for wanting
    pay, 86; and problems of support,
    86–87; education of, 88–89; attacked,
    104; black, 198–202, 218
Mission to Slaves, 137–50; origins of,
    138–40; as social order, 140–41;
    failure of, 148–50
Missionary mentality, 149, 205

Missionary societies attacked, 125–29
Moore, Richard Channing, 130
Moravians, 134–35
"More than conquerors," 219
Morris, Samuel, 15–16
Moses as deliverer, 220

New Birth, xvi–xviii, 13, 189
New Lights, 16, 17, 23–24
New-School Presbyterians, 164
Nurture, religious, and women, 112

Oglethorpe College, 90
Old-School Presbyterians, 163–64
Oral instruction of slaves, 145–46
Original sin and blacks, 215
Otherworldliness, as quality of
    Evangelicalism, 63–64
l'Ouverture, Toussaint, 177

Page, Anne Randolph, 116–19, 130
Paine, Thomas, 49
Persecution of black Christians, 194,
    198–200, 202–3
Personal conduct under surveillance,
    43–44
Personal holiness, 61–65; and
    emancipation, 68, 70; and blacks,
    226–28
Philemon, Letter to, as support for
    slavery, 176
Pianos as evidence of backsliding, 129
Piety, as an attribute of women, 113–14
"Poor," Methodists as preachers to, 66
"Popular talents" of clergy, 83–84
Preachers. See Ministers
Preachers' wives, 239
Preaching, 9, 10, 13, 14; Davies and,
    19; New Light Baptists and, 23, 24;
    as a gift, 84–85; as reconstitution of
    the community, 84; to blacks, 142,
    143–44; Africans' response to, 191;
    blacks' style of, 218
Presbyterian organization, 53
Presbyterians, 7, 14, 15–23, 49; and
    great revival, 51–53; on disestablish-
    ment, 56–58; against slavery, 69; and
    the ministry, 85, 86; on other
    Evangelicals' work with slaves, 145;
    schism of 1837, 63–64
Primitive Baptists, 128–29

Princeton, influence of on South, 88
Proslavery themes, 152, 156-57; and
    Bible, 157, 159; Federalist influence
    on writers of, 166-67; factors
    influencing, 166-67; and slave-
    holding ethic, 173; audience for,
    182-84
Protestant Episcopal Church, 129-31

Quakers, 7, 68-69, 77, 135

Race relations: affected by Evangelicals,
    67; blacks' impact on whites, 66-67,
    69-70, 70-71, 77-80, 114, 117; and
    missions to slaves, 140-41, 142, 143;
    church discipline and, 146-48, 173,
    174, 179, 225ff; as evidenced by
    black-white interaction in churches,
    193; and white support of black
    churches, 198-200; and blacks'
    independence, 203-5; changes in,
    within churches, 205ff, 248-50
Racial inferiority, belief in, 170, 171
Radin, Paul, 215
Randolph-Macon College, 89-90
Rape of black women, 107-8, 117, 180
Ravenscroft, John Stark, 92
Reforms of slavery suggested, 180-81
Religion and community, 2, 3, 4,
    17-23, 25-28. See also Community
"Religion and Patriotism, the Constitu-
    ents of a Good Soldier," 22
Religious controversy, 242, 243
Restraint, as an Evangelical value,
    241-42
Revivalistic preaching and "liberty,"
    245
Revivals, 27, 48-52, 88, 96, 243ff
Revolutionary ideology and slavery, 72,
    153
Richmond College, 90

Sandy Creek Baptist Church, 23
Schism, 14, 154, 160-64
Sectarian distinctiveness, 54-55
Self-control, related to social rank, 169
Self-discipline, 62-63, 70, 113, 114,
    121, 122, 144, 226ff, 240
Semple, Robert, 87
Separate Baptists, 23-28
Sexual abuse of women, 107-8

Sexuality, 62-63, 71-72, 105-6
Shakers, 51
Singing, congregational and African
    rites, 192
Slave codes, ecclesiastical, 247-48
Slaveholding: as a sin, 74; as not
    immoral, 151, 152; abolitionist
    condemnation of, 154; and ministry,
    158, 160, 161, 162, 163; ethic of,
    167-84; as social responsibility, 173;
    and Christian responsibility, 176-77
Slave insurrection: white fear of, 204.
    See Turner, Nat; Vesey, Denmark
Slavery: and Evangelicalism, 66-80,
    136-84; as burden, 152, 153; as
    government, 152; as part of social
    structure, 156-57; as beyond scope of
    church, 156-57; as means of convert-
    ing Africans, 157; as school, 173; as
    symbiotic with Christianity, 174-75;
    as objectification of human dilemma,
    178; and liberty, 243-44
Slaves: conversion of, 67; management
    of, 141, 142; as members of family,
    142; and obedience, 142, 144; family
    life of, 143; as beasts, 172; as
    children, 172, 174
Social distance, 25-26, 41-42
Social distinctions, 9, 10, 24, 26, 28;
    repudiated by Evangelicals, 34-35,
    36, 41
Social ethic of Evangelicalism, 41, 65,
    66-80
Social order, 14, 25, 40, 42, 177, 178;
    and discipline, 42-44, 52-55, 56;
    Evangelical education and, 94-97; of
    the mission to slaves, 140-41, 144;
    and proslavery thought, 167, 168
Social solidarity in Evangelicalism, 65
Social strain, 15
"Son of Thunder," 84
South, as more Christian than North,
    181-82
South Carolina Conference (Methodist)
    and founding of missions, 138
Southern Baptist Convention founded,
    163
Southern defeat as experience, 78-80
Southern Lady and the Evangelical
    ideal, 123-24
Spirits, realm of, 209-10

Stearns, Shubal, 23–24, 48, 250
Stone, Barton Warren, 51
Stowe, Harriet Beecher, 231
Submissiveness of women, 112, 113,
    119–21
Subordination of women and slaves,
    169–70
Superstition, 211, 212
Survival, as questionable analytical tool,
    230*ff*

Tanner, Elder John, 103
Theology, as issue among Evangelicals,
    30–34
Theft, as disciplinable offense, 147–48
The Saints' Everlasting Rest, 63–65, 77
Thornwell, James Henley, 155, 176
Thoughts on African Colonization, 154
Thoughts upon Slavery, 68
Tryon, Governor William, 28
Turner, Nat, 137, 177, 204, 231–35,
    236

Uncle Tom's Cabin, 184, 230
Union Theological Seminary
    (Richmond), 88
Usefulness, as a quality of ideal
    Evangelical woman, 114–16

Vesey, Denmark, 137, 204, 213, 230,
    231
"Voluntaryism," 57–58

Voluntary societies, growth of, 88
Voluptuousness, 62

Waddell, Moses, 87
Walker, David, 138
Washington College, 88
"Watchful care," 43
Wesley, John, 68
Wesleyan Female College, 90
White-black interaction. *See* Race
    relations
Whitefield, George, 13, 15
Wightman, William, 94
Wofford College, 94
Woolman, John, 68, 69
Worship: black, 197–98, 200, 214;
    black-white, 200; and self-esteem,
    220
Women: church activities of, 26, 109;
    as majority of church members,
    47–48, 102; as Evangelical ideal,
    101–24; and care for preachers, 102;
    sphere of, 111–20; attraction to
    young ministers, 105–6; as mothers,
    112–13; and domesticity, 112; and
    submissiveness, 112; and piety,
    113–14; place of, in slaveholding
    ethic, 169–70, 184
"World," 14, 20, 24, 26, 38, 40,
    41–42, 46, 123
Worldly women, 111, 112

DATE DUE

GAYLORD			PRINTED IN U.S.A.